"Become the News!"

Discover how to gain
Ongoing HIGH PROFIT
PR and Media Publicity for
your Business, Company,
Cause or Charity.

To the best editor
e copywriter I know.
Love Kevin!

by: Kevin Martyn

Dedicated to my adorable family:

My wife Tess, affectionately known as the 'Dragon Lady', she entered my life with the speed and fury of a force 8 tornado! As well as being the family 'Head Cook and bottle washer' she is my best friend, confidant and main supporter in life. She is my self appointed manager, trainer and accountant; she keeps me on my toes and never lets me get away with ANYTHING! ...exactly the sort of wife I needed, but best of all is she brings love and affection as bright as a ray of golden sunlight on a summer morning into my life every single day.

My lovely children, Lele and Ethan who make my life complete, and keep me young in spirit, test my referring skills to the maximum and ensure I am always tired enough for sleep when I retire at night.

My patient father who tirelessly kept me lubricated with cups of hot tea while putting this book together.

Thank you all for being there and believing in me!

Special thanks go to:

My good friend and PR guru Jeremy Fraser, who has been my main motivation and adviser while compiling this book.

Table of Contents

Notes:
Please use this margin for writing your ideas thoughts, inspirations and personal plan of action.

This Tutorial will then act as your route map to PR success!

Kevin Martyn

"The Journey Begins"

Welcome to the start of what is going to be a ***VERY*** profitable journey for you; in fact, after reading and digesting this material, the only thing that is going to stop you from generating new business from it, is ***YOU!*** – that is, more ***SPECIFICALLY***, if you ***DON'T*** use it!!!

There is nothing in this eTutorial that is based on theory; rather it is all formed from many years of practical experience. All of the techniques you will discover are tried tested and proven winners which will work for you regardless of your occupation, or your location in the World.

Depending upon your line of business, product, service or good cause what is suggested here may need a little adapting and adjusting, but the principles are exactly the same, and if used correctly WILL work well and return the results you are after.

The press and media the World over operate in ***EXACTLY*** the same way. They all have the same needs, and their number one requirement is an ongoing flow of quality public interest stories and articles for their publications, or programmes.

This is ***GREAT*** news for both you and your bank balance as you will not find it difficult to master the art of media promotion and PR marketing using the process you are about to learn.

Notes:
Please use this margin for writing your ideas thoughts, inspirations and personal plan of action.

This Tutorial will then act as your route map to PR success!

By the time you reach the end of this material you will possess ***ALL*** of the knowledge that you need to begin obtaining really ***GOOD*** results from your PR promotional efforts. You will be able to rapidly build on these foundation skills, tighten your focus and before long be obtaining even ***BETTER*** results from often quite moderate efforts.

The results you can expect...

The amount of publicity you can obtain for you or your company is not limited in any way, and neither is the amount of new targeted prospects that you can attract. Here in the UK there are thousands of publications and media outlets as well as hundreds of broadcast media opportunities which will keep you as busy as you wish to be. It's the same wherever in the World you live; if you then also turn your attention to online PR you will have access to a ***GLOBAL*** market place and audience numbering hundreds of ***MILLIONS.***

One thing these media outlets have in common is a hunger for QUALITY articles and news releases which will NEVER be satisfied!

PR marketing is a VERY creative outlet...

You will soon discover that there are some well defined, but unspoken regulations in dealing with the media. However, once understood you will find that these ***SYMBIOTIC*** rules are quite unrestrictive, and you are free to be as creative as you wish. You will discover that originality and artistic inspiration in PR marketing is often ***VERY*** well rewarded.

Notes:
Please use this margin for writing your ideas thoughts, inspirations and personal plan of action.

This Tutorial will then act as your route map to PR success!

In fact I often tell people that PR marketing is 85% creativity, or that my job requires 85% inspiration, and just 15 % perspiration.

But don't worry or panic, as although successful PR marketing requires you to think creatively, much of the time we follow tried and tested templates and a simple process that makes the formula for creating compelling articles and news releases as simple as painting by numbers.

As we progress I will give you the ***REALLY*** fast and ***EASY*** method that both Jeremy Fraser *(my friend and PR expert)* and I use to get an unlimited flow of creative ideas and inspiration in virtually all of our projects. With just a couple of minutes of thought followed by a little light testing you will be able to adapt this process to return results which are relevant to your own topics or focus. Within a very short period of time this process will have built you a small stockpile of practical and usable ideas for use in your PR and media promotion.

A journey of a thousand miles starts with the first step...

You will be discovering and learning many new techniques which **ALL** have the potential to bring positive financial improvement to your business ...***just so long as you use them.***

FAKE it until you MAKE it...

I recently heard the tale of the person who asked an exceptionally wealthy self-made entrepreneur what should be his first action if he won a £1,000,000 on the lottery? Without hesitation he replied; ***"start thinking like a millionaire!"***

This is really ***SMART*** advice for success, so I suggest that from this point forward you start thinking of yourself as a PR marketeer.

Notes:
Please use this margin for writing your ideas thoughts, inspirations and personal plan of action.

This Tutorial will then act as your route map to PR success!

There has never been a better time to master this skill...

97% of businesses still use traditional marketing methods to promote themselves which in general require some form of pursuit of your potential prospect to gain their attention. Unfortunately, and as many companies are discovering, this type of over-used marketing is becoming far less effective every day, whilst at the same time becoming more and more expensive to maintain.

So what makes PR marketing so different?

The simple answer to this question comes down to just one word ***"PERCEPTION!",*** ...let me explain.

The editorial you generate within your target publications may be selling the very same benefits as the advertisement of one of your competitors, who could be advertising on very the next page. The difference is that the viewing public know that first and foremost the advertisement is biased by it very nature, and has been specifically designed and written to promote and generate profits for the company which placed it.

Where as, and by contrast, your article or press release is ***PERCEIVED*** to have been written by a journalist who has ostensibly recognised that you and your story are of some ***IMPORTANCE*** ...otherwise he or she wouldn't have given it space!

> *Please remember this: In general the public believe that it is quite DIFFICULT to gain press and media coverage. And therefore tend take to far more notice of what is said.*

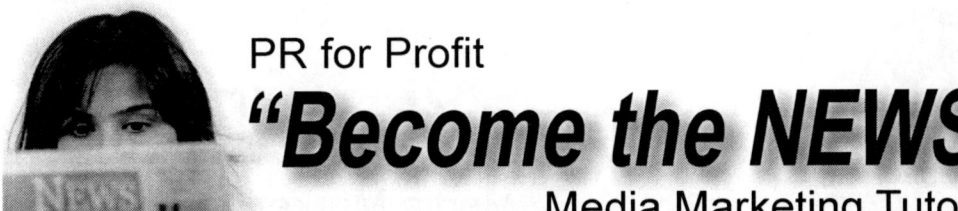

For that ***REASON:*** In the eyes of your potential prospects this type of exposure is a ***VERY POSITIVE*** thumbs up endorsement of quality information.

I would like to reinforce this fact by asking you a question. Let's imagine that two companies offer virtually the same product or service.
Company 'A' can be seen aggressively advertising and marketing their product ***EVERYWHERE.***

Company 'B' does very little traditional advertising, but regularly gains press or media coverage of some sort and then uses the fact that they are favoured by the media by showing the *(independent)* coverage they have received.
Which of these two companies' products or services would you ***PERCEIVE*** to be the best, or offer the best value?

- Company 'A' who advertises themselves?
- Company 'B' who are promoted by reliable, independent news sources?

Whatever ***YOUR*** answer, I don't think you would be surprised to discover that company 'B' will nearly ***ALWAYS*** be ***PERCEIVED*** to deliver better value and for that reason attract ***FAR*** more custom...

Notes:
Please use this margin for writing your ideas thoughts, inspirations and personal plan of action.

This Tutorial will then act as your route map to PR success!

Notes:
Please use this margin for writing your ideas thoughts, inspirations and personal plan of action.

This Tutorial will then act as your route map to PR success!

Can you see the potential?

By creating an ongoing PR campaign you will be able to stop chasing your target market, and begin attracting them instead.

When you keep on appearing in the press or media your company will start to be ***RECOGNISED*** as a leader or ***EXPERT*** within your specific market area. This then becomes a ***VERY*** positive cycle and the reason why you will be given so much more credibility by being seen in the media so regularly.

A sort of positive self reinforcing circle!

This process has been loosely termed ***MAGNETIC*** marketing as once it starts to builds momentum, it literally has the potential to ***ATTRACT*** high volumes of qualified prospects and leads to your company.

There is also an ADDITIONAL bonus...

Even when your media coverage is not selling for you, it is ***STILL*** positively positioning your company, product or service. Ongoing media coverage and publicity is accumulative, and the more you get, the more likely you are to become a permanent fixture in the minds of potential future prospects.

Eventually, and in the same way that when someone says 'Walkman' you may think of 'Sony' or, when they say 'vacuum cleaner' you may think of 'Hoover or Dyson', your company name becomes linked and synonymous with certain products or services.

Notes:
Please use this margin for writing your ideas thoughts, inspirations and personal plan of action.

This Tutorial will then act as your route map to PR success!

No PAIN no Gain...

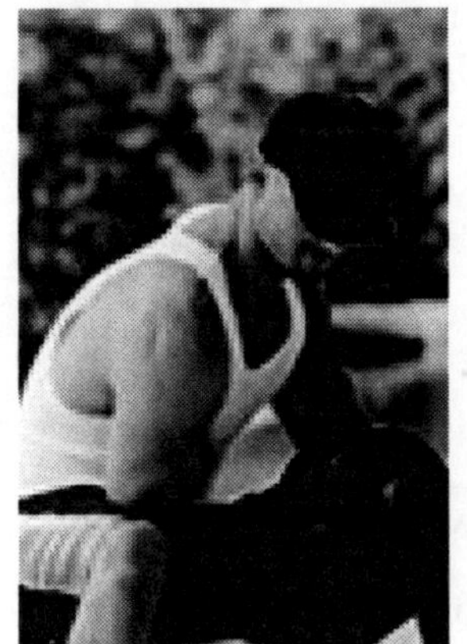

As a student of 'PR for Profit' we are really passionate that you gain good quality results as your success is our success also. However, just knowing what to do is ***NOT*** enough, you ***MUST*** take action and put your PR campaign into top gear to gain momentum just as soon as possible.

Like most things in life, PR marketing is a simple equation, the more ***EFFORT*** you put in, the more you will get back out.

Getting GREAT PR results is NOT difficult

I would like to reassure you right up front and before you really get started that none of what you are about to learn is difficult or hard to put into practice. Just follow the techniques and our examples you will discover in the rest of the course, and you should start getting results immediately.

Here is what you will learn...

Getting the odd bit of local paper publicity is one thing, but gaining ***ONGOING*** media coverage is another, so we will be introducing you to the complete PR process from start to finish. You are about to discover the ***EXACT*** techniques that we use on an almost ***DAILY*** basis to promote our own companies, products and services. We are going to tell you ***EVERYTHING!***

Here are some of the MAIN benefits you will receive when you master PR marketing...

PUBLIC AWARENESS – you will be quite amazed how easy it is to educate your potential customers to the benefits of your company, product or service via the press or media.

Notes:
Please use this margin for writing your ideas thoughts, inspirations and personal plan of action.

This Tutorial will then act as your route map to PR success!

There are dozens of different angles or themes to which public interest articles can be linked, and then associated with even the most commercial of products or services. Such articles can often ***MASSIVELY*** out-pull the response received from commercial advertisements promoting the very same subject.

ATTRACTING new and ***QUALIFIED*** prospects – There are many different direct-response mechanisms that can be disguised as ***QUALITY*** news articles. We are going to show how to use some of the better ones which will give you the vehicle with which to virtually turn on a new flow of prospects at will.

POSITIVELY POSITIONING and ***ASSOCIATION*** – For example: It's easy to obtain **TONS** of media exposure from supporting, helping, or being positively associated with a multitude of good causes or charities etc. Such associations are usually easy to achieve and manage, and are time effective and ***ABSOLUTE*** dynamite when it comes to gaining quality publicity for you. This is just ***ONE*** example out of many which could be provided!

SAVE MONEY – as well as bringing you new and higher levels of sales and custom, your PR will highlight how ineffective most traditional marketing forms really are, especially when compared to media promotion marketing. For that reason it is very likely you will be able to cut back on them leaving more money in your budget or perhaps even your own pocket.

BECOME a MARKET LEADER – as you can imagine every single article of media coverage you gain will go towards building your reputation.

Remember, the public believe that only significant people and companies offering quality products gain ***POSITIVE*** media coverage. Generally, and for that reason, the more coverage you gain, the more important you will be ***PERCEIVED*** to be.

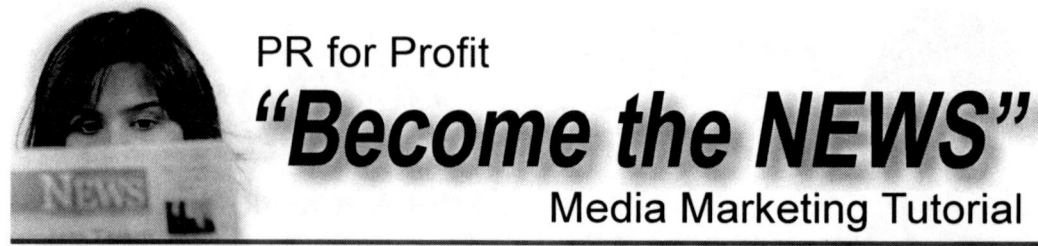

However, as we progress I will show you how to make every bit of media coverage you have ever gained, keep ***ON*** working for you for years and years.

Notes:
Please use this margin for writing your ideas thoughts, inspirations and personal plan of action.

This Tutorial will then act as your route map to PR success!

SWIMMING with the ***FLOW*** – as you progress and gain PR experience you will soon identify the easy opportunities which you could use to promote yourself via the media. In fact you will probably kick yourself for never noticing this valuable 'low hanging' fruit before. You will soon develop relationships with journalists at the publications and other media which are right for the product or service you offer, and as a result, find yourself attracting tons of new business the ***EASY*** way.

How to use this eTutorial

I have tried to write this material in a light and conversational style which I hope makes your progress simple, quick and enjoyable, and also encourages you to read it a number of times until you feel confident in using it.

As you will notice I have left a ***WIDE*** margin on every page for you to write down your thoughts, ideas, inspiration and the actions you plan to take as we progress. Used correctly, this margin, at the conclusion of your studies will contain your own hand written PR action plan ready for implementation.

> *A Friend who recently browsed my bookcase was HORRIFIED to discover how much I wrote, highlighted, underlined and made margin notes in many of the books I own. 'It's a SIN to disfigure good books in such a way' he protested.*

Notes:
Please use this margin for writing your ideas thoughts, inspirations and personal plan of action.

This Tutorial will then act as your route map to PR success!

I went on to point out that these were MY books and intended for my reference only, and it was such disfigurement that distinguished the books to be worthy of studying from those which were merely to be read.

I also told him that I believe you couldn't pay the author of the book a higher compliment than by using and studying his work in such detail.

Faced with this strong argument, my friend softened and after a little thought ended up nodding in agreement. So please feel free to pay us the same compliment by marking, underlining, highlighting and writing your ideas in the same way.

ALSO write down your questions...

How often has there been a question you would have liked to have found the answer to, but then forgot it, resulting in it remaining unanswered?

This used to happen to me all the time which I found frustrating until I started to write my questions in the margin of the book I was reading, in a different coloured ink to the rest of my markings. In this way, and at the conclusion of my read I could quickly go back over the book and find them.

Often, these questions would be answered as I progressed and gained a greater understanding of the subject I was studying. However, sometimes they were left totally unanswered and I always felt that an answer to that particular question may have been the ***VERY*** one that makes the biggest difference to my progress.

For that reason, I would like to encourage you ***ALSO*** to write your questions down as they come to you, preferably in a different coloured ink, as I do, for easy reference. Then, if these questions haven't been answered as we progress you may wish to visit our ***FAQ*** *(Frequently Asked Questions)* pages on the members resource site. You can see the link and the address at the bottom of each page. To remain current this is where all relevant updates to this material can be accessed.

If you don't find an answer there, please feel free to send an email to the address at the bottom of the notes margin.

A logical learning process...

As you will see from the 'bullet list' of contents below, the PR material you are about to assimilate has been written out in a very logical format. These are the ***BIG*** chunks which give you an idea of what you can expect.

- Understanding the PR game
- Idea generation & research
- Planning for success
- Writing news releases that ***GRAB*** attention
- Article delivery to the right people
- Feedback and improving your results
- Automation and making things easy
- Using the Internet to gain ***RAPID*** feedback
- Online PR

Notes:
Please use this margin for writing your ideas thoughts, inspirations and personal plan of action.

This Tutorial will then act as your route map to PR success!

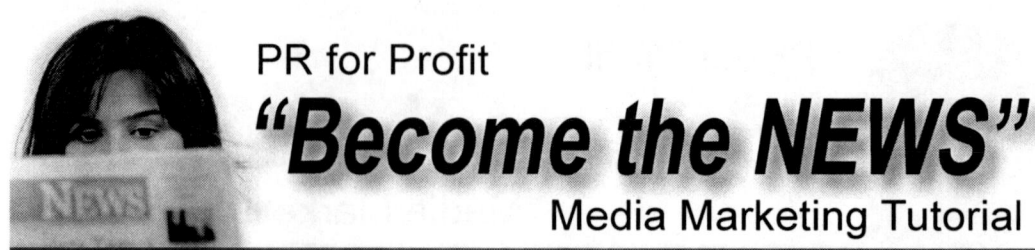

Notes:
Please use this margin for writing your ideas thoughts, inspirations and personal plan of action.

This Tutorial will then act as your route map to PR success!

Understandable PR worries

From the feedback we receive we know that the biggest concern which new students to PR have is writing their own news releases. So I want to tell you in this section that you will be surprised just how **EASY** this will be, when you have a template to follow. We will also give you many examples which you can copy, so don't give this any concern at this point, as in our opinion writing the release is the easiest bit of all.

Belief is *EVERYTHING*...

You may be a bit surprised to discover the following advice in a course about PR marketing and media promotion, but it is ***VERY*** necessary for your success. This short section is going to be the single most important piece of information you ever read, and could ***DRAMATICALLY*** improve every aspect of your life, if you act upon it!

READY?

Virtually 90% of your results at ***ANYTHING*** you do in life, including PR and media promotion will be regulated by just ***ONE VITALLY*** important mental element, over which you have ***TOTAL*** control, and that is your belief system!

EXAMPLE...

If you start out with the belief that gaining PR and media coverage will be difficult and hard work to obtain, I promise that you will not be disappointed, it will be!

Notes:
Please use this margin for writing your ideas thoughts, inspirations and personal plan of action.

This Tutorial will then act as your route map to PR success!

But you have a choice...

If you choose to believe it's going to be ***LOADS*** of creative fun to learn and master, and highly rewarding, you will also be correct.

Which of these two opposing beliefs do you think will best serve you and your advancement in life, or more specifically, in promoting your business?

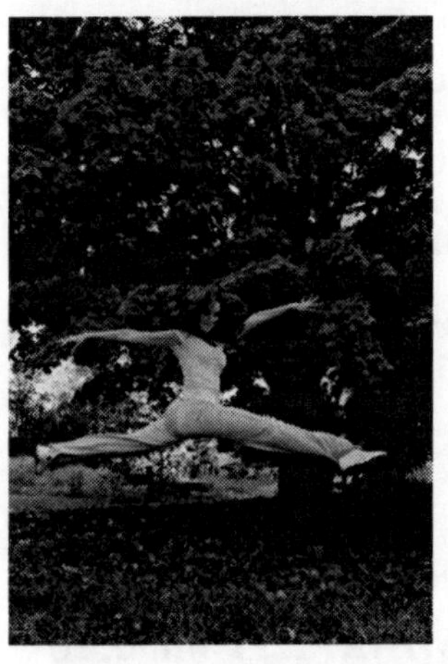

"If you 100% believe you can SUCCEED, then you WILL!"

Certainly, you may have a few set backs and learning curves to contend with along the way, we ***ALL*** do, and that's what makes life so interesting.

When you develop a ***CAST IRON*** belief system that you ***WILL*** succeed, at ***VIRTUALLY*** anything, very little short of death, incarceration, or severe injury can stop you! So start this journey by believing that nothing can ***STOP*** you from being a ***HUGE*** PR success, and you will be!

Action Plan

Well that's almost it for the introduction; you know what you are about to learn and the benefits you will receive from mastering this material – ***JUST SO LONG AS YOU USE IT!***

You will have a simple and complete system to attract as ***MUCH*** new business as you wish. So I have a few things for you to do before moving onto the next section where the real work and learning begins.

Notes:
Please use this margin for writing your ideas thoughts, inspirations and personal plan of action.

This Tutorial will then act as your route map to PR success!

BUY A BOOK TO RECORD YOUR IDEAS! – I would suggest you get a hard cover journal type book as once you start the creative thinking process for your news releases you will release a flood of creative ideas; they usually visit us for maybe just a moment or so before disappearing again. Ideas are like that so you ***MUST*** capture them as they come to you and record them for future use.

As you advance you will also discover that headlines and advertisements, topical news stories etc, will all spark, and cross-pollinate unique fertile ideas in your own mind, so don't waste them, ***CAPTURE*** them for future use. In my opinion, when you are looking for PR inspiration, your thoughts evolved for a reason. There is only one ***STUPID*** idea, and that's the one you fail to write down.

Please remember, that ***EVEN*** the ***DULLEST*** pencil is ***FAR*** more effective than the ***SHARPEST*** mind, so don't just think it – ***INK*** it, and get into the habit of writing down, or ***RECORDING*** your ideas in some way just as soon as you get them!

How fast can you ***WRITE?***

I find that the times when I get most, and ***ALWAYS*** the very ***BEST*** ideas are:

- When I am in the shower or bath
- When I have just woken up, or in the middle of the night
- When I am driving

I have to admit that these circumstances make writing down and capturing fertile and fleeting ideas ***VERY*** difficult, so I have discovered a great solution I will tell you about in just a moment.

Notes:
Please use this margin for writing your ideas thoughts, inspirations and personal plan of action.

This Tutorial will then act as your route map to PR success!

The other ***CREATIVITY*** problem I am ***GLAD*** to have, is this; often my ideas don't come in ones or twos', I get a ***STAMPEDE*** of them and can often get an almost overwhelming ***BLAST*** of inspiration which I know is going to contain some ***GREAT*** and very usable article material if only I can capture them before they dissolve from my mind as fast as water through a sieve.

So to overcome this ***VERY*** lucky situation I use a 'Dictaphone', in fact nowadays I use a 'Digital Dictaphone' which have today become ***VERY*** affordable and readily available from a variety of outlets including most electronic stores.

Armed with my 'Digital Dictaphone' I can capture ideas as they come to me, even when I am driving, where as writing them down *(even if I could)* would take ***FAR*** longer and would probably result in me losing a large percentage of them.

You might consider investing in a 'Digital Dictaphone' to carry around in your pocket or bag, in readiness for those little gems of inspiration that will come to you; I promise that when it comes to capturing ideas, you will not find a better way.

Once I get back in to my office I listen to my recordings, and expand upon them whilst at the same time transferring them to my permanent ideas book for future use.

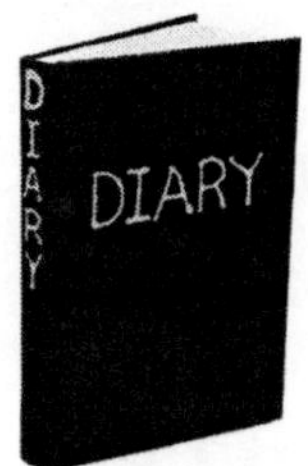

Whenever I am in need of an idea or inspiration for a new article or news release I open my book and moments later I am starting to jot down an outline for my next publicity action.

Notes:
Please use this margin for writing your ideas thoughts, inspirations and personal plan of action.

This Tutorial will then act as your route map to PR success!

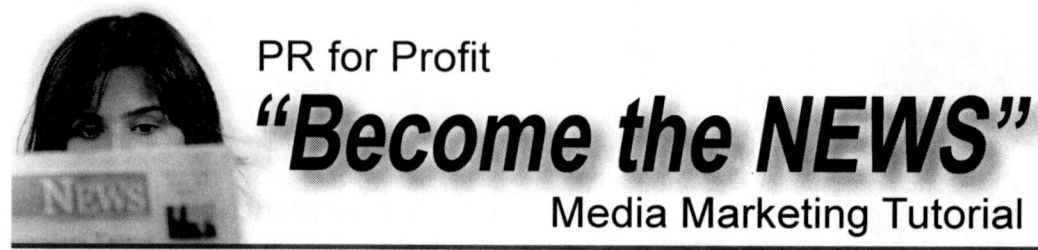

ALLOCATE TIME** for **ASSIMILATION of this material: Get out you diary ***RIGHT NOW*** and put some time on one side ***TODAY!*** I can tell you from experience the sooner you start using and practicing with this material the better your results are likely to be.

Not only are you generally more enthusiastic, but the sooner you take action with fresh knowledge the better, as you will be reinforcing what you have just learned and absorbed with first hand practical experience, for which there is no substitute.

Set yourself a GOAL!

Before you say anything, I know we're still in the introduction, but setting an ***ACHIEVABLE*** goal for yourself at this point will make a very ***BIG*** difference to your outcome.

You see at a subliminal level you'll know that you are working towards something tangible which you can visualise, and if you can visualise it you can achieve it!

Now please notice that I did say an ***ACHIEVABLE*** goal. So in your words write down what you want to achieve, *(remember your goal is something that you promise to yourself)*. So make it ***ACHIEVABLE*** and then sign it to seal your personal deal.

Now put it somewhere you can see it often *(remember it's hard to hit a target that you can't see)*. Most ***IMPORTANT*** of all is to have the 100% intention of achieving it ...and you will!

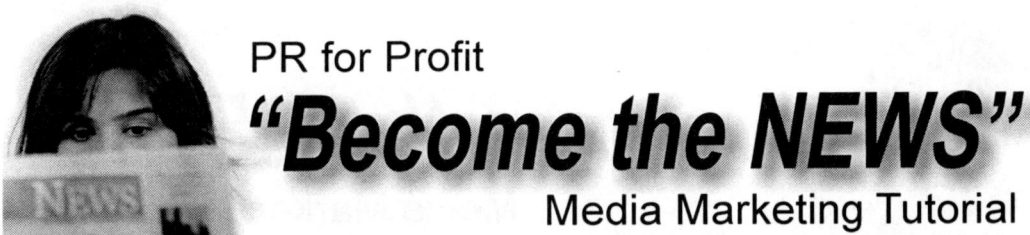

FINALLY - I almost forgot to say...

Congratulations! Purchasing 'PRfor Profit' is probably one of the wisest investments you will ever make, and once mastered it will go on paying you as long as you need to generate an income.

We look forward to helping you make a ***BIG*** and ***VERY*** profitable difference to your business...

Notes:
Please use this margin for writing your ideas thoughts, inspirations and personal plan of action.

This eTutorial will then act as your route map to PR success!

Support

If you have a question please
first check to see if you can find an answer by visiting our FAQ pages in the members resource section listed in the page footer.

If you can't find an answer send your question by email to:
support@PR-forProfit.Com

Notes:
Please use this margin for writing your ideas thoughts, inspirations and personal plan of action.

This Tutorial will then act as your route map to PR success!

Understanding PR...

This will be a very short section as understanding just how PR works is really quite simple and very straight forward. In the introduction chapter of this material I already mentioned that the media in general need you just as much as you need them, although they will never admit to this fact. However, if they had to find the material to fill their publications personally, rather than relying upon a very large proportion of it being submitted directly to them, they would be in ***BIG*** trouble; their publication would suddenly become very thin and meagre offerings indeed.

Fortunately for them, they are kept well supplied with an almost overwhelming abundance of material to power and fuel their publications. Their problem is that ***MOST*** of what is sent to them is of an ***EXTREMELY*** low quality and poorly presented or consists of blatant self-serving commercial promotions. Obviously most publications have a commercial advertisement section which they want you to use.

Now this is REALLY good news for us...

Getting noticed and having your article considered for publication is just a matter of being ***BETTER*** than the majority of others that are submitted to these very overworked news rooms. Making your news release ***STAND OUT*** and create interest is ***QUITE*** simple and a very important part of what you will be assimilating in this material.

Traditionally, PR is short for **'Public Relations',** however and by contrast and within this tutorial this abbreviation stands for **'Press Relations'** because much of what we are attempting to do is to develop ***GOOD*** and lasting relationships with the journalists, reporters and editors who have the power to publish the information we provide.

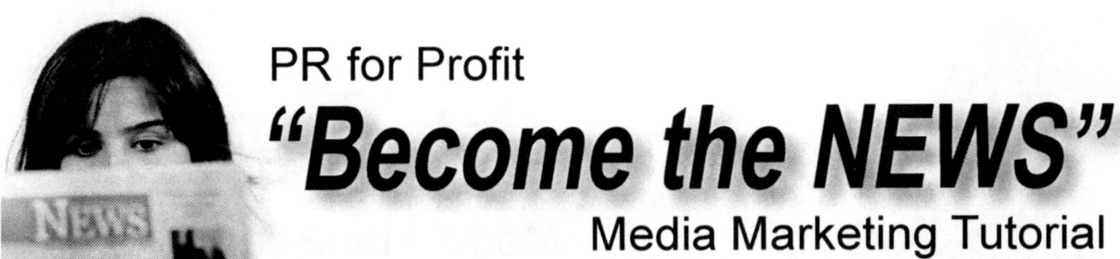

PR for Profit

"Become the NEWS"

Media Marketing Tutorial

We will be presenting ourselves as individuals who understand the needs of the media and for that reason will provide ***HIGHLY*** professional news releases and articles which deliver relevant quality public interest material. Our aim is to make a good and lasting impression in the mind of the journalist or editor to whom we submit our information. Our objective is to make them remember our name, and then recognise us as a future source for quality news material to whom they will want to speak and refer to in the future.

Although this desirable situation may take time to develop, you will eventually reach the point where getting your articles published is just a matter of calling your friendly journalist contacts, and pushing the send button on your email program. In fact they ***MAY*** even come knocking on your door looking for stories!

What a COINCIDENCE!

Just moments ago, and as I am writing this paragraph, I received a call from an article-hungry journalist concerning one of the subjects about which I regularly issue news releases. On this occasion he was looking to develop a story on this particular subject, but with a certain slant, and as you will have ***GUESSED***!
I have just made his job a whole lot simpler by offering to write this story for him.

He, of course readily accepted, and I am sure will almost certainly just add his name to the article before sending it for publication. But why should I worry? As this is an ideal win-win situation that couldn't get any better; he gets the story he wants for his paper, the public get an article of quality news information which they ***PERCEIVE*** to have been written by a independent journalist, and I will get a ***TON*** of response and new business which on this occasion I anticipate will be considerable.

Notes:
Please use this margin for writing your ideas thoughts, inspirations and personal plan of action.

This Tutorial will then act as your route map to PR success!

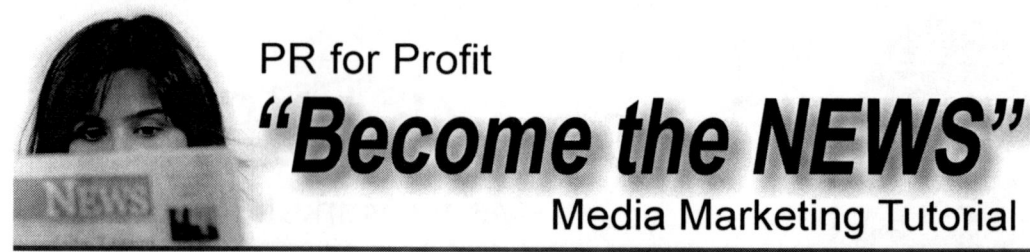

Notes:
Please use this margin for writing your ideas thoughts, inspirations and personal plan of action.

This Tutorial will then act as your route map to PR success!

Then there are the resultant press cuttings which give you far more credibility than a whole ***BOOK FULL*** of testimonials. These I can reproduce and use to support my marketing and sales material for literally years to come.

The PR game EXPLAINED...

Are you now starting to understand ***WHY*** the press and media ***NEED*** us?

You see there is ***NEVER ENOUGH*** high grade public interest material to satisfy their needs, or the public's appetite for news worthy information. For that reason the press and media create a proportion of their own material, but doing so is ***VERY*** expensive, time consuming and to find and create all their own news would probably not be financially viable. For that reason, many publications heavily rely upon what is submitted to them by those who fully understand the 'PR game'.

No one does ANYTHING for nothing...

Now virtually everyone who contacts the news room with a story is doing it for a reason which nearly always boils down to gaining attention and publicity for their products service or cause, and much of what is submitted to them is financially motivated.

Now this puts the press and media in a ***VERY*** difficult position, as we already know, most publications sell advertising space which accounts for a ***MAJOR*** part of their revenue. They ***WOULD*** definitely ***LIKE*** to use some of the articles and material which they have been sent because they ***OFTEN*** contain some ***EXCELLENT*** public interest substance. Unfortunately, they simply contain too ***MUCH*** commercial content.

However, and more importantly, if they published such material they will soon start to lose their advertising revenue.

Whilst at the same time, without the financial incentive ***NOBODY*** will take the time to create such quality articles for their use, and so a ***STALEMATE*** situation where everyone loses would ***SOON*** be reached.

For this reason, a very SATISFACTORY and workable solution has evolved...

...and this is what has been loosely termed media promotion or PR marketing and is the subject of this tutorial.

In a nut shell, PR marketing is the art of using the press and the media to promote you, your product or service without the use of blatant advertisements which would directly compete with the publications own commercial advertising revenue.

It's a true WIN-WIN, NO-LOSE situation...

The press and media receive ***QUALITY*** public interest information and articles, and in return you get media exposure which can be used in a ***HUGE*** variety of ways. It will also position you and your company as experts or market leaders and eventually result in ***MORE*** customers, ***MORE*** sales, and ***BEST*** of all, ***MORE*** income!

The results of modern PR can be quite spectacular, as many simple and creative ***HIGHLY EFFECTIVE*** methods and techniques of generating exposure have evolved.

Notes:
Please use this margin for writing your ideas thoughts, inspirations and personal plan of action.

This Tutorial will then act as your route map to PR success!

Notes:
Please use this margin for writing your ideas thoughts, inspirations and personal plan of action.

This Tutorial will then act as your route map to PR success!

Extremely subtle techniques, which very often ***DRAMATICALLY*** out-pull the results and the level of response which traditional advertisements, deliver. Cost just a ***FRACTION*** *(if anything at all)*, to produce. At the same time, you or your company are positively positioning as an ***EXPERT*** and market leader in your field, and a definite source which should be ***RESPECTED***.

EFFECTIVE promotional techniques...

In an upcoming chapter called **'Publicity Methods'** we will be looking at the specific workings of the publicity devices which we have used to great effect and have found to be ***MOST*** profitable. We use approximately 10 different tried and tested principles which fall into two different and distinct categories which we have called:

- Direct response
- Profile Building

Let me provide a brief outline explanation right now, so you can fully comprehend and appreciate the difference between these two categories, which will also help you understand the material which we will be covering.

First, and as its name suggests, the methods which fall into the 'Direct Response' category bring new prospects ***DIRECTLY*** back to you or your company, as the mechanisms they employ require the prospect to take some type of ***RESPONSIVE*** action. Generally, they will supply you their contact details in return for further information of some type which has an associated ***PERCEPTION*** of value.

Using one such method I built a list of ***HOT*** prospects in excess of 28,000 prospects in just 4 days! I hope this inspires you as we will be showing you ***EXACTLY*** how you can benefit from using the same technique.

Notes:
Please use this margin for writing your ideas thoughts, inspirations and personal plan of action.

This Tutorial will then act as your route map to PR success!

Now such spectacular results don't generally happen every week, but when they do occur you will know you have some ***VERY*** profitable times immediately ahead of you.

'Profile Building', our second category of publicity methods is generally far easier to achieve and usually the method which the uninitiated to PR marketing, associate with media publicity and PR in general.

Although much easier, 'Profile Building' PR, plays an equally important role in your ongoing PR campaign, as it this that keeps your, or your company name highlighted and fresh in the memory of the buying public, and your potential target prospects. However, the accumulative effect of PR marketing is extremely powerful, so as your PR campaign advances, 'Profile Building' is highly likely to return you very measurable and immediate results.

You can really have SOME FUN with the 'Profile Building' methods...

As you will soon discover, these are generally the techniques which are a little bit more zany, off-the-wall, and creative than those in the 'Direct Response' category; in fact just so long as it is in good taste, virtually anything goes. They will also involve and associate you with some really interesting and worthwhile people or causes if you follow this approach.

Developing the RIGHT habits to make PR HIGHLY profitable...

One of the ***BIG*** factors which determine our individual levels of success at ***ANYTHING*** is consistency. It's a ***VERY*** simple equation; if you consistently follow a successful recipe you are going to enjoy successful results. Below are four actions we encourage you to develop as habits which will go a long way towards helping you obtain ***CONSISTENTLY*** good results.

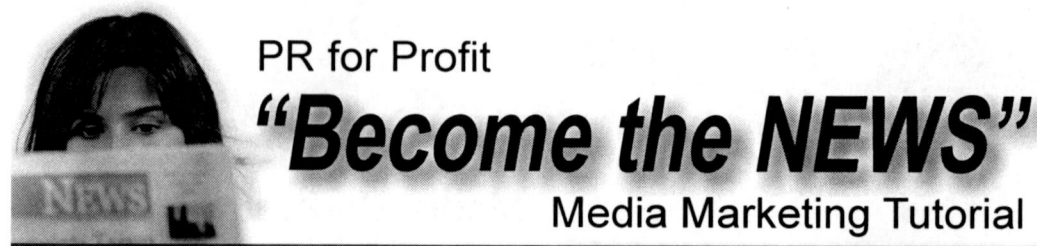

Notes:
Please use this margin for writing your ideas thoughts, inspirations and personal plan of action.

This Tutorial will then act as your route map to PR success!

Do ***SOMETHING*** every day – I usually create and despatch a new news article every week and because of the way in which we work find doing so quite effortless. The reason for this is that virtually every day we do something towards generating the next one.

It may just mean spending 10 minutes jotting down some outline ideas for the next release or researching a few facts that we will include, but we do ***SOMETHING!*** In this way we both have a number of articles in differing stages of completion and occasionally will be way ahead of ourselves and have a number of stories waiting patiently for timely dispatch, which will start generating us additional income.

Work well in advance – as I am ***CERTAIN*** you will already have heard said many times before, nobody ***EVER*** plans to ***FAIL!*** ...but those who do so should look closely at what went wrong for them, and learn from it ...very often they will discover it comes down to the fact that they totally "failed to ***PLAN***!"

Keep looking for stories – as you advance you will find inspiration for news articles ***EVERYWHERE,*** just stay alert! The best friend you have in your search is an open and enquiring mind and an attitude of positive expectation. With these tools firmly in place you will be well armed for success.

Study what others are doing – this is easily achieved by reading news papers, magazines and trade journals which are applicable to your area of business. After going through 'PR for Profit' you will gain a certain feel and understanding, and will soon spot which stories have been engineered, and the techniques which the writer has used to generate media and public interest. This is a ***GREAT*** opportunity and method of building your knowledge and adding new and usable tricks and methodology to your own growing toolbox.

Notes:
Please use this margin for writing your ideas thoughts, inspirations and personal plan of action.

This Tutorial will then act as your route map to PR success!

Idea Mining

It all starts with an IDEA...

I didn't start my career knowing that PR as a marketing tool had the potential

to generate large amounts of additional and ongoing income. It was only ***AFTER*** I personally benefited from the results of some ***CHANCE*** media promotion that I became aware of its true power; I experienced first hand, its income-generating potential, and wanted more of it.

So shortly afterwards, and with the very best of intentions and the right attitude I sat down to write my first news release. I knew what I wanted to achieve and that was another story in the press that would once again start my phone ringing. My first, chance press story, had resulted in me generating approximately six to eight months of my usual income in a matter of days and I ***OBVIOUSLY*** wanted to do the same again.

Two and a half hours, and *(in those pre-word-processor days)*, nearly a pad of note paper later, I was no further forward. I had been scribbling with gusto and writing without direction. Although I had committed a ***HUGE*** amount of energy and enthusiasm, it eventually became apparent to me that I was getting nowhere without a central idea or theme on which to hang my words.

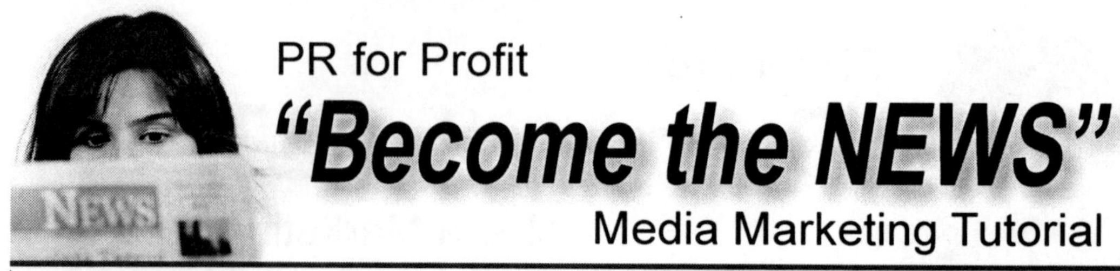

Notes:
Please use this margin for writing your ideas thoughts, inspirations and personal plan of action.

This Tutorial will then act as your route map to PR success!

Fortune favours the brave...

HIGHLY frustrated by this early failure, I started writing again, but this time it was to jot down ideas which I could write my release around. I did not have the benefit of the knowledge you are about to discover, but I am blessed with a very creative mind and the following day I sat down at the same table and started all over again. I still have my first effort at composing a news release, and today, 30 years later reading my first attempt makes me almost blush with embarrassment at just how poor it was. I am even more amazed that it was published at all, but fortune smiled upon me that day, and it was!

Was this BEGINNER'S luck?

Although the end results were not as good as the first professionally written article I benefited from a week or so earlier, it did get my phone ringing again, and more importantly fuelled me with a deep desire to get better at writing my own PR. The thought of gaining ongoing media coverage didn't even enter my mind at this stage; I just had a vague vision of the occasional article topping up my bank balance for me.

Everything happens for a reason...

In hindsight I realise that this early experience, which at the time I thought was a failure, was in fact a VERY fortunate success, inasmuch as it HIGHLIGHTED the importance of having a QUALITY idea to start off with, and BEFORE you try writing a news release.

Notes:
Please use this margin for writing your ideas thoughts, inspirations and personal plan of action.

This Tutorial will then act as your route map to PR success!

When you have the IDEA, the rest is quite easy.

There will always be an audience for creative news worthy articles and stories, so it's a simple equation; in general, the more ***QUALITY*** ideas you have the higher quality your PR is likely to be!

So what you are about to discover are my favourite idea- generating techniques. What we are attempting to do in this section is to get you thinking creatively and recording your ideas so by the time you start writing you are already well armed with a small arsenal of ***QUALITY*** PR inspiration which will fuel your successful launch into PR marketing.

As gaining ***GOOD*** ideas are so central to the generation of quality PR articles which get published, we have attempted to furnish you with a wide variety of ***IDEA*** generating-techniques for use in most types of businesses or situations where media exposure is required. To start the creative thought process we will be asking you a lot of questions which are designed to flush out dormant ideas and sparks of inspiration, that will grow into something bigger. At this point, don't dismiss ***ANY IDEAS*** that come to you, just record ***EVERYTHING***!

When it comes to getting your idea and an angle for writing your release there are ***NO*** ridged or hard and fast rules; anything goes, and it comes down to what works best for you. I suggest that you work though all the methods we will be sharing and become as familiar with as many of them as possible because they will all serve you well in the future.

Some of the techniques will directly apply to your product, service or particular line of business, and others will not, however, they may provide a structure that you can use to cross-pollinate ideas and techniques and develop some unusually creative results.

Notes:
Please use this margin for writing your ideas thoughts, inspirations and personal plan of action.

This Tutorial will then act as your route map to PR success!

As you progress in PR you will almost certainly develop many new and unique methods for generating ideas, and you will learn even more from other sources, which you will be able to add to your growing knowledge of how to think creatively and use to your advantage.

You already have lots of QUALITY public interest material...

This statement often startles those who are new to PR and media promotion,

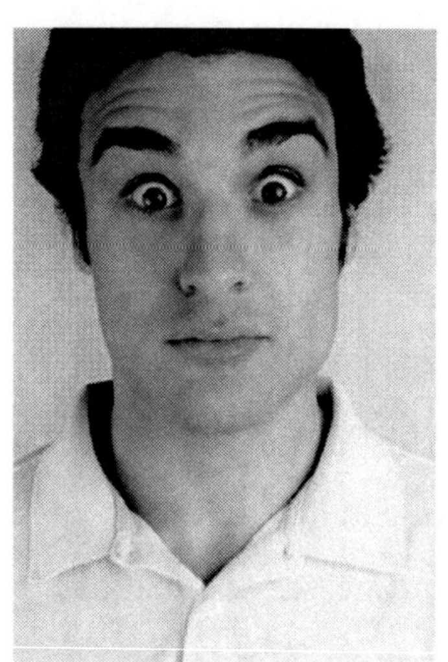

but by the time you get to the end of this section you should have a whole list of ready to use ideas for your own PR. As you gain experience and confidence using these techniques, you will find identifying usable PR ideas starts to become much quicker and easier. It's just a matter of developing a feel for what works and spotting the story or the angle for the idea you have, and that will come with experience.

EVERYONE has the wrong idea about this BIT!

Now let's get one ***MISCONCEPTION*** out of the way right now - You don't have to be ***ORIGINAL!*** There are very few original ideas or even unique angles on ideas, so don't think that you have to find one as you ***WILL NOT*** receive an award or recognition if you manage to do so. The media and press don't care if you are the first to come up with such a story, neither do the audience of their publications just so long as your article contains quality public interest information. Recycling ideas and borrowing inspiration from other sources is not cheating or classed as plagiarising unless you blatantly ***COPY*** large chunks of material created by someone else.

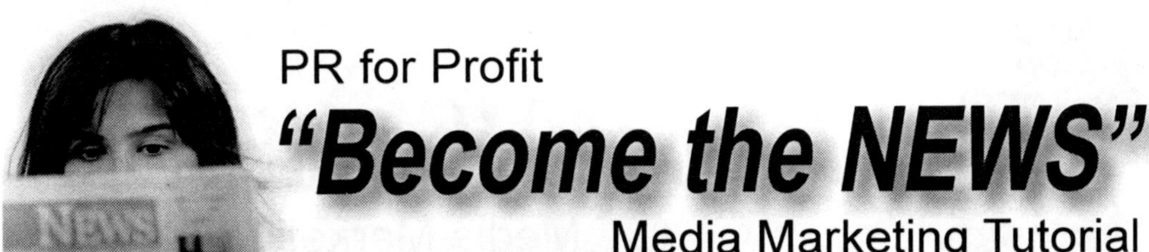

The people who matter in the PR industry will ***ALL*** tell you that reproducing a winning idea or formula in your own words or style is known as being ***SMART***. If you insist on cutting a new trail where no one else has trodden before, there are a few truths you should first know about being a pioneer. Generally, they have a very ***LOW*** life expectancy as ***MOST*** of them die of either starvation or from arrows in their back!

Notes:
Please use this margin for writing your ideas thoughts, inspirations and personal plan of action.

This Tutorial will then act as your route map to PR success!

Nowadays, writing in one form or other accounts for most of my work. Not just creative writing such as this PR material, but also what is known in the trade as 'Copywriting', which usually deals with creating written sales letters for websites and promotional material which usually persuades people to purchase something, or part with money in some way.

For many years I wondered how and why 'Copywriting' was so named, but after many years of practical experience the reason eventually became apparent.

It comes from COPYING the winning formulae of other writers! WHY? ...because it WORKS!

You see, in copywriting, like PR/news generation, there is very little that is new or original. Most sales copy employs proven mechanisms and tried and tested techniques which have been borrowed, copied and rehashed for ***MANY*** years. In fact, I have 'Copywriting' material, advertisements and books dating from the turn of the century and it may surprise you to discover that ***VERY*** little has changed in the past 100 years!

Notes:
Please use this margin for writing your ideas thoughts, inspirations and personal plan of action.

This Tutorial will then act as your route map to PR success!

Certainly, the language and sentiments that are used have been brought up to date and into the 21st century. However, the formula, arguments and mechanisms are ***ALL*** the ***SAME*** with very little that you could call new.

More recently, *(and mainly from television documentaries)* I have been studying the life and times of the Romans, and have discovered something ***EXTREMELY*** interesting. It seems that we share the same desires, worries, fears, wants and aspirations in life and from this perspective we have changed ***VERY*** little in the past two thousand years! Certainly, the way we live, quality of lifestyle and the technology that we have developed is very ***MUCH*** advanced, but we are still the same in almost every other way!

For that reason I believe that the sales copy and advertisements the Romans were using to persuade, lead and manipulate way back then, with just a little updating, would work just as well today.

So, what's all this leading up to?

One piece of GOLDEN advice, when it comes to PR creativity... *NEVER start with a BLANK canvas!*

Coming up with news worthy ideas is ***REALLY*** not difficult if you stick to the following process and use what is already working as inspiration and a template to develop your own ideas and PR news articles. Steal a little from here, and borrow a piece from there, and you will soon be credited in coming up with, and creating some ***HIGHLY*** original material and ***QUALITY*** news stories, although you will know differently!

Let me repeat, this is ***NOT*** cheating, almost ***EVERY*** successful copywriter and PR agent uses this technique and process, and builds *(what is known in the trade as)* a ***SWIPE*** file to refer to and learn from ...but more about that shortly.

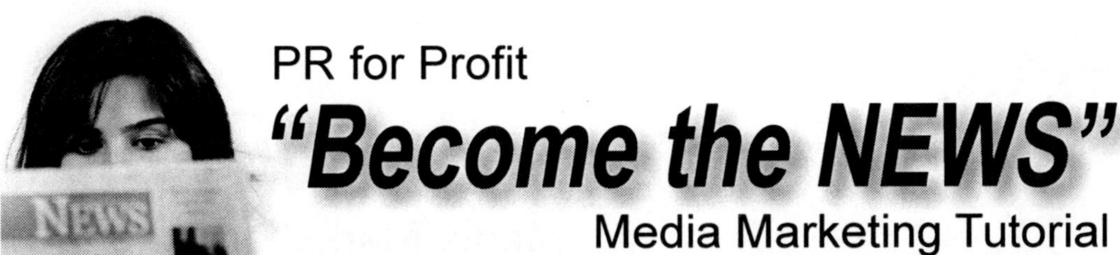

Notes:
Please use this margin for writing your ideas thoughts, inspirations and personal plan of action.

This Tutorial will then act as your route map to PR success!

How to get DOZENS of tried and tested PR ideas for just pennies...

Wherever you live in the world I am sure you have jumble, car boot and garage sales, charity shops, swap meets etc ...a place where unwanted, usually low value but still serviceable possessions end up being resold for next to nothing.

My wife and children ***JUST*** love spending a few hours on a warm sunny day visiting and spending a bit of their pocket money at such places mainly because they get the opportunity to indulge in a little hard bartering with a friendly opponent, and usually end up coming back with a box full of their purchases, which gives them the feeling they have found a ***BARGAIN***.

As far as I am concerned, and the frustrating part of this, most of what they buy ends up being given to the charity shop just a few weeks later.

On one such expedition, where, as usual, my wife had assigned me the dual role of taxi driver and baggage carrier, I waited patiently for her as she fiercely haggled with an equally stubborn seller over the difference of a few pence in exchange for yet another useless second hand item. As they were engaged in financial verbal combat, which was as aggressive as a pair of starving bull dogs fighting over a rat, it became obvious they were having ***GREAT FUN*** and this battle could take some time to reach its conclusion. So I wandered along to the next pile of rubbish which was heavily disguised as a second hand book store.

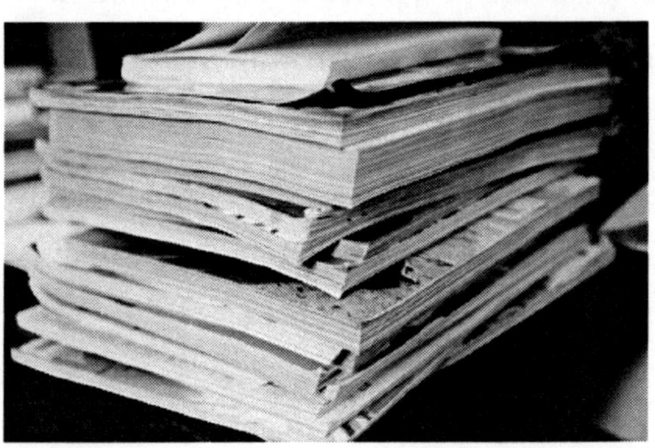

My attention was captured by piles of old glossy magazines which had been bound together with string. I noticed some of them where nearly 30 ***YEARS OLD*** and I picked up a loose copy.

Notes:
Please use this margin for writing your ideas thoughts, inspirations and personal plan of action.

This Tutorial will then act as your route map to PR success!

Thumbing my way through it I quickly spotted 3 or 4 ***VERY*** good and usable ideas for my own PR campaigns.

"Twenty pence" said a lady in hopeful anticipation! I playfully complained and pointed out that it was only 20 pence when it was new. *(Obviously some of my family's bartering skills must have rubbed off on me!)* "Okay 5 pence then" said the lady in readiness to do battle with me. "How much for the lot" I asked, and five minutes later, and at my wife's dismay, I was struggling away with four ***LARGE*** and ***EXTREMELY*** heavy bundles of glossy magazines for £5 ...I didn't even haggle over the price as I knew I was taking home a ***TRUE*** bargain.

Over the following month or so I slowly went through them all and found a quality supply of potential stories, ideas, inspiration and some great writing techniques which I knew would be worth a lot of money to me in future profits.

Since I discovered what an absolute ***GOLDMINE*** of useful information old magazines and similar publication can be, I never miss the opportunity of buying them when the opportunity arises. Some of them cost as much as £2 and £3 each, and all I need are the story and article ideas which they supply me with. So the fact that they are out of date does not matter at all.

Since recycling has become such a big issue here in the UK I have found that my local recycling centre *(Rubbish Dump)* is the best place to visit for old news papers and publications. Sometimes, and generally when their ***MASSIVE*** paper containers are full and well overdue for emptying, old papers and magazines due for recycling are piled high against their side. With a short explanation, and a kind word to the supervisor I have been allowed to take away what I want.

PICK the LOW hanging fruit first...

Your obvious starting point in your search for PR ideas is examining what's going on in your company, or in your life ***RIGHT NOW***, as this is ***MOST*** likely to be your best source of inspiration. Below are three simple section headings which we will be expanding upon in more detail to get your PR ideas flowing...

- What are you doing in your business?
- What *(public interest)* spin could you put on it?
- What ***COULD*** you be doing?

To start the creativity process, use the margin to scribble down any creative or possible ideas which come to you as you mentally answer and go over the following questions. If you run through this exercise regularly, you may well be ***AMAZED*** to see what emerges and develops. These questions are designed to make you think ***DEEPLY*** so take your time.

Just in case you are considering why I am asking all these questions, and the ones that follow, I would like to give you a brief explanation. If I asked you what special talents you possessed or what you are exceptionally good at, it's likely that you would, shrug your shoulders and say either NOTHING or 'I don't know'. However, if I asked your mother the same question, the answers would immediately start flowing and you would probably blush with embarrassment.

Notes:
Please use this margin for writing your ideas thoughts, inspirations and personal plan of action.

This Tutorial will then act as your route map to PR success!

Notes:
Please use this margin for writing your ideas thoughts, inspirations and personal plan of action.

This Tutorial will then act as your route map to PR success!

So these questions are serving the same purpose and are meant to highlight the things that others may feel you do differently, or better than your peers etc, in your business. Highlighting these points will give you a starting list of potential ideas for PR news releases and articles. If you don't immediately understand our objective you will as the mist clears and your understanding of PR grows and develops.

Just remember to write any ***IDEAS*** down as they ***COME TO YOU*** and in this way you should have a good selection for your new release all ready to go when we get to the chapter on writing. You could in fact say that this exercise is taking stock of your PR assets...

Q: What are you doing in your business right now?

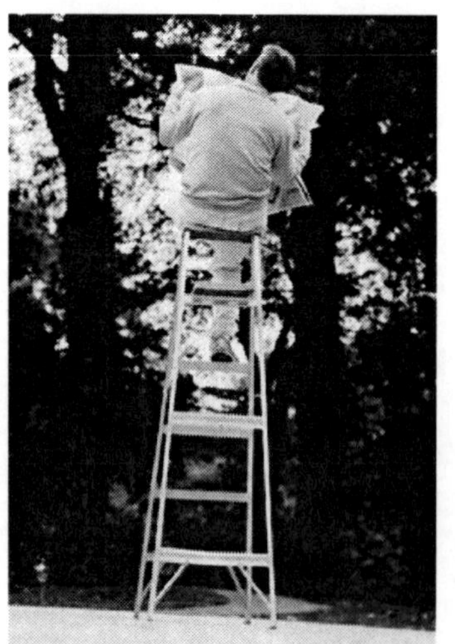

Is the way you do or conduct your business different or unusual to other companies with which you compete in any way? What have you heard others say in passing or directly about your business that you could now use to your advantage?

Presumably you have a business blueprint or outline *(business plan)* which covers all of your short, medium and long term goals and objectives etc. If so, this would be a good time to go over it to examine if there is anything here which you feel the public may be interested in, or which could be turned into an article.

By the way, this is not the time to be modest! When it comes to finding PR ideas to get your media coverage ball rolling you need to be ***OBJECTIVE***. You already ***KNOW*** if there are aspects that you and your company do differently, or ***EXCEL*** at, and it's these things we are looking for because they contain public interest.

> *Further more, as far as idea generation goes there is only one STUPID or silly idea, and that's the one you fail to WRITE down! If the idea came to you, presumably it came to you for a GOOD reason, and often ideas only stay in your conscious mind for just a few moments so it's up to you to capture them just as quickly as you can before they become lost, maybe forever!*

Q: What could you plan into your future business?

This is a great time to use your imagination and ask yourself what expansion ideas have appealed to you, or what have you dreamed about implementing into your business at some future point? Think ***BIG*** as this may create interesting ideas for public interest stories, especially if you start working towards achieving your dreams today.

Remember, we are just looking for a spark of an idea so have fun with this process, let your hair down and play full out as sparks of inspiration have the habit of developing into ideas, and ideas into news releases that convert into cash paying customers.

Notes:
Please use this margin for writing your ideas thoughts, inspirations and personal plan of action.

This Tutorial will then act as your route map to PR success!

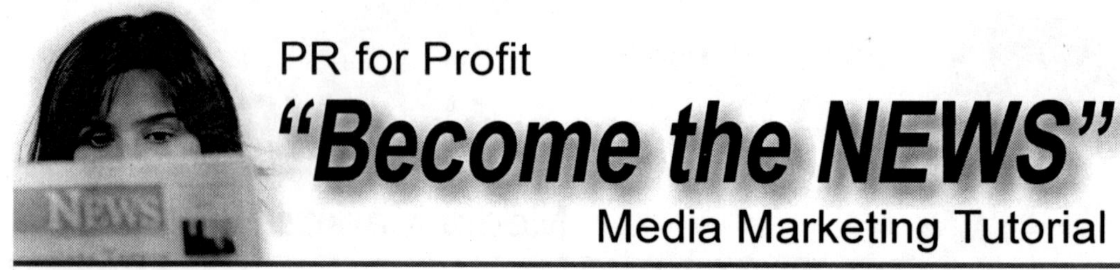

Notes:
Please use this margin for writing your ideas thoughts, inspirations and personal plan of action.

This Tutorial will then act as your route map to PR success!

Q: What are others in your industry doing?

Now this usually requires you to keep your eyes ***WIDE*** open to see what is going on, but I will be revealing an ***AMAZINGLY*** simple method for you to manage this process in just a few minutes or so per week. Knowing what is going on in your industry is ***REALLY*** important and you can learn a lot from being aware of what your competition is doing, and then quite often doing the very opposite.

Q: Development...

Are you planning any ***NEW*** products or services which a launch could be built around in the near future? Are you moving premises, building, expanding, making any major purchases or even planning to redecorate in the near future? Let's start building the idea list as all these have PR potential that we should consider...

Think about your products and services...

In your opinion what makes your products or services better than anyone elses? How do they differ and what makes them stand out? Price is important here, but quality and service are ***MORE*** important still. Is there anything you feel the public should or would like to know about your products or services?

Getting the idea?

Good, because now you have the idea of what we are looking for, below is a short bullet point list of questions for you to consider. These are ***FAR*** more difficult and answering them is likely to provide you with some powerful marketing insights.

List all of the benefits and features your company, service or product offers your target market. When you have listed them all, turn your attention to the features you have listed and convert them into benefits.

Notes:
Please use this margin for writing your ideas thoughts, inspirations and personal plan of action.

This Tutorial will then act as your route map to PR success!

Improve your USP *(Unique Selling Proposition)*. What are the ***SPECIFIC*** benefits that make your company, service or product a better purchase or investment than any similar in your market place? ...answer this from both your perspective and that of your potential target prospect.

1. Why would the public find your company, service or product interesting?
2. What is the ***SOLUTION*** you provide for your customers?
3. What are the things that your target market would like to know about your company, service or product?
4. What do you feel they should know, and be informed of concerning your business?
5. What are the long term implications of using your company, service or product?

How were they? Did you get some ideas? As well as providing some solid foundation for PR news release development, this exercise is ***LIKELY*** to highlight areas of weakness within your business, and others which need working on to take them into the next league and this action could be the very catalyst which generates your resulting PR ideas.

EVERYONE loves to get something of value for NOTHING...

"7 Profitable and FREE PR Tips That Will Make You Money"

As you are interested in learning and using PR within your business I am certain that this short and curiosity-raising headline grabbed your ***FULL*** attention.

This could have easily been the title of a simple and ***FREE*** report which would have delivered you to our 'PR for Profit' sales page, and would have been the catalyst for purchasing the material you are now reading.

Notes:
Please use this margin for writing your ideas thoughts, inspirations and personal plan of action.

This Tutorial will then act as your route map to PR success!

Most people just love free reports or tips booklets when the result is something that will make their life easier in some way. More importantly, giving something away that will provide a solution to a problem is ***ALWAYS*** a great way of gaining ***COMPELLING*** media exposure.

One of the reasons that they work so well is called reciprocity, which means if your information helped someone they may feel that they are in your debt, and this in turn means they are probably just a little bit more likely to become a customer if you have provided them with value. A much bigger and far longer lasting ***BENEFIT*** however, is the fact every time a prospect accepts your report etc, you have the opportunity to ***WOW*** the socks off them, and establish yourself or your company as an expert in your field.

Developing free reports, tips sheets and other easily produced incentives is an ***EXTREMELY*** powerful 'Direct Response' PR technique that I ***OFTEN*** use. I have dedicated a whole chapter to showing you exactly how you can create you own valuable giveaways to ***TURBO*** charge your PR campaign. At the moment however I feel that this is a good point at which to sow a few ***FERTILE SEEDS*** in your mind to germinate, so you start thinking about ideas and possible titles for such products for yourself.

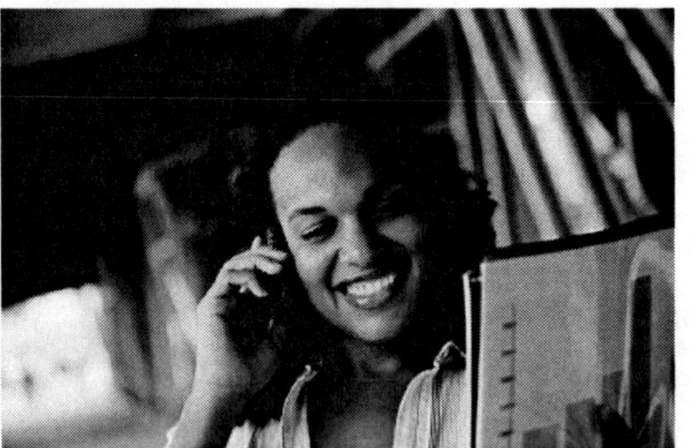

Action task...

Using the margin to record your ideas and consider creating a simple three or four page report of your own which offers, for example, 10 tips, or say '13 uses' for your product or service.

Notes:
Please use this margin for writing your ideas thoughts, inspirations and personal plan of action.

This Tutorial will then act as your route map to PR success!

If you would like to see one of the incentive reports which I created to promote this PR tutorial you can follow the link below. This particular one only took a few hours to prepare, and is responsible for attracting ***THOUSANDS*** of people to our web sites and building a ***VERY*** valuable mailing list ...you can download this one right now by going to:
www.pr-forprofit.com/report-thanks.htm

If you would like to see another example which is a little longer, below is another link to a report which I wrote on 'Web Site Profitability' called ***'JUMPSTART'*** and which has been ***HIGHLY SUCCESSFUL*** and more than served the purpose for which it was intended. You can download this report at:
www.pr-forprofit.com/jumpstart.htm

A good way of coming up with ideas for a report or tip sheet is to first write down your objective, know ***EXACTLY*** what you want this short report to achieve for you and then think of a headline as this is what will attract your potential prospects. Without over sensationalising, try to create an accurate and attractive headline which is compelling. Below I have given you 3 basic examples which will act as good template to build your ideas around.

- 9 ways to double your income in just 3 months!
- 7 things you ***ALWAYS*** wanted to know about [your product]!
- 11 quick and simple tips for [your service]!

Remember: reports and tip sheets are quick and simple to produce and have a VERY high perceived value, and can be used to attract new custom and also build an EXTREMELY valuable mailing list which will go on paying you for years to come.

Notes:
Please use this margin for writing your ideas thoughts, inspirations and personal plan of action.

This Tutorial will then act as your route map to PR success!

Now try coming up with 10 headline titles and report ideas of your own, and I promise you one of them, when you have read the chapter on creating products, will create a ***FIRST CLASS*** news article which you be able to use to attract a ***TSUNAMI*** sized wave of new interest.

Fast and EFFECTIVE research using the INTERNET

At the end of this section I am going to show you how to use the Internet to find a wealth of information, inspiration and an unlimited source of very relevant and usable PR ideas. Most people already know how to use the basic search engine functionality on Google or other search engines to find what they are looking for. However, and similar to an iceberg where you can only see the top 10% of its mass protruding above the water line, 90% of Google's ***POWER*** and functionality is generally left ***COMPLETELY*** unutilised and ***TOTALLY*** unexplored.

For this reason I am going to show you a few ***SIMPLE*** tricks and techniques that will forever change the way in which you use search engines and search the Internet. You are about to discover that a ***LITTLE*** research goes a ***LONG*** way, and that you will find a volume of quality ideas when you know where to look and search for them.

However, before we get to that point we are going to look at some ***VERY*** novel and ***FUN*** ideas for your PR news releases that will almost certainly bring you a ***HUGE*** amount of interest. You can also use the internet to search for similar ideas on the same general theme, however, I have given you many links to explore immediately and as an example of how easy it is to come up with such ideas.

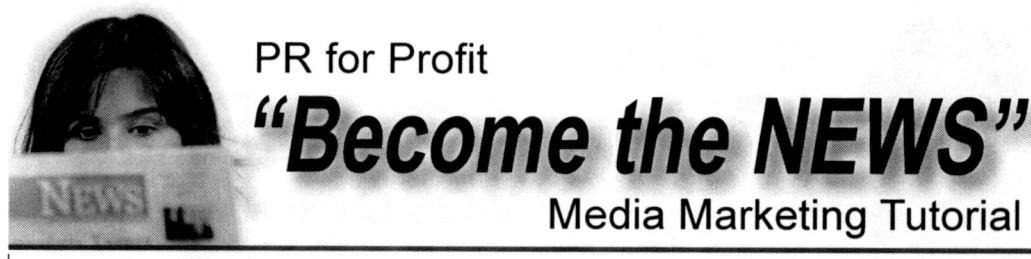

These suggestions won't be for everyone, as some of them are quite extreme and off the wall. However, if you have a fun or extrovert personality, having a good time with these ideas will certainly reinforce your reputation for enjoying the unusual and being a colourful character. If you have a more conservative nature you will still find a ***LOT*** of related ideas that you could use which will fit your ***SPECIFIC*** line of business, product or service as well as a made-to-measure glove!

Notes:
Please use this margin for writing your ideas thoughts, inspirations and personal plan of action.

This Tutorial will then act as your route map to PR success!

Going that EXTRA yard is REALLY worth it...

Take your time and have fun with the following ideas and you will soon discover you have one ***MASSIVE*** benefit and that is you will have little or no competition!

Hold SPECIAL fun days!

These could be virtually anything that the public and media would find interesting or which would add a bit of colour to your working day; and if they also lend themselves to a good photograph even better, as often a good picture can say a thousand words you simply wouldn't have the space for. Use the links I have provided below and on the resource page which accompany this material, and you will be spoilt for choice, and also, as I was, quite ***AMAZED*** that virtually every day of the year, and certainly every week has been designated for celebrating or remembering ***SOMETHING,*** or to mark and make you ***AWARE*** of a particularly ***GOOD*** cause!

Pick unusual and controversial topics that you believe are worthwhile and will enjoy having ***FUN*** with. Below are a few ideas I have just invented for such special days which you may wish to consider and could ignite your interest, all, without exception, correctly presented would lend themselves to the creation of ***GREAT*** PR articles. You can keep such an event confined to your business, or ask other local companies to become involved and turn it into a much larger occasion.

Notes:
Please use this margin for writing your ideas thoughts, inspirations and personal plan of action.

This Tutorial will then act as your route map to PR success!

"Countdown to spring" – Do you ever get the winter blues and are totally fed up with steel grey skies and dull weather? If so, you're not the only one, so take heart as by the time February arrives we are only a few weeks away from the start of ***SPRING***! So ***WHY NOT*** celebrate this fact by using some creativity to generate a ***REALLY*** newsworthy and fun day which will capture the attention of the press and media.

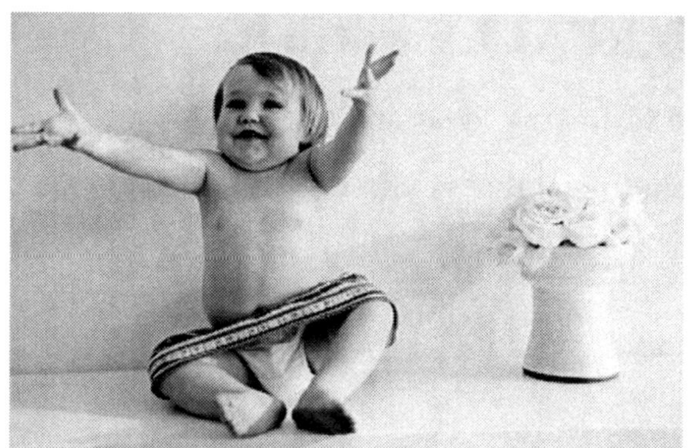

"Smile as much as possible day" - Have you ever heard it said that a smile is a curve that can straighten out many problems in life? – well it can! Wherever you live people ***NEVER*** smile enough, so why not have some fun with this fact and make a ***LOT*** of people happy by generating an idea which is related to your business, and ***WILL*** make people smile, I think the media will find this ***IRRESISTIBLE!***

"Appreciate your customer day" – As a rule, we could do much more to deserve and retain the loyalty of our customers. So start thinking up ways that you could ***WOW*** the socks of yours.

How about sending them all a personalised letter, card or emails simple saying that you appreciate their custom, and ask them if there is any way that they feel you could ***IMPROVE*** the service you offer them right now!
(Light blue touch paper at arms length and stand well back!)

There are dozens of way you could turn this into some EXCELLENT five star PR...

Notes:
Please use this margin for writing your ideas thoughts, inspirations and personal plan of action.

This Tutorial will then act as your route map to PR success!

"Donald Duck's Birthday" – Now here is a fun opportunity to get really silly and give people a good giggle. Put your imagination into top gear and come up with ten things you could do to make this day of interest to the media? It ***REALLY*** won't be difficult to turn this into a ***BIG*** winner for you. By the way I just Googled it and his official birthday is: June 9th 1934 which makes him 75 years old this year.

Half past Christmas day – Do you think people would possibly notice if they saw your staff walking around in a Santa suit on a warm 25c degree sunny summer's afternoon? The reason could be that you could be starting your Christmas sale early this year, or you could find a whole multitude of ***GREAT*** ideas to generate a first rate news release from.

Well there you have just five half decent possibilities which took just a few moments to come up with; how many could you come up with if you thought about it regularly? Let me answer that for you: more ideas than you could ever use, so why not give this a try and have some fun while generating your high effective media exposure.

Here's what I found by searching on the internet...

I have just spent 20 minutes searching on the Internet for ideas for PR articles and almost drowned as there are that many. What follows are a few of the rich mines of ideas which you may choose to investigate further.

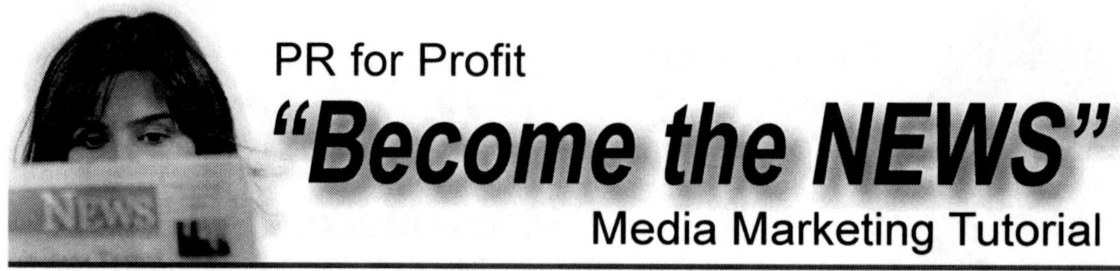

Notes:
Please use this margin for writing your ideas thoughts, inspirations and personal plan of action.

This Tutorial will then act as your route map to PR success!

What happened on this day in the past?

Now as I am writing this particular paragraph it is the 26th of February and with just a few minutes research on the Internet I have discovered that on this same day in the past it was the birthday of:

- Victor Hugo
- Johnny Cash
- Levi Strauss
- Fats Domino
- Buffalo Bill

Do you think that you could use this information to create a news release? I know I could and I am sure with just a little thought you could also see that the possibilities are many.

Also on this day:

- 1848: Karl Marx publishes the "Communist Manifesto" in London.
- 1919: The Grand Canyon is established as a national park.
- 1984: US troops withdraw from Beirut
- 1987: The Church of England's in favour of the ordination of women priests.

I can also see a couple of very interesting articles coming out of the above happenings. However ***TOMORROW*** would provide a ***GEM*** of a story which I could exploit in ***MANY*** different ways, here is what I discovered:

"Kissing Friday (the Friday after Ash Wednesday)...

On this Friday of Shrove Week, English schoolboys were once entitled to kiss girls without fear of punishment or rejection, a custom that lasted until at least the 1940s."

Finding such information is really not difficult...

Just to highlight this fact below are seven celebration day examples which I grabbed from the site link below under their month of January listings. You can see ***HUNDREDS*** more similar ideas by visiting:
http://www.louderbacks.com/home/dict/days.html

With a touch of your new found creativity, and presented correctly, I think you will find all of these examples have the potential to make ***VERY*** news worthy articles and keep your company in the news as well as getting press photographers knocking on your door for a photo quicker than you can say Jack Robinson.

7th January: Harlem Globetrotters Day – Whether you like basketball or not very few people are unaware of the Harlem Globe Trotters, so regardless of colour or race just imagine the office turning up as the favourite player of the past.

10th January: Peculiar People Day – Now we all know a few of these. So whether you decide to dress up and imitate one of our more notorious personalities from history or just be that character is up to you.

15th January: Hat Day – This is a great one for the ladies although it's a little more challenging for the men. Hats get noticed and make for ***GREAT*** photo opportunities.

18th January: Winnie the Pooh Day – Here is a ***FANTASTIC*** theme to link in with your favourite children's causes. Dress as Pooh, or one of his friends, or get the local children to so, or even turn the day into a teddy bears picnic and provide honey sandwiches, and I think you will be on to a winner!

Notes:
Please use this margin for writing your ideas thoughts, inspirations and personal plan of action.

This Tutorial will then act as your route map to PR success!

Notes:
Please use this margin for writing your ideas thoughts, inspirations and personal plan of action.

This Tutorial will then act as your route map to PR success!

21st January: National Hugging Day – It's funny how a hug lowers barriers and builds friendships and makes you feel great. *(Please ensure that the huggee is compliant as a punch in the mouth often offends!)*

25th January: Opposite Day – This one is really off the wall and something you could have real fun with. Just do everything backwards or the opposite to how you normally do them.

26th January: Australia Day – Now here is one I could take a particular fancy to. I can just see myself arriving at work as a swagman with corks hanging around my hat. Then having a barbi *(BBQ)* and a few cold tinnies *(Cans of larger)* to relax with after work.

Research Web sites

You will find a list of resources web sites which are kept current in the member resource area.

Local media just love local charity stories...

When you do something for your local area and adopt a community spirited attitude you immediately open yourself to the opportunity of receiving huge amounts of publicity and media exposure. If your local community are also your main source of customers this is the very place where you should get started on your PR campaign and be seen to be giving back and becoming involved as much as possible.

Being seen to be community spirited doesn't mean you have to give a penny in cash unless you wish to do so. It's simply a case of becoming ***ACTIVE*** in your area by supporting the local needy cause.

Action task...

Notes:
Please use this margin for writing your ideas thoughts, inspirations and personal plan of action.

This Tutorial will then act as your route map to PR success!

Make a list of ideas and ways in which you or your company could help:

- Old people's homes
- Toddlers groups and nurseries
- RSPCA
- Charity shops
- Emergency services
- Local schools
- Local produce

What do they want and what do they need? Ask them what they are trying to achieve. Remember you don't have to do it all yourself, you can organise other people to become involved and still get the majority of the publicity as the person or organisation which took the incentive and got the action started.

It's exactly the same associating yourself with a charity; they are always keen on attracting ***HIGH PROFILE*** exposure and publicity for their cause and of course they are always grateful for help with fund raising, and you can do virtually anything that you wish on your own terms so long as you both profit from the experience.

Notes:
Please use this margin for writing your ideas thoughts, inspirations and personal plan of action.

This Tutorial will then act as your route map to PR success!

TWO MORE rather UNUSUAL processes for generating PR ideas...

Experiment with doing things DIFFERENTLY...

A few years ago I attended a seminar where the main speaker said that 'humans are creatures of habit, and we are at our ***HAPPIEST*** when we are doing things with which we have become comfortable and familiar'. He went on to deliver a few interesting facts, the first being that the more successful business people and entrepreneurs in our society are generally the ones who embrace and adapt to change the quickest.

However, at the very pinnacle of achievement, the most successful of all are those who constantly test and experiment with their actions by stepping out of their comfort zones and finding new and possibly better ways of doing things.

Now this really made sense to me and inspired my imagination, so I decided to do a little testing and experimenting of my own by every day committing to doing ***AT LEAST*** one thing in a different way to normal. Now in the beginning these were mostly small actions such as cleaning my teeth with my left hand rather than my right, or driving a different route to my destination etc. Right from the start I found the process an interesting and fun experience, and I ***DID*** find lasting improvements that I am still using today.

However, as my confidence grew I also experimented with the way in which I conducted my business, and by doing so discovered ***TWO*** actions that increased my productivity by at least two or three times.

Notes:
Please use this margin for writing your ideas thoughts, inspirations and personal plan of action.

This Tutorial will then act as your route map to PR success!

WOW! Now let's put that into perspective... That's a 100% - 200% improvement from two simple changes! Although on this occasion *(for personal reasons)* I never used these discoveries for PR purposes, they in fact would have made ***EXCELLENT*** PR articles.

Now you have probably ALREADY guessed what is coming next?

So what would happen if ***YOU*** started experimenting with the way in which you do things in your company? Perhaps the way in which you deliver your service or sell your products?

I am willing to bet that if you experimented with ***JUST ONE*** new action every week you will not only find ***IMPROVED*** ways and methods of operating your business, but also discover some real PR ***GEM*** ideas. Often, controversial subjects heavily laced with public interest, will result in the development of ***HIGH*** quality articles which may attract volumes of new qualified prospects to your company.

There is one thing I can say for certain, and that is: if you don't try it you will ***NEVER*** know what ***COULD*** have happened or emerged from this ***FUN*** exercise! In the same way as I did, you also could discover an improvement which may make your life ***MUCH*** easier and ***VERY*** much more profitable, as well as striking some PR nuggets. Commit to giving it a go for a few weeks and just see what happens, you have ***NOTHING*** to lose – but ***EVERYTHING*** to gain!

This is a 'Thinking Outside of the Box' type exercise and if there are others who are involved in your business why not include them also by inviting them to have fun with this simple but ***VERY*** obvious idea. As the old saying goes, "two heads are better than one, and three heads are better then two" ...and so on!

Notes:
Please use this margin for writing your ideas thoughts, inspirations and personal plan of action.

This Tutorial will then act as your route map to PR success!

Just experiment; I think I am fairly safe in saying that once tried, this is the type of activity which will become a regular feature in your creativity process.

Here is yet another UNUSUAL method to add to your collection...

A few years ago I ran and facilitated a number of creativity workshops, and one ***FUN*** item became a ***BIG*** hit with the delegates and resulted in the generation of some ***VERY*** good and ***HIGHLY*** profitable ideas. This process would also work well for generating a profusion of quality PR material.

It works work best with a larger group of people from 6 – 20. Just in case your volunteers are unfamiliar with your business, or what you are trying to achieve, you will need to give them a quick verbal tour and outline. I would also suggest that you either video or audio record the entire session and you will understand why I suggest this in just a moment.

Next, and as fast as possible to make answers spontaneous, move from person to person and ***ALWAYS*** ask the following question: "What would happen if?" Then they complete the sentence with an answer of their choosing, and their response can be ***ANYTHING*** from the obvious, to the creative or the ***TOTALLY CRAZY,*** so your session may go something like this.

1. **What would happen if?** - You let your customers name the price they are willing to pay.
2. **What would happen if?** – You asked you prospects how, from their perspective, you would improve your product or service.
3. **What would happen if?** – You doubled the price of your service.
4. **What would happen if?** – You only worked two days a week.
5. **What would happen if?** – You gave your services for nothing and asked for donations instead.
6. **What would happen if?** – You let your prospects try your product or service before they purchased.

Notes:
Please use this margin for writing your ideas thoughts, inspirations and personal plan of action.

This Tutorial will then act as your route map to PR success!

I am sure you have got the idea!

Keep this going as long as your group can keep coming up with spontaneous and original replies. Then the ***FUN*** really starts as you listen to the recording and either capture their questions on paper for later consideration, or answer them directly. Now I promise you that most of these questions they have given you will be rubbish and offer no usable results. However, you will also get some really strange and quirky answers, and perhaps a ***FEW*** really inspired ones, which will be ***PURE PLATINUM!***

Let's use that first answer as an example:

You let your custumer's name the price they are willing to pay. Well what would happen if you did this for a limited period of time, perhaps a day? Now you didn't say you were going to let your products or services go for silly money, or at a loss. Only that they tell you ***WHAT*** price they are prepared to pay, and perhaps you could find out ***WHY*** this price, and not more or less, or even what they consider ***WOULD*** make it more valuable to them. You could not put a price on this type of ***VALUABLE*** information and feedback from paying customers.

It would also make an EXCELLENT PR news release...

On the following page is a rapidly drafted headline and first paragraph which I believe would immediately capture the attention of the press and media and start your phone ringing with excitement.

Notes:
Please use this margin for writing your ideas thoughts, inspirations and personal plan of action.

This Tutorial will then act as your route map to PR success!

"The Recession is not all bad news!"

To combat the ongoing credit crunch a local and forward looking company had decided to apply a unique and novel twist by offering their customers the opportunity to tell them the price they are prepared to pay for their services...

Watching the HEADLINES...

When I first started producing my own PR I soon discovered that there was a very distinct lack of educational material from which a beginner such as I could learn about it. For that reason I had to learn alone and it seemed that the obvious place to get started was by studying exactly what was already working successfully in my local news paper, and then trying to reproduce their style of article.

This was really great fun, and by studying and 'reverse-engineering', what I believed to be the better news articles, I slowly started to recognise, and then reproduce what I thought the press were looking for, and therefore how I should write my news releases. I cut out all the articles which were similar in style and technique to what I was trying to write, and later *(after a little research)* realised that these in general were the articles which had been produced by PR agencies and consultants, so I knew I was on the right track.

However, and far more importantly were the ideas that reading the newspapers and magazines with an open mind, generated for me. As I scanned the papers it was the headlines which would catch my attention first, and I realised that if the headline worked for me, it would probably work on other people also;

so I started experimenting by altering them to work and fit into my own news releases and was impressed by the results.

Scanning local papers for ideas is ***STILL*** to this day an ***EXCELLENT*** way of gaining and recycling ideas which have proved to be a success, as well as getting a good feel for what your local paper wants and the type of news *(if any)* they favour publishing. So I suggest that you spend a little time every week researching the publications in which you are most interested.

Action Task...

Locate a regular source of old news papers *(no need to buy)* them both local and national. Then every few weeks take an hour or so to study them carefully to increase your feel and understanding of what works, and also what doesn't. You ***DON'T*** need to read everything, but rather only that which is relevant to you.

So begin by ***SCANNING*** the headlines and see if any capture your attention. When you spot something interesting, either highlight the article with a highlighting pen, or, cut it out of the publication for future reference. Study it carefully and learn what makes it work. Ask yourself how you could use this article idea, and how you could alter or even improve upon it for your own news release. By doing this your PR skills will expand and grow considerably.

Remember to have a pen and pad at your side and write brief outlines of the ideas which come to you for your own PR; make them expansive enough that the next time you read them you will still fully understand them.
After a little practice your speed will increase to the point where you can scan the relevant areas of the publication in just a few minutes, and a whole armful of old newspapers in just an hour or so.

Notes:
Please use this margin for writing your ideas thoughts, inspirations and personal plan of action.

This Tutorial will then act as your route map to PR success!

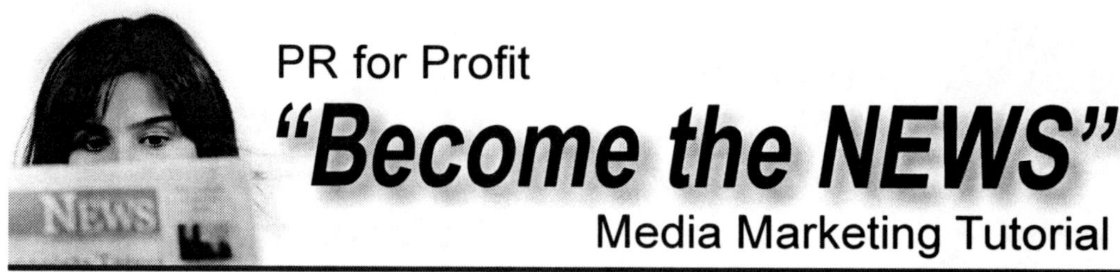

Notes:
Please use this margin for writing your ideas thoughts, inspirations and personal plan of action.

This Tutorial will then act as your route map to PR success!

Just the HEADlines...

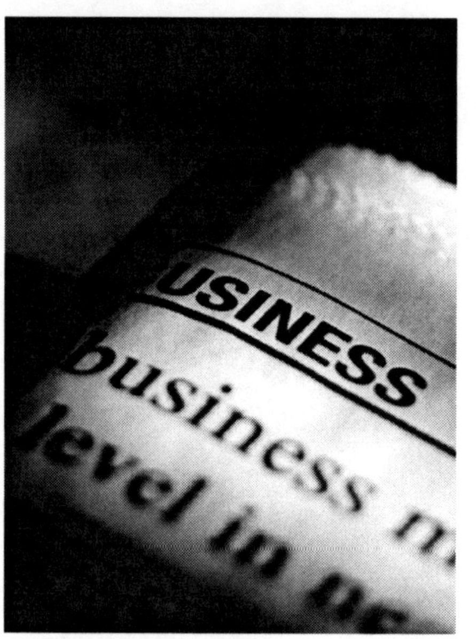

At this point in time, I am most interested in just reading the major headline stories to discover if there is anyway I can use or tap into these hot topics and the news items. As 'Stock Market' education is the theme of one of my main websites, watching and staying current with the headlines, and the specific stories related to the present economic climate, and the credit crunch is providing me with ***VOLUMES*** of very ***USABLE*** ideas, which are proving exceptionally profitable. The same may apply to your theme or line of business.

To read the main headlines I used to have to race out and buy a newspaper, but not anymore, as all of the headlines are delivered to my computer desktop totally free of charge, and are ***INSTANTLY*** updated, or appear on my screen within minutes of happening. We now have an exceptionally ***WIDE*** variety of free and competing news services from which we can pick. I use "Yahoo" for no particular reason other than this service is the one which was provided by my ISP *(Internet Service Provider)* BT, *(British Telecom)*, and is a quality service which I have become used to and familiar with.

Notes:
Please use this margin for writing your ideas thoughts, inspirations and personal plan of action.

This Tutorial will then act as your route map to PR success!

As you can see from the above screen-grab of one of the panels, it provides me with all the top and breaking headlines in just one compact panel. I can see everything I need at a glance, and then just click on it to expand and read the full story if I wish; I can also see larger pictures, and accompanying video clips.

What I find particularly convenient about the "BT Yahoo" interface at: http://home.bt.yahoo.com is that it gives me a ***RANGE*** of ***HUGELY*** versatile and personalise-able news tools in ***JUST ONE*** place. 'Yahoo' also allow me to bring all my favourite 'RSS' feeds to the same page and read them from there. Now if the terms 'RSS' or 'News Reader' are alien to you, don't worry as I am about to reveal all, and 'RSS' and 'News Readers' are about to become your newest best friends, and an amazing source of high quality information and inspiration.

This powerful interface allows me to stay up-to-date with all the latest information which is relevant to me. I am sure there are many other services which offer a similar service of equal quality; I have listed a few which you may want to explore below and will keep them current on the resource website.

http://news.yahoo.com
http://www.cnn.com
http://news.bbc.co.uk
http://news.google.com
http://www.foxnews.com
http://abcnews.go.com

Notes:
Please use this margin for writing your ideas thoughts, inspirations and personal plan of action.

This Tutorial will then act as your route map to PR success!

The SWIPE File...

This is a very opportune time to introduce you to another new term 'Swipe File'; the name, I think, is American and I was using one long before I ever heard this term mentioned. Basically a 'Swipe File' is your own collection of what you believe to be successful cuttings of PR articles etc, or PR techniques and examples to which you can refer as and when you need inspiration, or to generate ideas.

Over the years I have collected a number of quite extensive 'Swipe Files' on different subjects such as copywriting and writing headlines. Years ago I realised that there was a ***PRICELESS*** ongoing copywriting education literally dropping through my letter box virtually every morning. I am referring to what usual recipients of such correspondence may refer to as 'Junk Mail'; to me it was a way of generating an income! Much of what arrived had been written by some of the World's top copywriters, who regularly held seminars which would cost thousands to attend as a delegate, and here was their very best material being conveniently delivered directly to my home for me to study - and I was ***VERY*** grateful!

I used newspapers, magazines and trade journals in very much the same way and soon I possessed a number of very messy boxes and loose folders of cuttings, and different 'Swipe Files'.

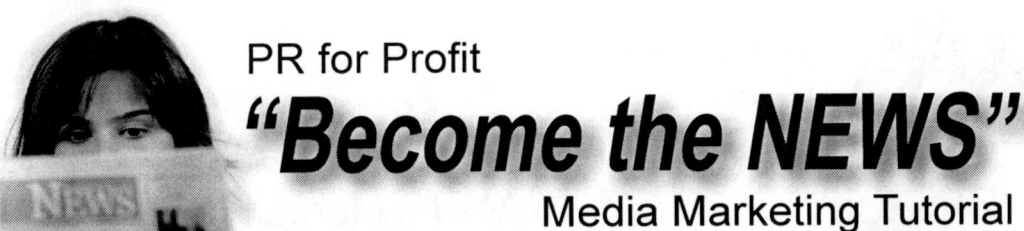

This CONSTANTLY growing fire hazard did not please my wife...

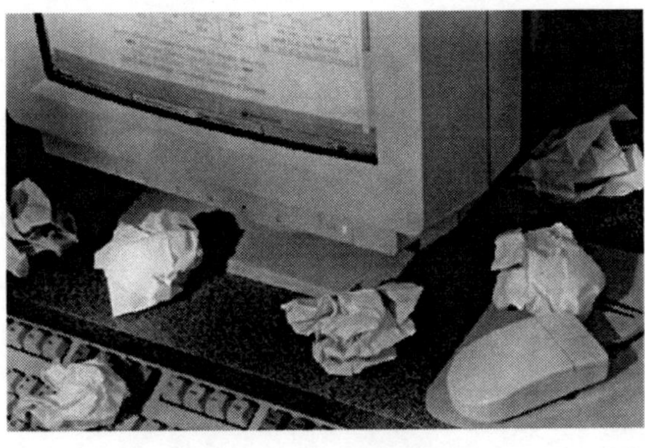

Although 'Swipe Files' are a ***VERY*** valuable and necessary asset for the serious student of PR or copywriting to possess, they were, and still are ***EXCEPTIONALLY*** awkward to store effectively as they mainly consist of loose cuttings and ripped out pages. Neither were they simple to search through or index and as a result I would have small piles of them which I was using or referring to, scattered untidily across my desk; many others could be found lying carelessly around my office. In the early days I referred to them so often, it was difficult to keep my office tidy, and definitely ***NOT*** the way my wife would like to have seen it kept! First time visitors to my working environment would be forgiven for thinking that a small, but powerful ***TORNADO*** had just blown through the place moments earlier.

In frustration, my wife took ***DECISIVE*** action by photocopying and organising my clipping collection. She placed as many as possible on one page, indexed them into strong and thick 4D ring lever arch files which made everything much easier, and kept the office tidy. In just a few years I had collected ***DOZENS*** of such volumes.

Notes:
Please use this margin for writing your ideas thoughts, inspirations and personal plan of action.

This Tutorial will then act as your route map to PR success!

Notes:
Please use this margin for writing your ideas thoughts, inspirations and personal plan of action.

This Tutorial will then act as your route map to PR success!

Then Came the digital scanner...

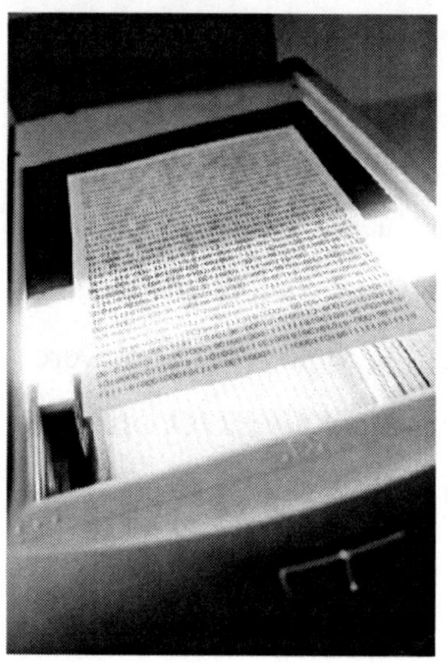

In the mid nineties I invested in an image scanner which made our old photocopier fondly named 'Old Inky' for the toner it generously shared with all users and some passers by, totally redundant. Inspired by this revolutionary new technology my wife started working again on the ***MAMMOTH*** task of scanning and indexing my ***NOW*** considerable volume of 'Swipe Files'.

To make referencing simple I had a second monitor fitted to my computer which allowed me to search my 'Swipe Files', and then display the articles I was studying and had borrowed ideas from on one screen, whilst using my word processor to write on the other. I certainly think that a digitised 'Swipe File' is the best way to go as I can keep ***EVERYTHING*** that I have collected neatly stored on the hard drive of my laptop, and then take it with me wherever I travel and refer to it at will.

An ESSENTIAL piece of software...

Nowadays 98% of my searching is done on line and I have discovered what I believe to be the ideal tool to maintain and build a digitised 'Swipe File'.

It's called 'Snag It' and you can find a link to the very latest version of this software in the resource pages which accompany this material. We are now on version 9 as it just keeps getting better and so there may be a higher version available when you read this. *(At the time of writing they offer a 30 day FREE trial of this software).*

Notes:
Please use this margin for writing your ideas thoughts, inspirations and personal plan of action.

This Tutorial will then act as your route map to PR success!

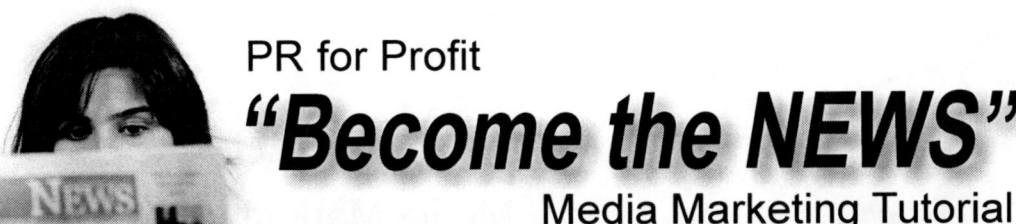

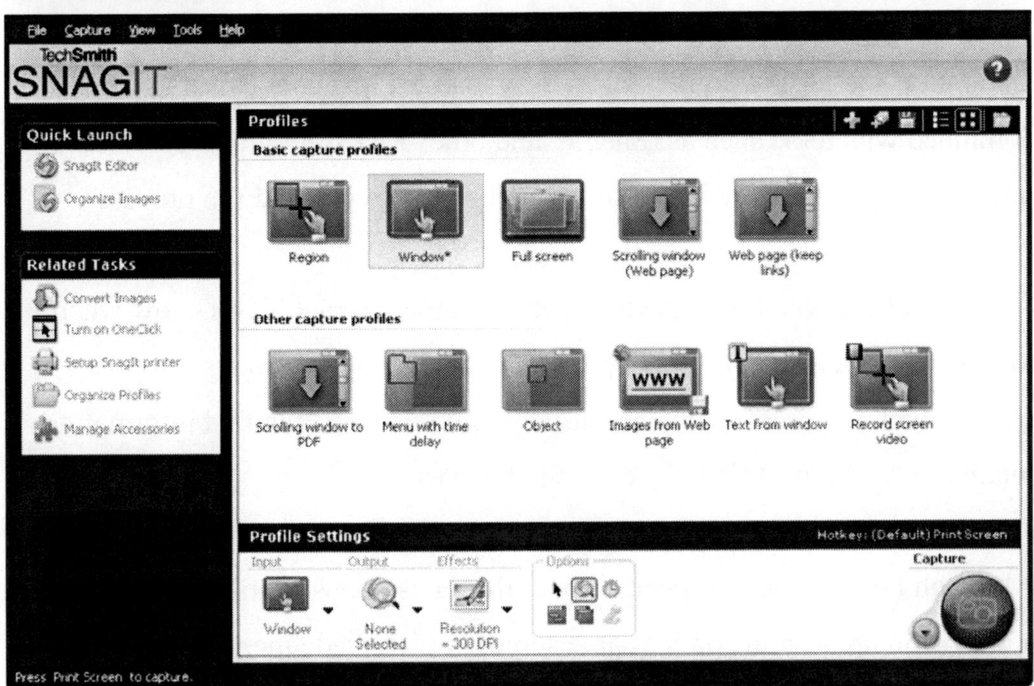

As you can see 'Snag It' is a simple and quick to use application for capturing virtually anything you see on your computer monitor. In fact, many of the illustrations you see in this tutorial have been captured using 'Snag It', including the one above of the 'Snag It' capture screen.

It can also be used to store and organise the images which you capture as well as editing and embellishing them in a variety of ways if you so desire. I use 'Snag It' to highlight paragraphs of text on my screen-grabs, or add notes and my own ideas directly to them.

'Snag It' has become one of my very favourite software tools as it makes collecting and storing PR ideas quick, fun and effective. To learn more about this useful software go to: www.techsmith.com

To conclude this section of 'PR for Profits' which we have called 'Idea Mining', I would now like to show you how you can find a ***WEALTH*** of PR ideas from searching the Internet at any time of the day or night you choose, because remember it's always open 24/7, 365 days a year.

Notes:
Please use this margin for writing your ideas thoughts, inspirations and personal plan of action.

This Tutorial will then act as your route map to PR success!

Using the Internet has certainly become my favourite way of gaining inspiration and ideas simply because it is so quick and convenient to use. When combined with tools such as 'Snag it' and other ***FREE*** programs I will be introducing you to shortly, it becomes a highly effective and fun process.

A wealth of ideas can **ALWAYS** be found on the Internet if you know where to look. Unfortunately, most people don't and for that reason tend to give up easily which is a great shame because it is said that you can find information relating to virtually ***ANY*** subject on the Internet.

Although I can't be more specific about the dates, a few years ago I watched a television programme on the same subject which made the very same claim; this was back in the days when the Internet was still being referred to as the 'Information Super Highway'. To prove this point a ***PROFESSIONAL RESEARCHER*** looked for the specific information needed to build a nuclear explosive device! ***AMAZINGLY***, all of the necessary and required information was ***QUICKLY*** found using the internet and he **DID** indeed possess all of the knowledge he needed to become a **ONE MAN** super power. **FRIGHTENING!**

With this in mind, finding inspiration for PR articles and relevant supporting information for you to write quality news stories should not be difficult, in fact I am living proof that it is not.

Now an entire book could be dedicated to the subject of searching for information on the internet. However, a little knowledge can go a very long way and make a **REALLY BIG** difference to the results you are likely to return. So what follows will put you **LIGHT YEARS** ahead of 97% of the people who use the Internet as well as making it a whole lot more fun.

Notes:
Please use this margin for writing your ideas thoughts, inspirations and personal plan of action.

This Tutorial will then act as your route map to PR success!

Which search engine should you use?

Now this section could date in the future and so you will need to use the information that you are about to learn to keep your knowledge current. I would like to start by examining four terms which are **HIGHLY** relevant to this subject and which you will find useful when searching or surfing on the Internet:

- Directories
- PPC (Pay per click)
- Search engines
- Meta search engines

Let's take them one at a time...

Directories...

A little like the yellow pages directories which you will find in most countries, Internet directories are generally filled to bursting point with relevant entries for your search term, and often results which are ***NOT*** so relevant. You see the motivation for offering listings in a directory is usually financial which nearly always compromises integrity.

The top directories which are most used by Internet surfers charge a fee just to get a listing, often regardless of the relevancy of what advertisers have on offer. At the time of writing the cost for one year's ***BRIEF*** entry in the Yahoo directory is $299 which tells you there is '***GOLD*** in them ***THAR*** hills!' For that reason, I only use directories for searching as a **VERY** last resort, and you will discover the reason why very soon.

Notes:
Please use this margin for writing your ideas thoughts, inspirations and personal plan of action.

This Tutorial will then act as your route map to PR success!

PPC – 'Pay Per Click'...

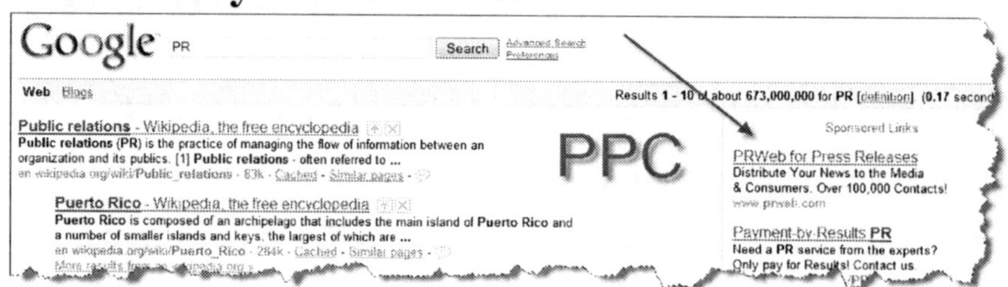

Most people familiar with the Internet, and search engines in general, have seen these mini-advertisements cleverly placed to catch your eye. As you can see, they generally appear on the right hand side of the SERPs *(Search Engine Result Pages)*. If your search term is a popular one with financial implications you may be returned as many as 8 or 10 PPC advertisements per page.

If it's not such a popular term there may only be one or two PPC adverts present, or even none at all. So the first thing we can learn from PPC is that it gives us a ***VERY*** good indication as to the popularity of the subject and search term you are using. This in turn may also give us a suggestion of the level of interest which may be shown in a news article on the same specific subject.

PPC advertisements are one of the means by which the search engines generate their revenue. You will also see them situated on some website pages.

They can be identified easily as they always carry a heading of either **'Sponsored Links'** as on this example, or, **'AdWords by Google'**

Notes:
Please use this margin for writing your ideas thoughts, inspirations and personal plan of action.

This Tutorial will then act as your route map to PR success!

As the name implies every time these short and direct adverts are clicked upon there is a cost for the privilege of doing so, but don't worry, it's not you who has to pay it!

It's the advertiser who uses the PPC system to generate a flow of traffic to their website in the hope that a proportion of visitors will convert into paying customers.

Generally, the higher the position of the PPC listing on the SERPs page, the higher the cost per individual click also, and some of the more popular search terms can cost $5 or $10 ***PER CLICK***. A few, such as the search term 'Mortgages', which obviously have ***HIGH*** earning potential associated to them, can cost as much as $25 ***PER CLICK***.

As far as using PPC ads for research is concerned, and as they only offer the advertisers a minimal amount of space to capture the attention of surfers, they tend to be quite accurate and highly focused, and from a research perspective can return some very specific search results.

However, there is one moral problem now that you know how 'Pay Per Click 'works, and that is this: is it fair to cost the PPC advertiser money by clicking upon their links when ***YOUR ONLY*** interest is that of research for your own PR ideas?

I have never felt comfortable with this fact so I am going to show you how you can get to their website and the information you need without it costing them a penny.

Notes:
Please use this margin for writing your ideas thoughts, inspirations and personal plan of action.

This Tutorial will then act as your route map to PR success!

This is what you do...

With your mouse '***RIGHT CLICK***' on the AdWord of your interest, and a dropdown box offering you many options will appear; select the **'Copy Link Location'** choice which will copy this information to your computer's 'Clip Board'

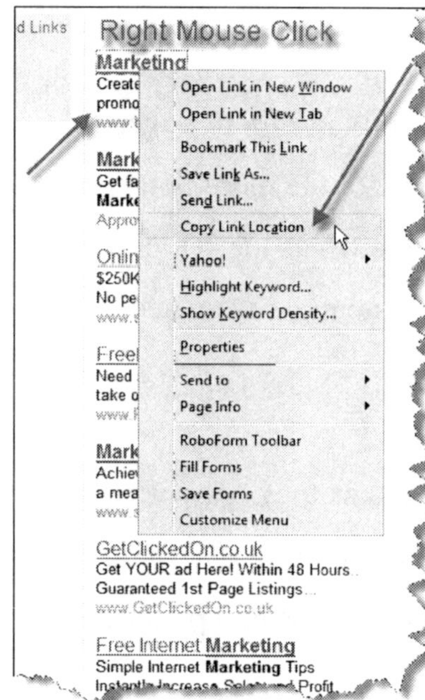

Then place your mouse cursor in the address bar of your Internet browser and '***RIGHT CLICK***' once again and another drop down selection box will appear. This time click on **'Paste'** link, or if you are already an experienced PC user you will know that you can use the shortcut commands 'Ctrl C' and 'Ctrl V' to achieve the same outcome!

This will paste the exact destination URL *(website address)* details into the address bar for you and all you have to do is hit the enter key on your keyboard to navigate to this site without it costing the website owner a penny in advertising charges. It only takes a second to do this, so if you are using the PPC link for research purposes this is a good and ***VERY FAIR*** habit to develop.

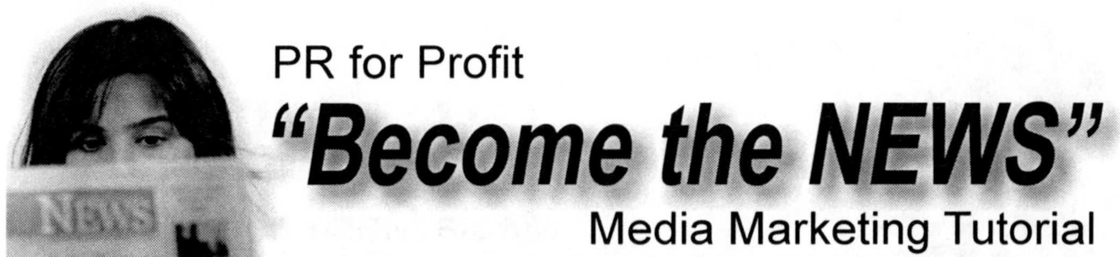

Notes:
Please use this margin for writing your ideas thoughts, inspirations and personal plan of action.

This Tutorial will then act as your route map to PR success!

Search engines...

I wanted to explain PPC to you before we got to search engines so you would understand that most ***MAJOR*** search engines provide both free and paid listings. The free listings are generally on the left hand side of the page which the ***SERPs*** *(Search Engine Result Pages)* are returned upon.

Depending upon the search term you are using there could be ***THOUSANDS*** of pages indexed in the search engine's database that use that keyword or keywords phrase. ***GENERALLY***, the more relevant the website to your search term, the higher they are likely to rank in the search engines ***FREE*** listing.

As someone who has spent many years studying and practising ***SEO*** *(Search Engine Optimisation)* from the web developers point of view, please believe me when I tell you that gaining and then maintaining a ***PAGE ONE*** listing in a major search engine with a competitive keyword phrase, is not an easy thing to achieve.

The search engine algorithms can't be fooled and for that reason the only certain way to achieve a first page listing is to put in the necessary ***HARD WORK*** by providing ***EXCELLENT*** user-friendly content upon your website, and ***EXACTLY*** what your visitors are looking for.

The reason that I have explained all of this for you is so you understand that the free search engine listings will ***NEARLY ALWAYS*** return the best quality search results for you and you will understand ***EXACTLY*** why in just a moment as we go into far more depth.

Notes:
Please use this margin for writing your ideas thoughts, inspirations and personal plan of action.

This Tutorial will then act as your route map to PR success!

Meta search engines...

Unlike the traditional search engines which are constantly referencing websites, the meta search engine only searches the top results supplied by other major search engines; in the past, and in my opinion, these resulted in too much reproduction of rather shallow results.

However, and by contrast, one meta search engine which we will be taking a look at shortly searches news sites, blogs and social book marking sites and well as what has become to be known as 'Tweets' which are basically 140 character micro blogs and can lead you to some ***EXCELLENT*** veins of information. At the moment, this new-to-the-scene meta search engine is my main starting point for ideas generation, and for that reason I will be sharing its secrets with you.

How many MAJOR search engines are there?

As is the nature of the Internet this information may change quite rapidly so it is really worth keeping abreast of changes; however, at the moment, there are just 3 main search engine players – Google, Yahoo and MSN!

However, and in my opinion, the one which provides the ***VERY BEST*** search results is Google and the only major search engine that I am going to focus on from this point forward for 4 main reasons.

- They are the ***BIGGEST***.
- They are likely to ***KEEP*** this lead.
- They are the most ***RELEVANT***.
- They make gaining ***QUALITY*** search results simple.

Notes:
Please use this margin for writing your ideas thoughts, inspirations and personal plan of action.

This Tutorial will then act as your route map to PR success!

There are also a few more benefits to using Google which we will be imminently exploring. However, the most important aspect of their service to users is ***RELEVANCY***! There is nothing worse than typing in a specific keyword and then being returned results which offer no value, or relate to something else.

My time, like yours, is finite and so I know I can rely upon Google to provide the ***BEST*** source of information on the subjects for which I am looking for.

Wherever you live in the World, and as you will see from the Google UK logo above, they also have regional specific databases across the world, which may help to make your searching even more focused and accurate.

How the search engines work...

The reason the Internet is often referred to as the ***NET*** or ***WEB*** is because websites all have links either to, or from them provided by other website or indexes of some type. This countless number of links which crisscross and makes up the Internet, resembles a spider's web making access to any part of it both quick and simple.

To keep the search engines results up-to-date with what's going on and happening on the web, Google employs what are known as ***SPIDERS*** which follow hyperlinks across the web and visit websites of all types. The spider may just spend fractions of a second on a website exploring the content and links before moving to the next website.

The spiders index pages rather than websites, the information from which they add to their ***HUGE*** database, and after being filtered by the search engine algorithms, each page is assigned a certain rank and relevancy which determines the pages placement in the SERPs *(Search Engine Results Pages)*.

Notes:
Please use this margin for writing your ideas thoughts, inspirations and personal plan of action.

This Tutorial will then act as your route map to PR success!

The more relevant their algorithms show it to be, the greater the value and trust given to that page.

However, it indexes and returns results on far more than just web pages; it also searches files which it finds that contains text such as PDFs *(Portable Document Format)* etc, as well as finding and returning other relevant results in blogs, videos and a whole host of other formats.

Your UNDERSTANDING for just a moment please...

Now if you already know and fully understand the following snippet of information which I am going to share, please forgive me, as I know for most people it is quite obvious. However, my motivation to explain it comes from a fairly recent telephone conversation with a ***HIGHLY*** intelligent friend who was trying to navigate his way to a new website I had just built and placed on the Internet. However, try as he might he ***COULD*** not find it and asked for my help...

Patiently, I kept on spelling out the website address as he kept on typing it in to his ancient computer, to be told that the site didn't exist! As he became more and more irate at the lack of success, so did I also, as I ***COULD NOT*** understand what was going wrong. Eventually, I asked him where exactly he was typing the web address into, to discover that after typing in the address he was clicking on the search button!

EUREKA! – it then became ***PAINFULLY*** obvious what he was doing wrong; he was typing the address into Google rather than the address bar.

Notes:
Please use this margin for writing your ideas thoughts, inspirations and personal plan of action.

This Tutorial will then act as your route map to PR success!

Google will only find the pages which it has indexed into its database. Now getting indexed in the first place can be a very frustrating task for webmasters and can take ***MONTHS*** to achieve. ***SOME*** websites ***NEVER*** get indexed at all and for that reason will never be listed in search engine results.

A simple and frustrating mistake to make and I want to ensure you don’t do the same...

Let’s perform a Google search...

The best way to begin a search is to start broad and then refine it until you discover the information or website which you wanted. For this example I am going to use the keyword ‘Judo’ because it is a sport in which all of my family participates and has a strong interest in. I am also going to use the geographical location of my nearest city so we can see what is going on in the area, so in the search box I am going to type my keyword phrase ‘Judo in Bristol’.

Results **1** - **10** of about **32,400** for **judo in bristol**. (**0.17** seconds)

The first thing that I would like to draw your attention to is the Google results bar which tells us that it has found 32,400 results with both the keywords ‘Judo’ and ‘Bristol’ in it.

Notes:
Please use this margin for writing your ideas thoughts, inspirations and personal plan of action.

This Tutorial will then act as your route map to PR success!

Now that is a lot of pages to search through so I am going to show you how to refine this search in just a few moments. First however, let's look at the results because there are a few things which I would like to highlight.

Please notice that I clicked the 'Pages from the UK' button as this is where I live and will make the search more relevant. The first listing returned in the search I have highlighted with a red box as this is another type of PPC advertisement; sometimes you will find as many as three of them at the top of the listings. They usually have a different coloured background to differentiate them from the organic search results *(Optimised free listings)* and also are marked as 'Sponsored Listings'!

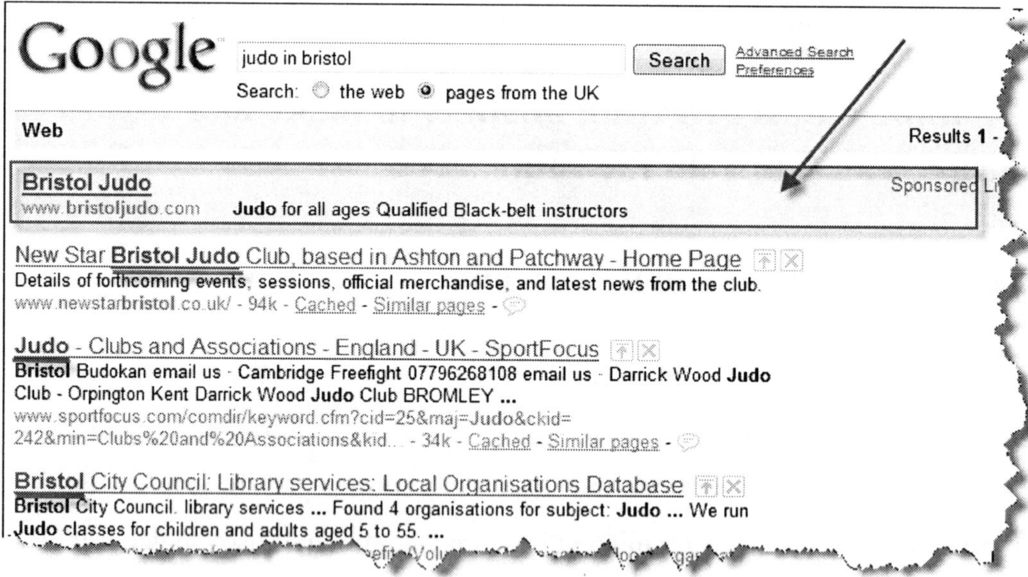

The first line of text which you see highlighted in blue is the page title, and the black text underneath is the page description; these are often referred to as meta tags. The green text at the bottom of the listing is the page URL *(website address).*

The first listing underneath this is for the 'New Star' club at which my children sometimes train. You will notice that the keywords 'Judo' and 'Bristol' have been highlighted, and to emphasise this I have given them an additional red underline.

Please Note that only the ***FIRST*** organic search result has returned both keywords in the title. The two below have the keywords either in the title or the description and after the first three listings, the results become very irrelevant as they are about 'Judo' in general, or 'Bristol' in general, and of no specific interest.

Let's tighten up the search...

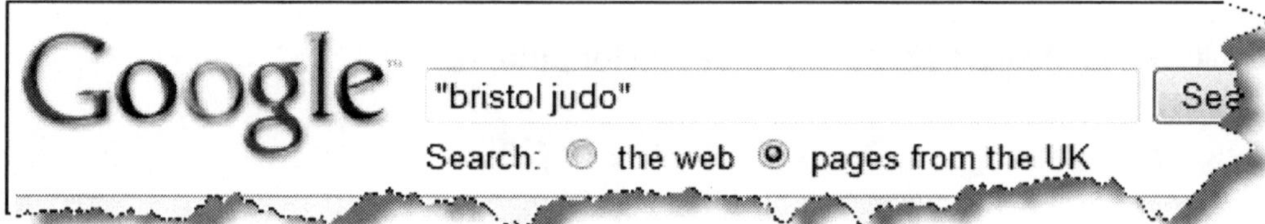

This time I am going to use just the two main keywords, but place them between "inverted commas" so the search looks like this "Bristol Judo" and I have also reversed the order of the keywords as "Bristol Judo" sounds more logical. Now the inverted commas tell Google to ***ONLY*** return listings with the words "Bristol Judo" together and in this order, let's see what happens...

Results **1** - **10** of about **222** for "**bristol judo**". (**0.22** seconds

As you may expect this refined search returns a ***MUCH*** smaller number of results and "Bristol Judo" will appear in every result. Now this is a very much more focused search and is returning far higher quality results.

Notes:
Please use this margin for writing your ideas thoughts, inspirations and personal plan of action.

This Tutorial will then act as your route map to PR success!

Notes:
Please use this margin for writing your ideas thoughts, inspirations and personal plan of action.

This Tutorial will then act as your route map to PR success!

Now try this...

In the address bar type 'allintitle:' and the key words of your choice.

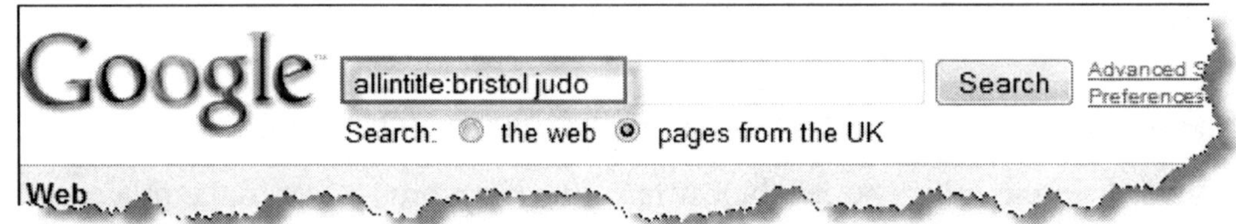

What this has forced Google to do, is search ***ONLY*** the title of the pages it has indexed that include your keywords; the reason for doing this is so that pages with your keywords in the 'Page Title' are likely to be more focused and relevant, as webmasters have obviously made an attempt at optimising this page to be found for those keywords.

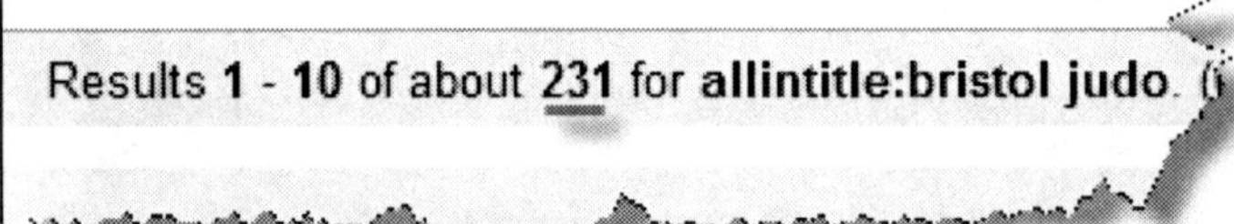

On this occasion the 'allintitle:' search returned just a few more results that a search using inverted comas. However, this exercise is not about the ***QUANTITY*** of results which we are returning, so much as the ***QUALITY*** and ***RELEVANCY*** of the results to help with PR idea generation, and finding supporting information when writing news articles.

Four other helpful shortcuts for searching...

I am now going to introduce you to four characters which I have found make searching Google ***MUCH*** simpler. For this example I am going to use the search term 'Currant' because my wife has just placed a small piece of delicious looking birthday cake by my side which has been sent to me by a friend. It smells lovely and I am almost drooling over the thought of the rich fruit cake hiding under the sweet icing. So I am going to type this keyword into Google and search before taking a bite...

Notes:
Please use this margin for writing your ideas thoughts, inspirations and personal plan of action.

This Tutorial will then act as your route map to PR success!

Google currant Search
Search: the web pages from the UK
Web
Currant Shortbread Recipe
Currant Shortbread Recipe, a classic dish from Scottish.
www.celtnet.org.uk/recipes/miscellaneous/fetch-recipe.php?rid=misc-currant-shortb
- Cached - Similar pages
currant - Hutchinson encyclopedia article about currant
Hutchinson encyclopedia article about currant. currant. Information about currant in
Hutchinson encyclopedia. black currant, red currant, currant bush, ...

You will notice that the first listing it has returned for me is a recipe for currant shortbread, so lets imagine that I would like more recipes or information which contain both the keyword 'Currant' and 'Shortbread'; now as you already know, I could type both keywords in between inverted commas but that would force results with the two keywords placed together, with is not what I want.

So on this occasion I am going to use a + plus sign which would make the search look like this: 'Currant +Shortbread'. Please note, I ***HAVEN'T*** left a gap between the plus sign and the word Shortbread.

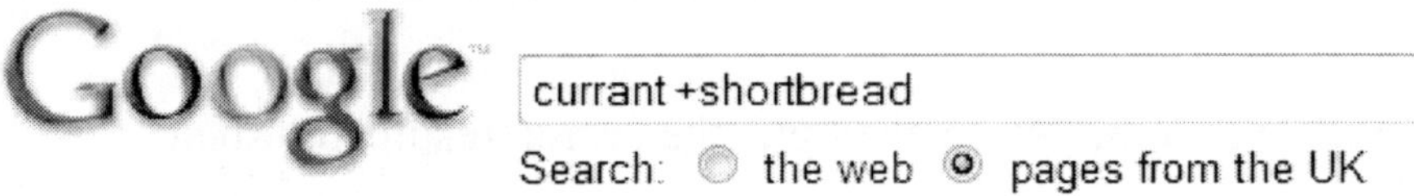

As you can see it has returned a ***TON*** of results and I can tell you that most of them in the first few pages are virtually all dedicated to 'Currant Shortbread' recipes.

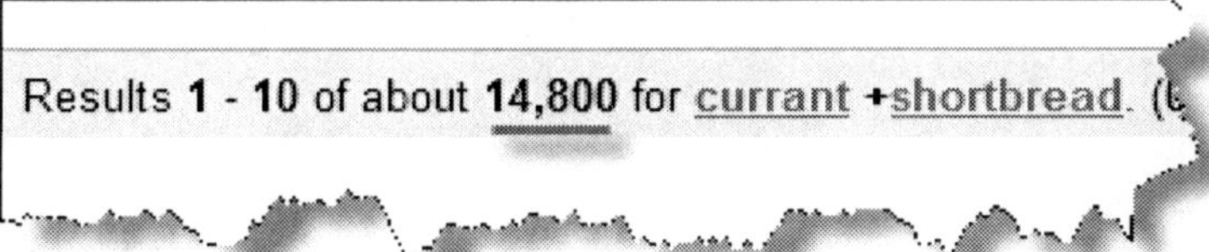

However, it could be that I ***HATE*** shortbread and for that reason ***DON'T*** want results which contain anything to do with it.

Notes:
Please use this margin for writing your ideas thoughts, inspirations and personal plan of action.

This Tutorial will then act as your route map to PR success!

Now I am sure you are already ahead of me at this point. If you just thought I should place a – minus sign in front of 'Shortbread' like this –Shortbread, ***WELL DONE***, you are correct!

Google
currant -shortbread
Search: the web pages from the UK

The search using the minus or subtract sign has returned lots of relevant results and not one of them contains the word 'Shortbread'.

Results 1 - 10 of about 192,000 for currant -shortbrea

Another useful character that you may find the need for is the *star or multiplication symbol which you will find situated on the number 8 key. This symbol acts as a 'Wild Card' when you are unsure of a word which may belong between two others, or are looking for alternatives.

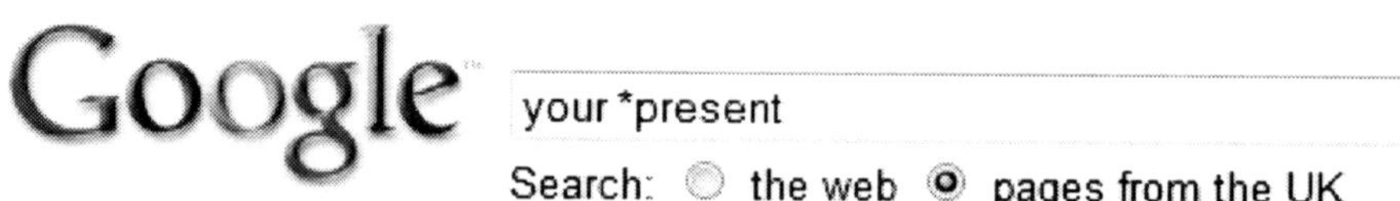

On this occasion, and in the above example, the search results returned:

- Your ***BIRTHDAY*** present
- Your ***CHRISTMAS*** present
- Your ***ANNIVERSARY*** present
- Your ***RETIREMENT*** present

Etc, I am sure you have got the idea...

Notes:
Please use this margin for writing your ideas thoughts, inspirations and personal plan of action.

This Tutorial will then act as your route map to PR success!

Just occasionally I get ***REALLY*** stuck for ideas on a certain theme and that is when the use of this final character could be useful.

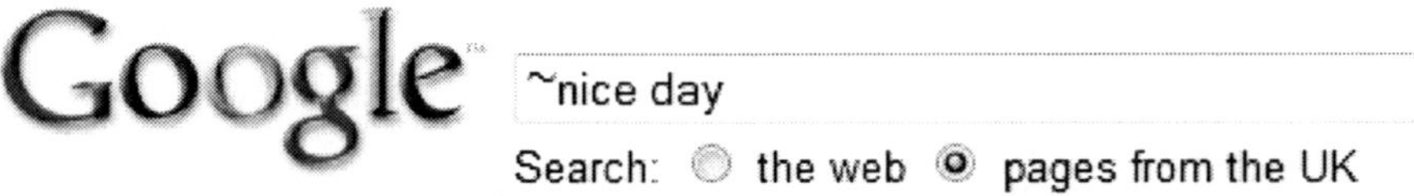

On my keyboard this character shares the home of the hash key # next to the return key. What this character does is to look for alternatives or 'Synonyms' to your keyword or key phrase; for example this search provided the following results:

- ~nice day
- ~good day
- ~pleasant day
- ~cold day

Why not experiment and try it out for yourself.

Or, if you don't like messing around with these characters, or find them difficult to remember, you could use the Google 'Advanced Search'

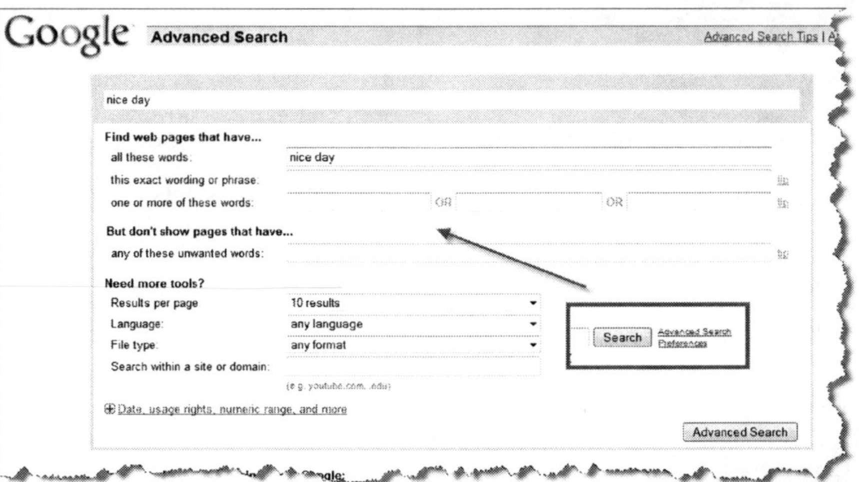

You will find the 'Advanced Search' link to the right of the Google search box. It does exactly the same thing as using the shortcut characters but the boxes take ***MUCH*** longer to fill in, which can be a pain if you are making a lot of searches.

Notes:
Please use this margin for writing your ideas thoughts, inspirations and personal plan of action.

This Tutorial will then act as your route map to PR success!

Book marking your results...

This is just another snippet which you may well already know, but just in case you don't, I am including it for completeness...

I quite regularly come across websites which prove to be really ***GREAT*** resources for idea generation on a particular theme on which I am gaining PR and media exposure. When this happens, and as I know I will want to refer to that website or blog etc, again, I find it best to bookmark the site. If you are using Firefox as your browser you can either click on the bookmark link, or press on the 'Ctrl+D' key as a shortcut.

If you are using 'Microsoft Explorer' as your web browser, the process looks slightly different but still uses the same shortcut key which is 'Ctrl+D'.

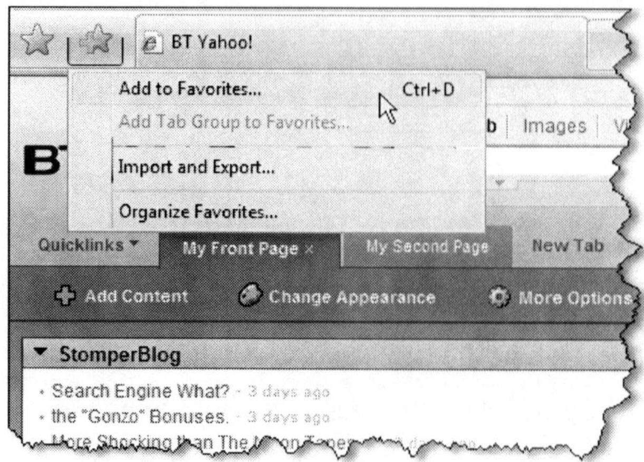

I have found the best practice to adopt is to create a 'New Folder' for each of my projects and in this way I can always find what I am look for again quickly. I also rename my book marks and links for my benefit as I will be the only one using this system so I can call them anything I wish that will help my efficiency.

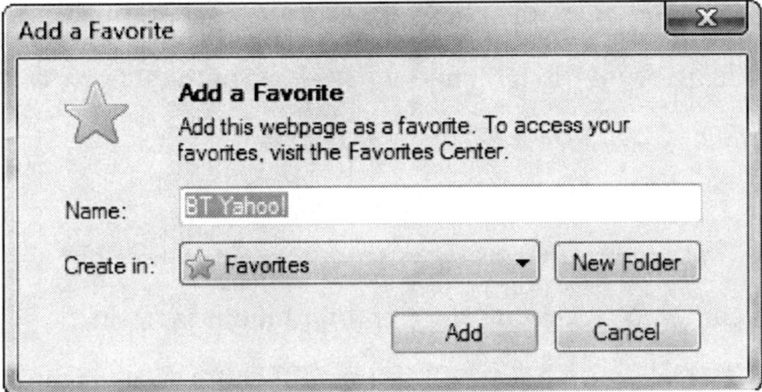

Action plan...

Now you have just covered a ***MASSIVE*** amount of information a ***LOT*** of which may be new to you, so it is important to try it out by experimenting and playing with what you have learned before moving on.

Use your new skills to research subjects in which you have a particular interest, using all of the special characters I have shared with you to refine and focus your search.

Research companies which you consider to be your opposition by typing their company URLs; if you don't know their address, use what you have just learned to find them and see if what they are doing in their business ignites any ideas for use in your PR.

Research the competition you may not yet be aware of by making a list of the keywords your customers may use to find other companies which are similar to yours. Then search using these keywords, make a list of these companies by starting a new bookmark folder so you can go back and visit them at will.

Notes:
Please use this margin for writing your ideas thoughts, inspirations and personal plan of action.

This Tutorial will then act as your route map to PR success!

Notes:
Please use this margin for writing your ideas thoughts, inspirations and personal plan of action.

This Tutorial will then act as your route map to PR success!

(I'll shortly be showing you a way of spying on your opposition which takes next to no time at all to set up and follow).

What are other companies in the same line of business as you, but who are located in other countries, can you find? ...and ***WHAT*** are they doing differently? What can you learn from them? ...and what ideas can you borrow to make a good news story?

Remember to record ideas and inspirations as they occur to you in the right hand notes margin so you can ***EASILY*** come back and find them later on. When you have a hot idea ***DON'T*** stop because I promise there is another one hot on its heels, and another one close behind that also, so just record your idea as quickly as you can, and keep going.

Research where your target market is likely to hang out and what attracts them as well as the type of websites they are likely to visit. What does your target market have in common? Now I promise you it's a lot more than you presently think it is, and as you identify these distinctions you can use your new searching skills to find these places where they congregate, and then write ***HIGHLY*** focused PR that will capture their attention.

So what did you discover? From going through this 'Action Plan' I know you will have started to see the true potential and value of using the Internet for research purposes.

Three more ***INSPIRATIONAL*** gems...

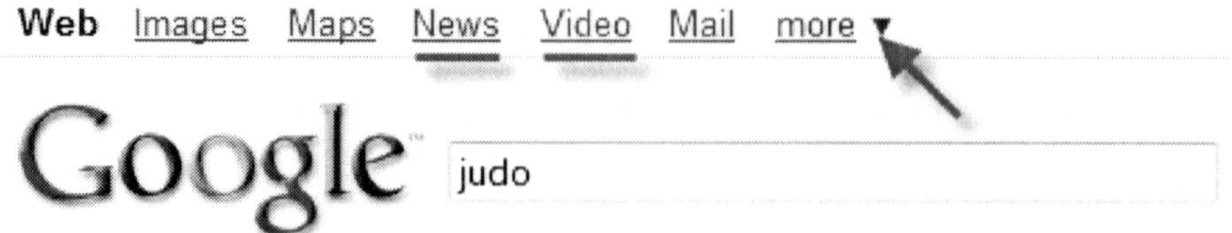

Now you are going to love what follows, and I have saved it until this point because if I had showed you them first, you may well not have read any further.

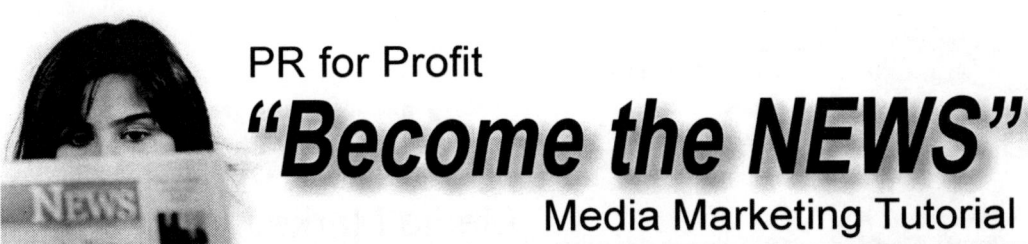

As you can see, immediately above the Google search box are a row of links and a dropdown box which ***HIGHLIGHTS*** even more search options.

News results
Browse Top Stories

Recent
Last hour
Last day
Past week
Past month

Archives
All dates
2008
2002-07
1999-2001
1990-98
1960-69
Other dates

Blogs

News Alerts

RSS | Atom
About Feeds

Start by clicking on the 'NEWS' link and you discover a ***WHOLE*** page of news items dedicated to your search criteria, and access to a whole archive of additional material on the same subject, and it gets better still.

You will be able to search what has happened over the last hour, day, week, or month as well as going back to previous years. As you can see from the 'News Results' screen grab, I can search as far back as 1960.

WOW!

As you can see, you can also subscribe to news alerts and RSS feeds from the very same window, and we will be coming to them shortly.

Then when you reach the bottom of this page you will be offered a variety of links to related searches on the same subject.

Searches related to: **judo**

bronze	**kilogram**	**ippon**
mongolia	**xian dongmei**	**keiji suzuki**

Stay up to date on these results:
- Create an email alert for **judo**
- Add a custom section for **judo** to Google News
- Search blogs for **judo**
- Add a news gadget for **judo** to your Google homepage
- Subscribe to a news feed for **judo** in Google Reader

Notes:
Please use this margin for writing your ideas thoughts, inspirations and personal plan of action.

This Tutorial will then act as your route map to PR success!

Notes:
Please use this margin for writing your ideas thoughts, inspirations and personal plan of action.

This Tutorial will then act as your route map to PR success!

Video news articles...

Now if you are uncertain about searching videos to gain inspiration and ideas for PR and media exposure, I really can't blame you, as I was also, until more recently, because video seemed a very slow and such an unreliable media for the internet. It just kept starting and stopping and frankly frustrated me with all of that waiting and hanging about.

However things have ***CHANGED*** a lot and now *(apart from peak Internet traffic times)* I have found viewing video has become quite reliable and smooth running. Now before you jump to the conclusion that I have an ***ULTRA*** high speed Internet connection, let me inform you that I live in a ***VERY*** small village way out in the sticks which is situated next to the sea, and I probably have one of the slowest connections you will find ***ANYWHERE***, but I still gain a ***LOT*** of value from searching for ideas using Internet video.

The visual aspect makes me think in a different way and ideas come flooding to me and I believe that they will to you also. Internet videos tend just to be a minute or so in length and load quickly, so if you wish, you can scan through them only stopping at what captures your attention.

Notes:
Please use this margin for writing your ideas thoughts, inspirations and personal plan of action.

This Tutorial will then act as your route map to PR success!

Not only that, I now maintain my blog, using video because it has become so quick and easy to distribute, and guess what, it ***ATTRACTS*** far more visitors and potential custom. This is the way of the future and it is here to stay so adapt and grow with this fast moving new trend.

So what is a BLOG?

The term blog is a contraction of two words which are 'Web and Log' and as the term suggests it is really a simple online diary of events. However, they are in fact far more than just this and the blogging culture is growing rapidly.

The best way for me to explain the ***FULL*** benefits of a blog is first of all from my point of view as someone who creates material for three blogs on a regular basis, and then from your perspective as someone who may read them in search of ideas to power their own PR campaign and for providing supporting content.

First, the difference between the way in which I plan and create a blog or conventional web page is ***VAST***. Perhaps it's just me, and the way in which I think, but if I decide to write a new web site page I already have an idea of how it should look, and what length the content should be well before I start; this is the planning stage. I also have to then give consideration as to how I will link this new page in with my existing website and how visitors will find and navigate it for it to be of value to them, and just as importantly, of value to me. Remember, although I really love what I do, my primary motivation is financial, and this is a fact I must not lose sight of.

By contrast, when I decide to make a new blog entry there is very little planning involved other than a firm and definite idea of what I will write about and the motivation to make an entry often comes from a simple action or discovery which I find interesting enough to move me to 'blog composing mode'.

Notes:
Please use this margin for writing your ideas thoughts, inspirations and personal plan of action.

This Tutorial will then act as your route map to PR success!

The blog has no set rules and my entries can be ***VERY*** brief, or as long as I and the subject about which I am writing, dictates it must be. I can make, and often do, multiple entries in the same day as I take ***'BLOG BREAKS'*** in much the same way that some people may take coffee or tea breaks to give their minds a little light relief and diversion. They provide me with a little alternative distraction away from the main theme on which I am concentrating. I both write, and more recently, make short videos for my blogs.

From a webmaster's point of view, blogs are ***EXCEPTIONALLY*** easy to optimise for the search engines to index, and often I write short keyword-optimised entries which appear on the first page of Google within half an hour of their creation and publication upon the Internet. I am sure you are starting to understand my enthusiasm for them.

From the point of view of the researcher, especially for PR material, blogs can be a ***FANTASTIC*** source of inspiration because there are so many of them. Remember, in general, blog entries are short and easy to search and snatch ideas from. But the ***GREATEST*** of all the benefits that they offer is that most of them provide an RSS feed. Now if you don't already know what RSS feeds are we will be coming to them next.

Notes:
Please use this margin for writing your ideas thoughts, inspirations and personal plan of action.

This Tutorial will then act as your route map to PR success!

The best way to search blogs at Google is to first complete your search, and then use the dropdown additional choices box, and click on the 'Blogs' link. As you can see I am using my 'Judo' example again.

Browse Top Stories New!

Published
Last hour
Last 12 hours
Last day
Past week
Past month
→Anytime
Choose Dates

Subscribe:
Blogs Alerts
Atom | RSS

The first thing that you will notice when this page opens is that it now offers you the option to browse the top stories; now this is a brand new feature to me also. However, let's think about this option for a moment and the ***HUGE*** benefit and possibilities which it offers the budding PR marketeer.

If these have become top Internet stories it is ***HIGHLY POSSIBLE*** that a news article on the same subject will be ***EQUALLY*** as popular.

This offers ***SMART*** PR students an additional advantage to stay ahead of the game by writing articles which are ***MORE LIKELY*** than the average news releases to be picked up and run with by other publications.

You will also notice that you have the facility to search blog entries by the time which the entry was created. This is a really useful facility to have which you should experiment with.

Notes:
Please use this margin for writing your ideas thoughts, inspirations and personal plan of action.

This Tutorial will then act as your route map to PR success!

Remote-Controlled Hairbrush: WANDERING **JUDO**
6 hours ago by Mike Ellis, The Jolly Reprobate
WANDERING **JUDO**. Angry after the breakup and spoiling for a fight, Brandon helmeted up and headed out to deliberately violate Starbuck's "no shoes, no shirt, no service" policy. Views as of now: 58911. Posted by Mike Ellis, ...
Remote-Controlled Hairbrush - http://rc-hairbrush.blogspot.com/

Judo in Richmond Va - JudoForum.com
4 Mar 2009
looked on the judoinfo site, and see mma institute has **Judo** in Richmond. The others don't have a website showing times etc. Any suggestions **Judo** is preferred or BJJ in the Richmond area. Thanks in advance. COJudoka ...
JudoForum RSS Feed - http://judoforum.com/index.php?showtopic=32520&st=0&gopid=437606&
[More results from JudoForum RSS Feed]

Download King Toryumon - **Judo** Suwa mp3 free download
6 hours ago
Download King - Toryumon - **Judo** Suwa mp3 for free.
Latest Mp3 Additions at mp3INT.com - http://www.mp3int.com/latest_mp3_additions/
[More results from Latest Mp3 Additions at mp3INT.com]

The search results also are slightly different as you will notice I have highlighted in red, the time when they where first published to the internet. The description also is far longer than the one used in website listings where only approximately 170 characters are displayed.

Quite interestingly, and from just a few minutes following the search result links, most judo related blogs seem to be used like press releases, which makes them really useful when looking for ideas.

What is an RSS feed?

RSS stands for 'Really Simple Syndication' and is a commonly used protocol for syndication and sharing of content, originally developed to facilitate the syndication of news articles, although it is now widely available on most blogs and some websites.

Notes:
Please use this margin for writing your ideas thoughts, inspirations and personal plan of action.

This Tutorial will then act as your route map to PR success!

The simple explanation and ***BIG*** benefit of RSS is that you can have all of the news content which is published by a specific blog delivered directly to your desktop it becomes immediately available as it is published, rather than you having to visit that particular blog or website to read it.

What AMAZING technology...

So let's consider the implications for a moment. This means you can benefit from many blogs or RSS 'News Feeds' all delivered to a convenient location of your choosing! Now before your imagination starts to run wild and you start imagining this is going to take up a load of space, or a lot of time to monitor, it ***DOESN'T!***

You see, when you subscribe to an RSS feed, you decide how many current stories or entries you wish to see on view, and it only displays the title of the blog entry; let me show you...

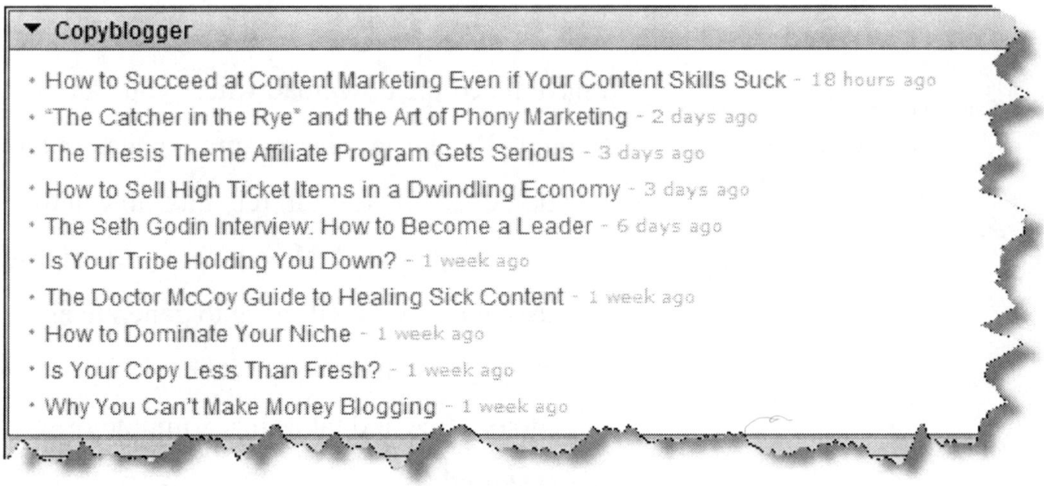

▾ Copyblogger

- How to Succeed at Content Marketing Even if Your Content Skills Suck - 18 hours ago
- "The Catcher in the Rye" and the Art of Phony Marketing - 2 days ago
- The Thesis Theme Affiliate Program Gets Serious - 3 days ago
- How to Sell High Ticket Items in a Dwindling Economy - 3 days ago
- The Seth Godin Interview: How to Become a Leader - 6 days ago
- Is Your Tribe Holding You Down? - 1 week ago
- The Doctor McCoy Guide to Healing Sick Content - 1 week ago
- How to Dominate Your Niche - 1 week ago
- Is Your Copy Less Than Fresh? - 1 week ago
- Why You Can't Make Money Blogging - 1 week ago

The above selection of blog entries are delivered to my 'Yahoo' news reader which I have already mentioned. 'Copyblogger' is the name of the RSS blog feed. On this occasion, because I find the author's content so usable and valuable, I have elected to see 10 entries at the same time. These dropdown by one place every time a new article is published, until they are completely replaced by newer entries and are no longer visible.

Notes:
Please use this margin for writing your ideas thoughts, inspirations and personal plan of action.

This Tutorial will then act as your route map to PR success!

I can see exactly how fresh the article is, and if I want to read it, I simply click upon the headline which is also a link to the article. This may open the blog article for me to read on the same page, or it may open another browser window for me to read it.

RSS feed News readers

There are many different and FREE news readers as I have already discussed, but there is one I would like to show you in a little bit more detail because of the amazing features it offers us when searching for PR news release ideas and inspiration.

By the way, 'Google Reader' is completely free...

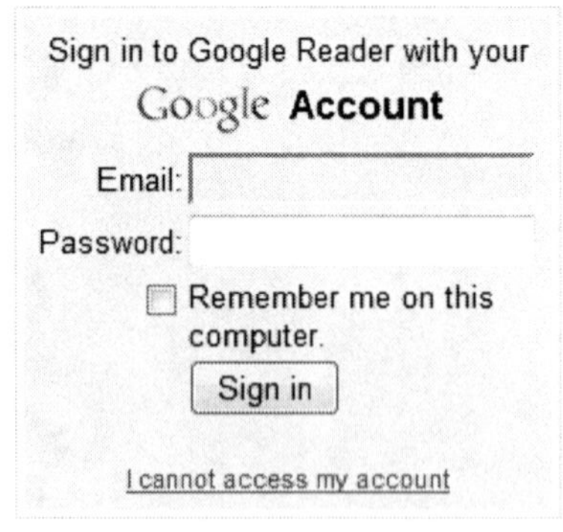

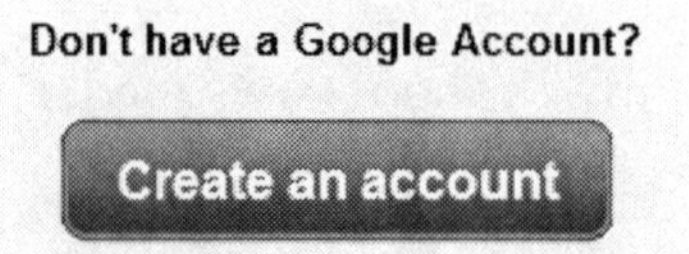

I have listed the download where you can find 'Google Reader' on the resources pages as the location does not seem to remain stable and tends to jump around. Now before you can use this useful tool you will have to generate an account, but as already mentioned, it's completely free and takes just a minute or so to get started.

For maximum efficiency, bookmark your 'Google Reader' page and ask the computer to remember your access details, and then you will only have to do it once.

Now your reader will be blank when you start your account as you have not yet added any RSS feeds, but I will show you how to do this in just a moment or two. For now I will show you inside my 'Google Reader', which I use to monitor blogs on heath, fitness and weight loss! It seems, that you have cunningly unearthed my secret and discovered I am in fact ***FAT***!

You can play for hours with all the useful features Google provides you with, so all I am going to show you are the basics, and then you can explore when you get your own Reader.

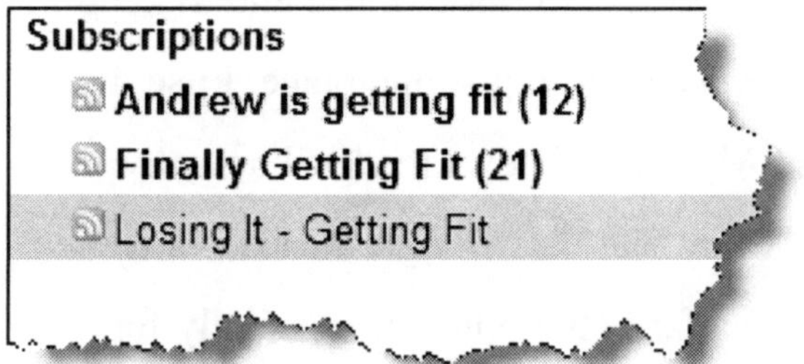

In my 'Weight loss' news reader, I have subscribed to just 3 feeds so far, but there is no restriction and I could have in fact subscribed to 300 or 3,000.

The numbers which are in *(brackets)* at the end of the first two feed titles are informing me how many ***NEW*** articles this blog has published since the last time I visited, of which I am not yet aware. Now I can click to open any specific feed I wish. Or I can select to see all of them in the same panel.

As a rule it is going to be the headline title of the blog entry which is likely to be the deciding factor whether I should open the article or not, as generally, I am spoiled for choice at the sheer volume of information that is available.

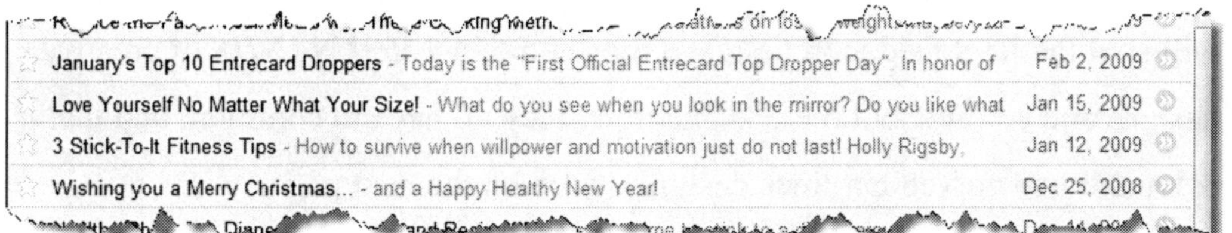

This is what the rest of the page looks like; a long list of the headline titles from which you can gain ideas and inspiration.

Notes:
Please use this margin for writing your ideas thoughts, inspirations and personal plan of action.

This Tutorial will then act as your route map to PR success!

Notes:
Please use this margin for writing your ideas thoughts, inspirations and personal plan of action.

This Tutorial will then act as your route map to PR success!

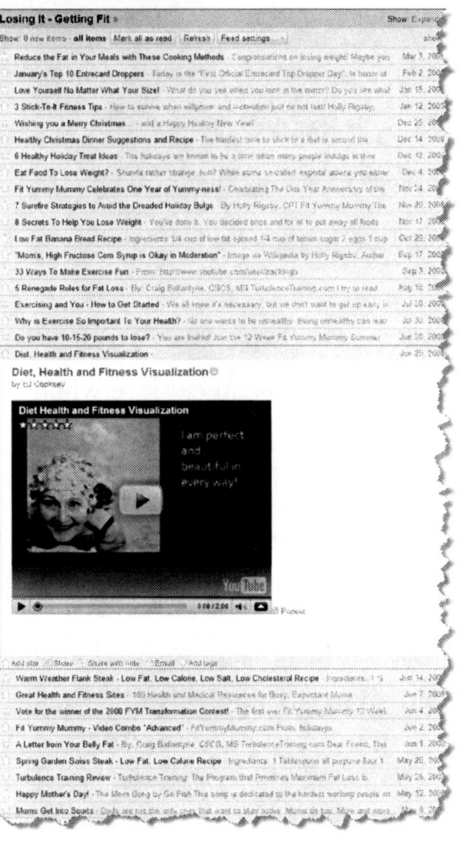

If one of the titles captures your attention, such as the one to left which captured mine, you only need to click on it for it to expand out for easy reading.

Or, and as happened on this occasion, for it to reveal a video which can be viewed directly from this location.

Although, for ease of use and to keep everything in just one place, I use the 'My Yahoo' news reader, I actually think that the 'Google Reader' seen here is a far better choice, especially for beginners to PR.

How to accept an RSS feed...

When you know where you are going to read your RSS feed, the rest is fairly simple; so let's go through the process of grabbing your first feed right now...

Spotting where you can obtain your feed is not difficult either, if the website or blog has one, it is unlikely to be kept a secret, and it may be as easy as spotting the link that says 'Get your RSS feed here'. More likely however, is that you will spot the RSS feed icon first, and they come in ***THOUSANDS*** of creative designs and colours, but there is one thing they all have in common, and that is a dot and two curved bar lines design as seen on the next page.

Notes:
Please use this margin for writing your ideas thoughts, inspirations and personal plan of action.

This Tutorial will then act as your route map to PR success!

So look out for this design and then click on that link and it is likely to open up a screen such as the one below, which offers you a wide range of different ways in which you can accept the feed.

If you are using the 'Google Reader', or 'My Yahoo', it will be as simple as clicking on the link of your choice and then following the on-screen instructions. Sometimes you will see lots of these links in the margins of the blog page you are reading and all you will need to do is click on the one of your choice.

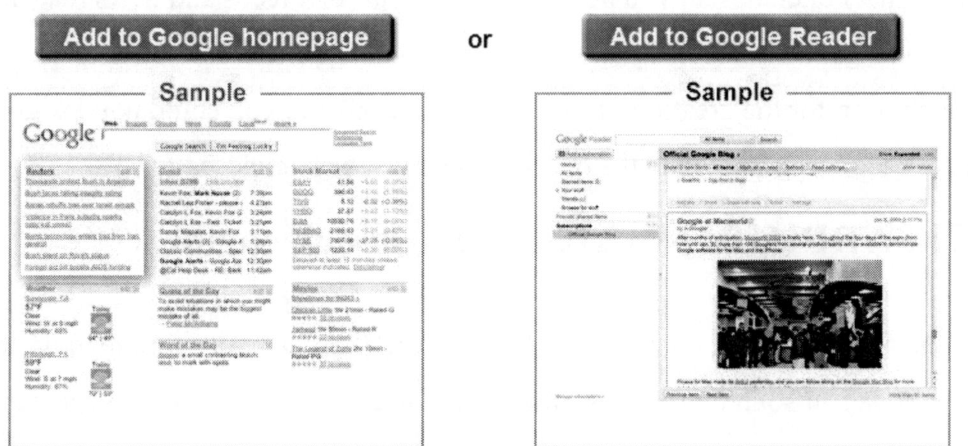

If you click on the Google link it will take you to a page which offers you the above choices; if you have a 'Google Reader' account click on this choice to complete the process and the feed will have been added to your Reader ready for you to begin to benefit from the very next time you open this program.

Notes:
Please use this margin for writing your ideas thoughts, inspirations and personal plan of action.

This Tutorial will then act as your route map to PR success!

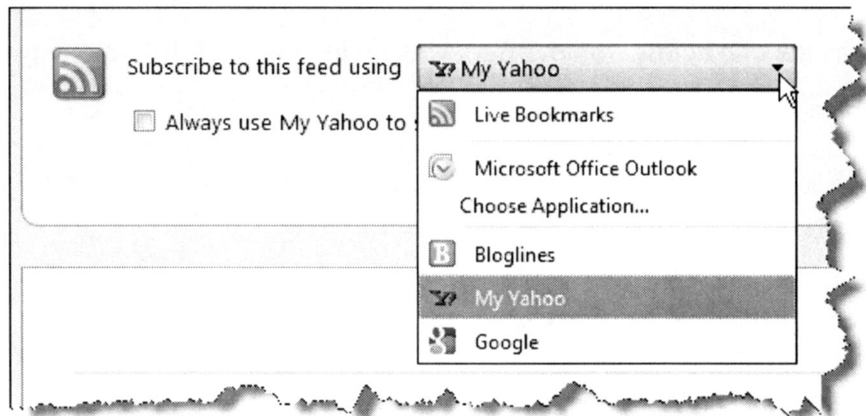

However, sometimes when you click upon the RSS feed link you may be confronted with a different screen such as the one above, and a dropdown box with additional choices. Again, just click the one which best suits you; I am fairly sure that the choice of application you will be offered will differ from the one that you see above. I believe the reason for this is that it is a ***SMART*** application, which takes a quick look inside your computer to see which feeds you are equipped to accept before offering you options that will work.

Well that concludes all you need to know about RSS feeds and news readers, so have fun with them. If you were to design an application to offer ideas and inspiration for the creation of PR and media exposure you could not design a better tool or system than the one you have just been exposed to.

The ADDICT-O-MATIC meta search engine...

This is going to be a quick one as the following tool is really simple to use but is a powerful source of PR inspiration and often my starting point when setting out on a new information gathering expedition for the next news release.

As already mentioned this is what is known as a 'Meta Search Engine'and can be located at: www.addictomatic.com However, unlike other so called 'Meta Search Engines' this one searches a collection of the top social bookmarking,

Notes:
Please use this margin for writing your ideas thoughts, inspirations and personal plan of action.

This Tutorial will then act as your route map to PR success!

video and blog websites as well as news sources, which makes it quite 'Cutting Edge'.

Even if you don't have a topic in mind it offers you the option right on the very front page of searching a ***TON*** of different news sites by clicking on any of the links. However, I <u>do</u> have a topic in mind and I bet you already have a fairly good idea as to what it may be...

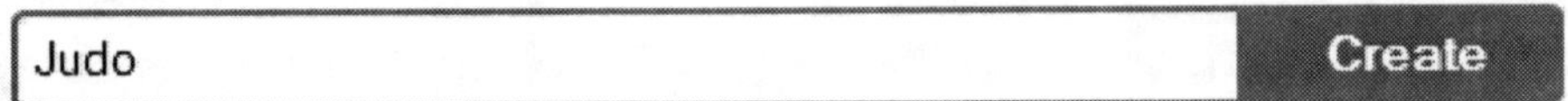

Now I am not going to delve very deeply into this page because it can become ***HUGE*** and we can see from the screen grab that it is returning the ***TOP*** results from a wide variety of different information websites. This is an ***EXCELLENT*** source of news ideas and inspiration from which you can benefit, so have fun with it.

Notes:
Please use this margin for writing your ideas thoughts, inspirations and personal plan of action.

This Tutorial will then act as your route map to PR success!

Twitter Search

- Mat leggen en dan clinic judo geven in Rilland
- @VictorianSquid Not sure which I prefer...Judo or Rugby...they both hurt, but make you feel alive. Black belt here I come.
- @dpwalsh I eat about 2 hours before judo, always have... You'll learn... :-)
- Martial Arts: Physical Techniques And Mental Discipline http://www.budosite.com/judo/martial-arts-physical-techniques-and-mental-discipline
- stalemate!...I aint budging an inch!.....wonder if he had any judo lessons?...could be in danger here

More at Twitter Search »

Friendfeed

- Massimiliano Badolati: Auguri Di Buon Compleanno A Giulia Quintavalle, Campionessa Olimpica Di Judo (via YouTub..Italiano)
- Kurt: Good Judo session tonight. My cardio sucks sooooo bad, though. Need to get in shape if I'm gonna compete in May. (via Twitter)
- Noah Coffey: Just got to see my wife's belly move a little for the first time from a baby judo chop! :D :D :D (via Twitter)
- GOD: I always get super anxious before Judo tests... I know my stuff, but I can't help but get... (via Reverend Nick)
- FriendFeed Times: Martial Arts | Karate | Self Defense (berkeley) (via craigslist | all community in SF bay area)

More at Friendfeed »

Addicto Top Blogs - Bloglines

- Cheers and Jeers: Wednesday
- Cheers and Jeers: Thursday
- Sue Decker's Downfall (YHOO)
- Prime Minister Fitness DVDs - Vladimir Putin Releases Martial Arts...
- Ten questions for Vladimir Putin

More at Addicto Top Blogs - Bloglines »

Tr... Video Search

Live.com News

- Musing The Week's Media - Cricket365.com
- Russia seeks to join cycling elite with Katusha's firepower - International Herald Tribune
- THIS DAY IN HISTORY: FRED BLASSIE VS. ROCKY JOHNSON, PUBLIC ENEMY WIN ... - Pro Wrestling Insider
- Abhinav Bindra to train ITBP men - MSN India Cricket
- Youth wrestlers celebrate winning season - Barnstable Patriot

More at Live.com News »

YouTube

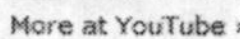

More at YouTube »

Twingly Blog Search

- Friday Night Video 3/6/09
- PPC Tip: When to Use Negative Exact and Negative Phrase Match
- Friday March 6, 2009 Annabel Michaels
- Ben bu yaz nerdeydim? Futbol Maçında.
- Asian Americans in Football

More at Twingly Blog Search »

Ask.com News

- JUDO: U.S. Athletes Earn World Rankings After Warsaw and Prague ...
- Doctor dumps dying Coventry judo champ Ian Thompson
- Second largest judo event in Asia kick off in Taipei in May
- Judo squad leaves for Iran on March 7

Google Blog Search

- **Judo**: Ana Azevedo sagrou-se campeã nacional em -70 kg - Rádio Trofa
- kumo-**judo** - onze poils en KUMOno - Cowblog
- Slow motion **judo** | Best Funny Animate Gifs Updated Daily - Gif Bin
- MI **JUDO**: CAMPEONATO DE ESPAÑA SUB-20
- MI **JUDO**: UNA PREGUNTA AL DALAI LAMA

More at Google Blog Search »

Digg

No results found.

Flickr

More at Flickr »

Delicious Tags

- Video judo-educazione
- http://www.fpjj.com.br/
- Confederação Brasileira de Jiu-Jitsu
- Faculty profile: Jiwhan Han - News
- Tour de Lisp: Lisper's first look at Haskell

More at Delicious Tags »

Blinkx Mainstream Vid News

- Aikido ~ First UK Film 1963
- Lakers' Mbenga Wears Purple, Gold Plus Black Belt
- The Effectiveness of Morote Gari Part II

How to receive INSPIRATION by email....

Can you imagine how easy the process of gaining ongoing ideas and inspiration would be if you were delivered a daily dose of motivation and PR ideas by email? Well, now I am going to show you how to achieve this. Unsurprisingly, what I am going to show you is yet another Google product known as ***'Google Alerts'*** and again they are free.

This is how Google 'Alerts' work...

Basically you choose a keyword or phrase on any subject that you wish and type it into the ***'Google Alert'*** set up panel, and from that point forward Google sorts, filters and dispatches every bit of information which it can find on that specific subject.

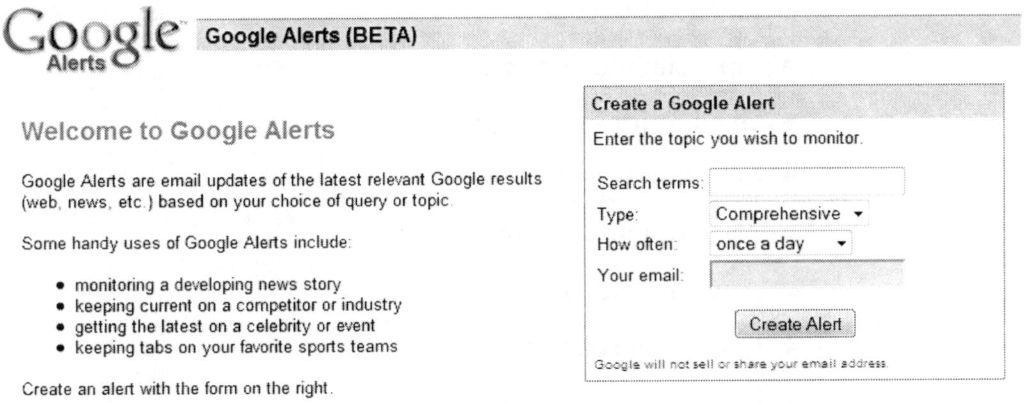

Google Alerts | Google Alerts (BETA)

Welcome to Google Alerts

Google Alerts are email updates of the latest relevant Google results (web, news, etc.) based on your choice of query or topic.

Some handy uses of Google Alerts include:

- monitoring a developing news story
- keeping current on a competitor or industry
- getting the latest on a celebrity or event
- keeping tabs on your favorite sports teams

Create an alert with the form on the right.

Create a Google Alert

Enter the topic you wish to monitor.

Search terms:
Type: Comprehensive
How often: once a day
Your email:

Create Alert

Google will not sell or share your email address.

As you can see it really is a ***VERY*** simple panel and takes just moments to set up.

You are not restricted as to how many ***'Alerts'*** you can set up. To get started, you need to think about the keywords and keyword phrases which your potential prospects might use if they were searching on the Internet to find a company such as yours. Make a list of these words as you will need them in just a few moments.

Notes:
Please use this margin for writing your ideas thoughts, inspirations and personal plan of action.

This Tutorial will then act as your route map to PR success!

Notes:
Please use this margin for writing your ideas thoughts, inspirations and personal plan of action.

This Tutorial will then act as your route map to PR success!

For example:

Let's imagine you run a website which specialises in stock market education for beginners. What keywords, keyword-phrases or associations can you think of that might lead people to look for such a website?

Here is a short list of keywords which I thought of for this example; in reality I would come up with many more.

- Pension fund shortfalls
- Pension crisis
- Early retirement
- Financial security
- Financial freedom
- Financial independence
- Great returns on investments
- Investing wisely
- An additional income
- A second income
- Long term security
- Financial responsibility
- Capitalising upon investments
- Saving money
- How to save money
- High returns on your savings

Now these keywords and phrases, and others like them are likely to return ***LOADS*** of interesting news story ideas, from which you can borrow, adapt or perhaps with a creative rewrite even duplicate without the fear of being accused of plagiarising.

You see the ***'Alerts'*** which arrive in your inbox will be made up from news articles, blogs and search engine listings from across the globe, so it is highly unlikely you will ***EVER*** borrow from anything that is happening locally.

Some of these ***'Alerts'*** will bring back a ***LOT*** of quality inspiration and will result in you generating ***MANY*** good news articles, whereas others may be ***TOTALLY*** useless and never provide you with even ***ONE.*** So you will have to be prepared to ***EXPERIMENT*** to find the words and phrases that work the very best for you.

In general, I have found that the longer keyword phrases return better quality material which result in good ideas being generated for me; but experiment, because this may vary for other phrases.

Let's now set up an example alert so you understand the process...

Simply type one phrase for every new ***'Alert'*** you decide to try out; I have used the 'Word' golf in this example.

Create a Google Alert

Enter the topic you wish to monitor.

Search terms: golf
Type: Comprehensive
How often: once a day
Your email:

Create Alert

Google will not sell or share your email address.

The next box down is the ***'Type'*** box and lists ***"Comprehensive"*** as the default setting. However, if you click on the dropdown it will offer you a much wider selection of search options.

Notes:
Please use this margin for writing your ideas thoughts, inspirations and personal plan of action.

This Tutorial will then act as your route map to PR success!

Notes:
Please use this margin for writing your ideas thoughts, inspirations and personal plan of action.

This Tutorial will then act as your route map to PR success!

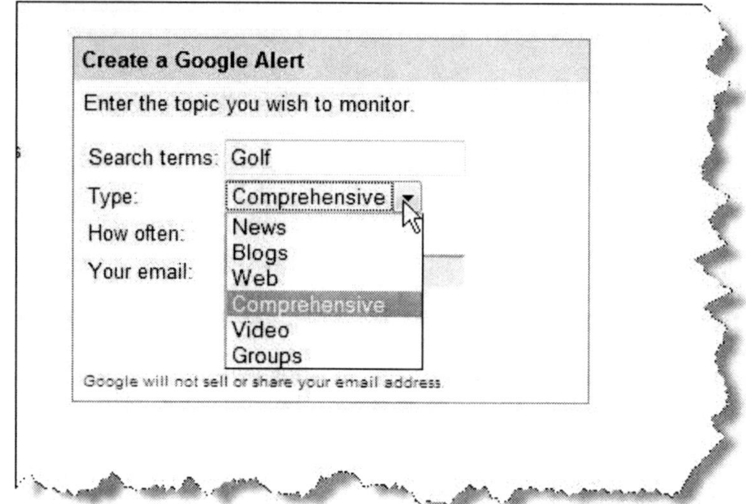

Google offers you a total of five different choices of locations from where it can source and filter your results, and they all have specific benefits; again I suggest that you ***EXPERIMENT*** with all of them to see which serve you best.

I generally select ***'Comprehensive'*** as this retrieves data from ***ALL*** of the different sources in just one email.

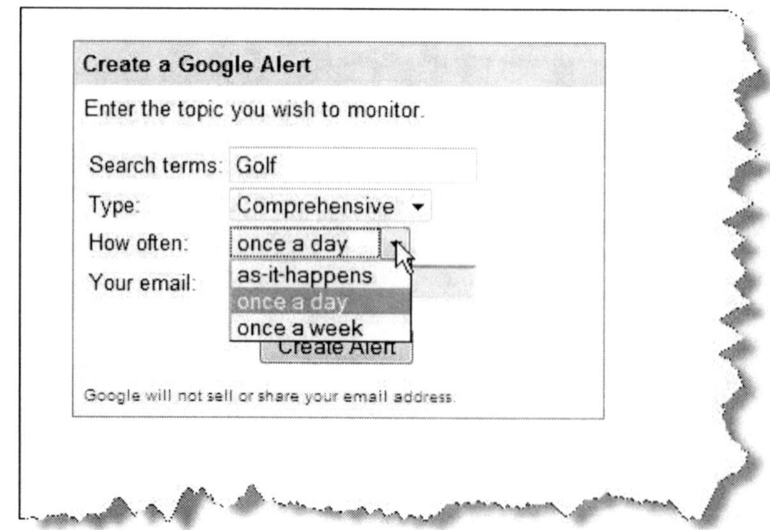

The next consideration is how often you want your ***'Alerts'*** to be delivered?

Notes:
Please use this margin for writing your ideas thoughts, inspirations and personal plan of action.

This Tutorial will then act as your route map to PR success!

If you are keen to start getting ideas you may wish to set the ***'Alert'*** to ***"as-it-happens"*** or ***"daily"***. You can alter the delivery schedule at any time with just a click of a few buttons, so at a later date, when you have a store of ideas, you may wish to change the schedule to weekly, or even suspend it for a while.

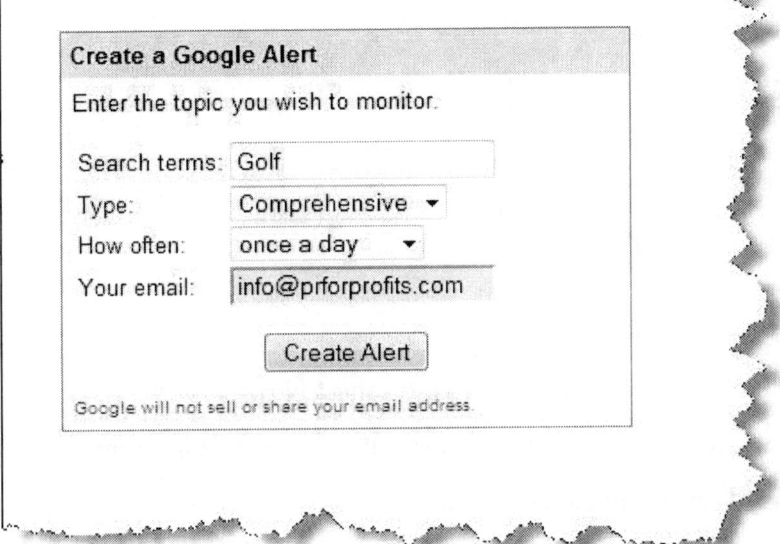

The penultimate task in the setting up of your 'Alert' is to type in your email address and click the ***'Create Alert'*** button.

You will not receive Google Alerts on this topic until you click the link in the verification email and confirm your request.

Google then displays the message above which tells you that there is one action left to take and that is confirming your new ***'Alert'***; so go directly to your inbox and there should be a confirmation link waiting for you, because Google is very quick and efficient when it comes to sending emails.

Notes:
Please use this margin for writing your ideas thoughts, inspirations and personal plan of action.

This Tutorial will then act as your route map to PR success!

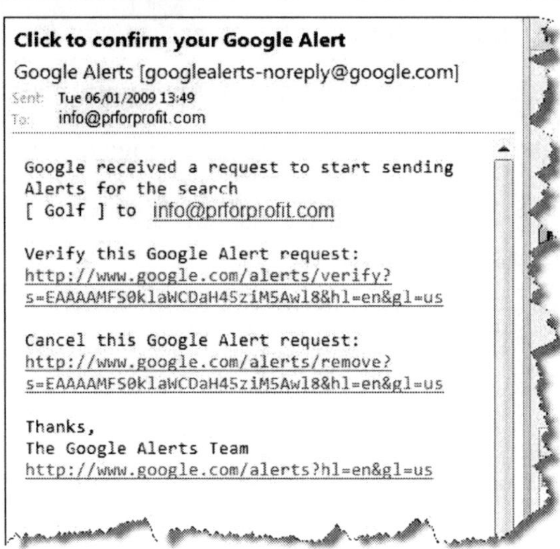

Click to confirm your Google Alert
Google Alerts [googlealerts-noreply@google.com]
Sent: Tue 06/01/2009 13:49
To: info@prforprofit.com

Google received a request to start sending Alerts for the search [Golf] to info@prforprofit.com

Verify this Google Alert request:
http://www.google.com/alerts/verify?s=EAAAAMFS0klaWCDaH45ziM5Aw18&hl=en&gl=us

Cancel this Google Alert request:
http://www.google.com/alerts/remove?s=EAAAAMFS0klaWCDaH45ziM5Aw18&hl=en&gl=us

Thanks,
The Google Alerts Team
http://www.google.com/alerts?hl=en&gl=us

As soon as you receive this confirmation, click on the ***"Verify Google Alert request"*** link and you are up and running and should start receiving your alerts from this point forward until you cancel them.

On the next page is an email of ***'Alerts'*** I received today relating to my local town 'Weston Super Mare' as I like to stay up-to-date with what is happening there, and the ***'Alerts'*** deliver every latest piece of news.

If you see anything which interests you in your ***'Alerts'***, just click on the link and it will take you directly to the blog or news article from which it was sourced.

Notes:
Please use this margin for writing your ideas thoughts, inspirations and personal plan of action.

This Tutorial will then act as your route map to PR success!

Google Alert - Weston Super Mare
Google Alerts [googlealerts-noreply@google.com]
Sent: Fri 06/03/2009 13:22
To: action@kevinmartyn.com

Google News Alert for: **Weston Super Mare**

Dons receive injury boost
Kingston Guardian - UK
Both are in contention for a return to action in Saturday's clash at **Weston-Super-Mare**, where Lee could return in the role vacated by jake Leberl, ...
See all stories on this topic

Bristol local rugby fixtures in full
Evening Post - Bristol,England,UK
Somerset Two South: Bridgwater & Albion III v Minehead Barbarians II, Martock v **Weston-super-Mare** II, Somerton v Crewkerne, Wellington II v Taunton III, ...
See all stories on this topic

Pats looking up table rather than down
Gloucestershire Echo - Cheltenham,England,UK
A WIN at **Weston-Super-Mare** tomorrow should secure Old Patesians' place in the South West One top four at the end of the season. Fourth side Pats are three ...
See all stories on this topic

South West One rugby team news
Western Daily Press - Bristol,Bristol,UK
Weston-super-Mare (home v old Patesians, 2.30pm): C Crichton; K Middlemiss, D Sanft, S Bennett, P Sprague; J Mackey, R Bennett; D Price, D Burge (capt), ...
See all stories on this topic

Google Blogs Alert for: **Weston Super Mare**

Fight at Asda in Phillips Road, **Weston-super-Mare**| Bristol News ...
A man was left with head injuries after a fight at a **Weston-super-Mare** supermarket.
This Is Bristol channel feed - http://www.thisisbristol.co.uk/news/rss.html

Blackpool stag weekend - UK-Muscle Body Building Community ...
By bigbob33
Old Today, 10:13 AM. bigbob33. Trying hard!! bigbob33's Avatar. Join Date: Jan 2009. Location: **Weston super mare**. Posts: 176. Total: 6571. Talking Blackpool stag weekend. Hi guys, I'm going on a stag weekend in Blackpool in a couple of ...
UK-Muscle Body Building Community... - http://www.uk-muscle.co.uk/

The Cheerful Insanity of Me - How Cheesy Can Magic Stunts Get?
By Owen
Would love to see this, but suspect chances of me being anywhere near **Weston-super-Mare** on 20th are fairly minimal (especially with it being a Friday and me being at work in London). Oh well, ho-hum. EDIT: Just noticed the year of the ...
The Cheerful Insanity of Me - http://hmmm-tea.livejournal.com/

Engineer's Daughter: up, up and away
By Ms Heidi
For instance, we're putting a 60m wheel up at the seafront in **Weston-super-Mare** in May, which is just the thing the place needs after the pier burned down last year. Even though they aren't designed as permanent structures, people often ...
Engineer's Daughter - http://engineersdaughter.typepad.com/engineers_daughter/

This once a day Google Alert is brought to you by Google.

Remove this alert.
Create another alert.
Manage your alerts.

I would just like to draw your attention to the area to which the arrow is pointing, as this is how to control or adapt your ***'Alerts'***.

So there you have it...

An ***AMAZINGLY*** simple and ***RICH*** source of idea-generating material that will ensure you never run short of PR material to promote you, your business, product or service ***EVER*** again!

This brings us to the end of the chapter on finding ideas for news articles.

Notes:
Please use this margin for writing your ideas thoughts, inspirations and personal plan of action.

This Tutorial will then act as your route map to PR success!

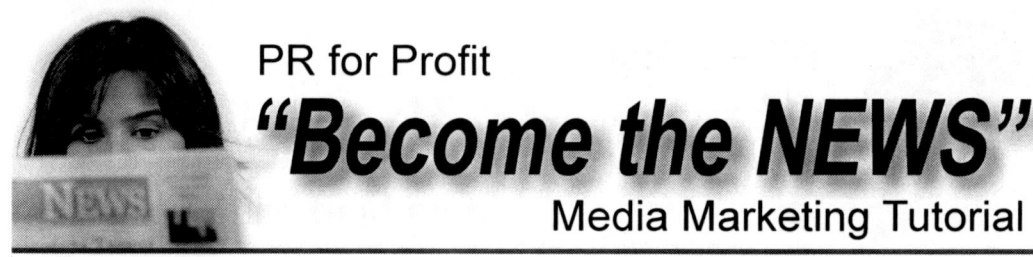

Media formats and outlets...

In this section I would like to explain the many different types of media exposure that are available for you to gain and take advantage of. This will enable you to start giving some consideration to specifically what you are trying to achieve with PR marketing; also you will see which of these possibilities would suit you and your company best, as well as identifying the most logical starting point for you.

BIG and glossy always sounds nice, but it is not necessarily the most profitable type of PR or media exposure, nor is it the easiest or quickest to obtain. In the previous section of this tutorial you have already heard me use the expression ***'Low Hanging Fruit'***, and that is what should ***ALWAYS*** be our objective; the biggest and most profitable returns for the smallest investment of our time and resources.

There are no limitations...

If you like working, and making money, you are about to discover that there are no shortage of press or media outlets you can use as often as you wish; for this reason you can stay as ***BUSY*** and productive as you want to be.
Once you have established the methods you are going to use, and outlets you feel are most profitable, you are free to use them just as regularly as you desire.

Notes:
Please use this margin for writing your ideas thoughts, inspirations and personal plan of action.

This Tutorial will then act as your route map to PR success!

At the very end of this tutorial I will be sharing the time saving system that I use to deliver my PR news releases and maintain relationships with our media contacts. This simple system has the ability to really turbo charge your PR output and start attracting extremely high volumes of new prospects whatever your line of business.

You have probably already started to build ideas on which to write your news releases, so knowing ***WHERE*** you will send them is the next logical step and that's what we will be covering in this section. First let's examine the type of media you should be considering using...

The local press...

Now for most people gaining exposure in their local press, this is the natural starting point to their PR journey, as it is always a good idea to learn to walk before you try running. There is ***NOTHING DIFFICULT*** in gaining ongoing media exposure in local press or publications, and most small towns have at least one local paper which is always ***HUNGRY*** for quality news items with a local flavour. Here in the UK there are hundreds if not thousands of local papers and with experience you could get relevant articles into many if not most of them.

As you gain skill and experience you may well be able to craft and create news stories that will be of interest and offer benefit to the local press across the country. To make this possibility more practical, later in the tutorial I will show you a method of localising your article by 'Form Feeding' relevant information, which means that these ***AUTOMATED*** alterations will allow you to use the ***VERY SAME*** news article to send to every publication, and they will believe it has been written specifically for them.

Notes:
Please use this margin for writing your ideas thoughts, inspirations and personal plan of action.

This Tutorial will then act as your route map to PR success!

The National Press...

Writing for the National press is not really any different or any more difficult

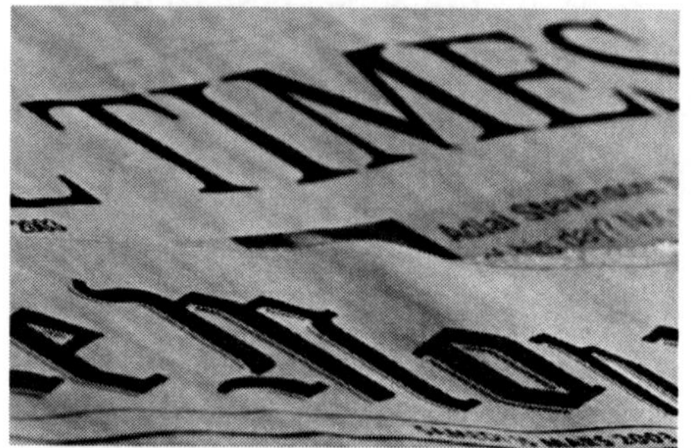

than for the local papers. It's just that far more people are likely to read them and as an obvious result see your article. So it stands to reason that gaining National media exposure is perceived as being ***MORE VALUABLE***, and for this reason the National press have far more news articles sent to them in the hope of publication. This means that they can be ***HIGHLY*** selective in what they accept for publication, so make sure your offering is good.

If you feel your article has National appeal you should send it in for consideration and potential publication and see what happens, as you have ***EVERYTHING*** to gain, and ***NOTHING*** to lose. Remember, that in the same way "a faint heart never won fair lady" un-submitted news releases never get published. Even if your article isn't published, all is not lost as you may be able to speak to a journalist and find out ***EXACTLY*** why they are not going to use it, or even how they think you should improve it so that they ***WOULD*** publish it. This would be really ***VALUABLE*** feedback of the highest quality.

Remember there could be a ***WIDE*** variety of reasons why it wasn't published that have ***NOTHING*** at all to do with the news article quality. So, you could ***ALWAYS*** alter or even ***REWRITE*** your article with a slightly different spin and then re-present it which ***MAY*** result in it getting published.

Another possibility could be that your story is picked up from another publication or one of the National papers which could run with it, which does happen, and is a ***BIG BONUS,*** and this is what we are constantly hoping for.

Parish Magazines...

From ***BIG*** and brave to small and humble; if I had written this PR tutorial a year previously you wouldn't have found this section, and I would have left out what for some of you will become an ***ENORMOUS*** and highly profitable opportunity; let me explain.

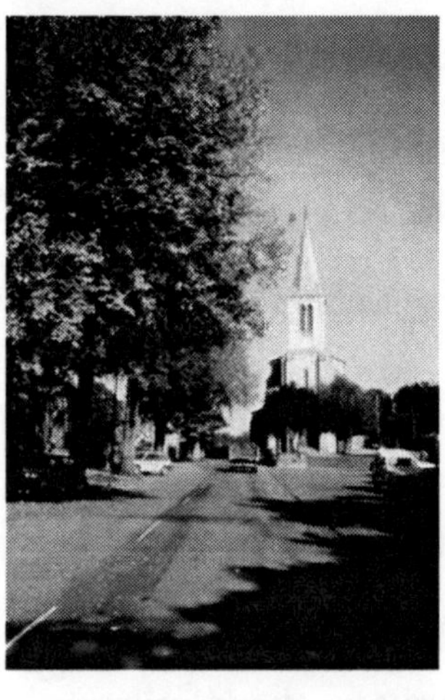

I live in a small village where four times a year we receive a small, unprofessionally produced parish magazine which varies in length from 12 to 20 pages depending upon the time of year. Every time this *(quite amateurish)* magazine is published and delivered, it is read by most members of my family because it contains a lot of ***VERY LOCAL*** news and bits of gossip from on our own doorstep.

A year or so ago I noticed that an electrician friend of mine ***ALWAYS*** advertised in it, and rather than a little ad, he took a half a page advert, so the next time I saw him, I asked him how well his advertisement worked for him. I was ***VERY*** surprised to hear that 'Parish Magazines' were his ***ONLY*** source of advertising!

He went on to tell me that he advertises in fifteen of them in the local area and it cost him no more than £200 a year to advertise in the ***LOT!*** ...and that this advertising was responsible for keeping him ***REALLY BUSY*** throughout the year!

It was ***NOT ONLY*** the response he generated which caught my interest, but also how ***MANY*** little magazines there were being published in such a small area, and that most churches or parishes have one of their own. Although there is a ***VAST*** difference in the quality of the finished product, which range from those printed on the home computer, to others which are professionally printed.

Notes:
Please use this margin for writing your ideas thoughts, inspirations and personal plan of action.

This Tutorial will then act as your route map to PR success!

Notes:
Please use this margin for writing your ideas thoughts, inspirations and personal plan of action.

This Tutorial will then act as your route map to PR success!

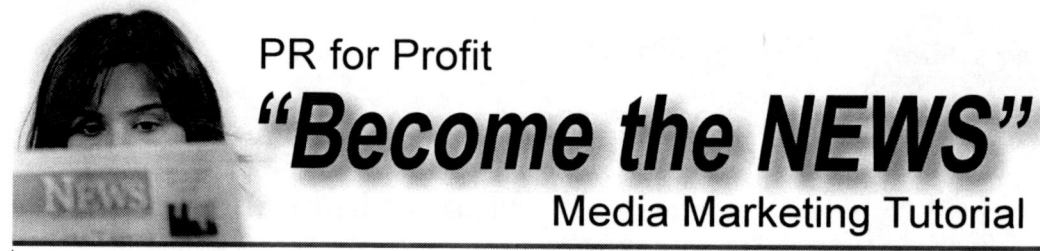

After a few months I had quite a collection of these little publications cluttering my office bookshelves, and two things became very apparent.

First; they were all ***VERY*** inexpensive to advertise in.
Second; they could benefit from some professional content.

This really got me thinking, so I decided to try a little experiment. I wrote a short and compelling article on the subject of using the computer to make money from home, and an additional income, which at the conclusion offered further information and the download of a full report from one of my websites in return for the visitor's email address.

By this time I had built a short email list of about thirty five such publications, so I emailed a short covering letter plus the article to include in their magazine if they wished to do so. As the report had already been written, the whole process only took me an hour or so to complete from start to finish. To this day I am not certain just ***HOW MANY*** of these parish magazines actually published my article, but I waited in patient anticipation and over the following 3 months my efforts were rewarded as I had "1,893" people who read this article and then submitted their email to download the ***FREE*** report I had produced.

These were people who had qualified themselves as individuals who were interested in the type of products and services I had for sale, and I was now free to follow up and market to them at will.

Notes:
Please use this margin for writing your ideas thoughts, inspirations and personal plan of action.

This Tutorial will then act as your route map to PR success!

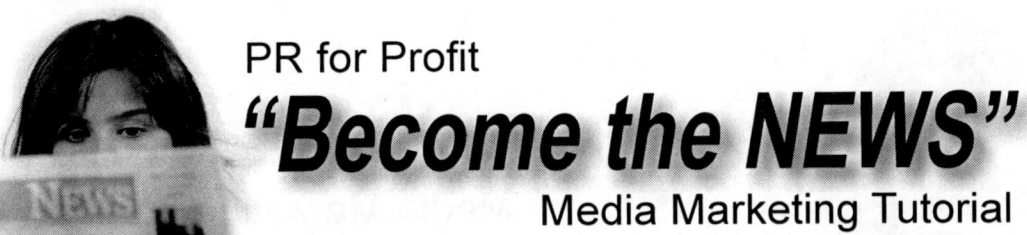

I had just struck GOLD!

...and it's a gold rush you can now capitalise upon if you offer the right product or service, or can design one which will work within this market place.

Now before you become cynical and begin thinking this could have just have been ***BEGINNERS LUCK***, I did also, and for this reason I repeated the same experiment using a different article and tip sheet on a slightly different subject which I had prepared. ***BINGO***! My second attempt enjoyed a much ***LARGER*** success than the first time around. As you can imagine I will be exploring the commercial aspect of this discovery as we move forward.

I have considered the possibility of building an email list of all such magazines across the country and then a resource website which I would populate with updated topical articles, which editors of such magazines could freely use to make them more interesting. Obviously, such articles and stories would be heavily laced with links to my websites which would result in financial reward.

Of course, someone may decide to do this before me, and it could be you!

Notes:
Please use this margin for writing your ideas thoughts, inspirations and personal plan of action.

This Tutorial will then act as your route map to PR success!

Community magazines...

During my search for these potentially profitable little magazines I discovered that ***MOST*** areas also have many competing ***MINI*** commercial, or so called 'Community Magazines'. These are generally A5 sized, like a piece of letter-sized paper, which has been folded in half, and I found no less that 5 of these which were published on a monthly basis and delivered around different areas of my local town which has a population of approximately 50,000 people, ie; it is not a large town!

I discovered that all these 'Mini Mags' were ***VERY*** commercially focused, approximately 50 % or more being dedicated to local adverts, and it was blatantly apparent that they ***ALL*** suffered from a lack of ***PERSONALITY*** and well written content. I would like to bet that the editors of these magazines, who generally consist of entrepreneur/stop-at-home-mums, would ***BITE*** your hand off for an ongoing supply of short and compelling articles to ***BEEF OUT*** their magazines!

Remember the LOW HANGING fruit? Are you seeing the potential?

Now this figure may be wildly inaccurate, but from the number of community, church and parish magazines and publications which I found in my area alone, I conservatively calculate there could be many thousands of them across the UK; perhaps as many as 5 – 10 for every newspaper and I have a list of over 1,600! This could mean 8,000 – 16,000 little magazines all looking for quality content ***EVERY*** month or so! ...even if this figure is much lower than estimated, it is ***STILL*** one ***WELL WORTH*** exploring further as it offers PR marketeers who are armed with the right product or service, great ***FINANCIAL*** opportunity and reward.

Notes:
Please use this margin for writing your ideas thoughts, inspirations and personal plan of action.

This Tutorial will then act as your route map to PR success!

How to find them...

Church or parish magazines should not be difficult to find in your own area, and I will put a link to a community magazines franchise I found on the resource website...

Glossy magazines and trade journals...

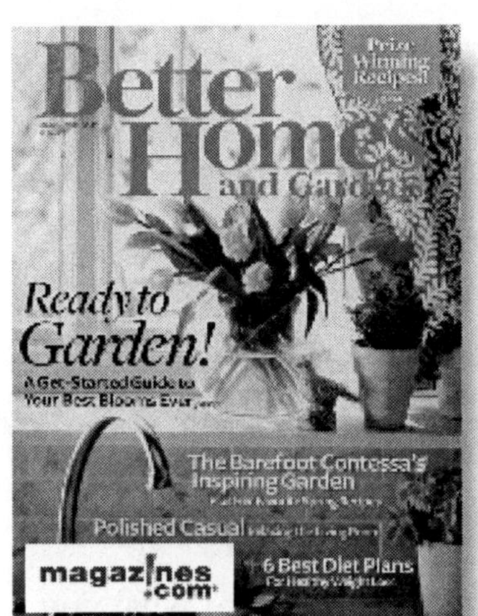

By glossy magazines I mean the sort you may find in the news racks of your local newsagents, and as you know there are ***HUNDREDS*** of different titles available on most subjects; in fact I will be showing you how to find the details of approximately 1,900 of those in the UK at the end of this section.

Such magazines generally have a very specifically defined target market of consumers and will be mainly interested in well written quality articles. Now here is a ***BONUS***; you may in fact be offered payment for writing for these magazines; more about that in a moment.

Before you start writing your article though, be certain to contact the publication which most captures your interest to make sure they would be interested in receiving something from you. You also need to be aware that such magazines may be working ***MANY*** months in advance, and so if they accept your article for publication you may not benefit from the results for some time.

Notes:
Please use this margin for writing your ideas thoughts, inspirations and personal plan of action.

This Tutorial will then act as your route map to PR success!

Do you fancy getting paid to *WRITE* articles?

WANT TO SELL A STORY TO THE PRESS BUT NOT SURE HOW?
1 TELL US YOUR STORY. FILL OUT OUR ONLINE FORM
2 WE TELL YOU HOW MUCH YOUR STORY IS WORTH
3 IF YOU'RE HAPPY TO GO AHEAD, WE GET YOU THE BEST DEAL FOR YOUR STORY

If so, you may be interested in checking out 'Famous Features' at: www.famousfeatures.co.uk where there is a ***VERY*** good income to be made from freelance writing for publications which may be of interest to you. If so, this could be a good starting point, where you can discover much of what you need to know to get started immediately.

PR marketing and Radio exposure...

Strangely, most people don't think of the radio as providing an opportunity for getting media exposure, so if you also think in this way it is time to

RECONSIDER. As well as entertaining their listeners with music and keeping them up to date with local, and national news items, many stations also run a variety of topical head-to-head type magazine programs which are ***ALWAYS*** on the lookout for someone with a good topic or story to tell, and who would make a good interviewee for their station.

Usually such interviews last just 3 or 4 minutes in length, longer if the journalist thinks you can handle it, or if they know you well; but as a rule of thumb they are short, brief and very much to the point.

Neither is there necessarily any particular need for you to visit the radio station studio, as they may agree to call you at a convenient location, usually your home or office, and interview you there by phone. Now here is the best bit; if you furnish them in advance with a list of the questions you would like them to ask, they will usually do so because they know these are the questions which you have come prepared to answer. Just think about the radio journalist's requirements which are simple; they want to look professional, and provide a smooth running and entertaining interview for their listeners.

Now if the idea of conducting a radio interview makes you a little nervous let me tell you that it is ***DEAD EASY!*** I have been conducting radio interviews for 30 or more years and when I first started I ***ALSO*** was petrified at the idea of a large listening audience which I couldn't see. However, I had no need to be as I have always found radio journalists to be kind and helpful people who will work at relaxing you and making the interview enjoyable and as easy as possible for you.

Once they are familiar with you as someone who knows what they are talking about they are likely to remember and recommend you to their colleagues, and you are likely to find yourself being asked back for follow up interviews.

Best of all, with the right topics, radio publicity is ***VERY*** easy to obtain, and I have found on many occasions, and within just minutes of receiving my email news release, radio station programmers call me back to arrange the interview or to investigate further.

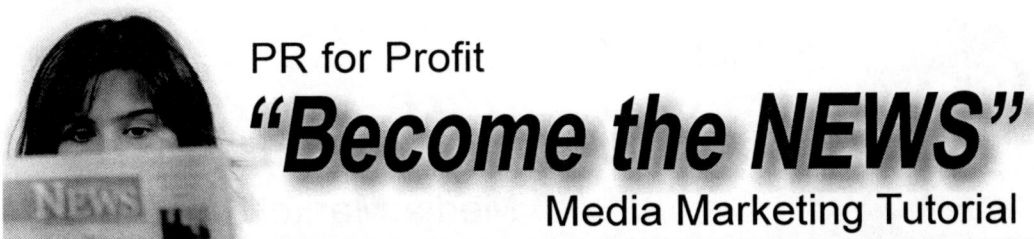

Notes:
Please use this margin for writing your ideas thoughts, inspirations and personal plan of action.

This Tutorial will then act as your route map to PR success!

Notes:
Please use this margin for writing your ideas thoughts, inspirations and personal plan of action.

This Tutorial will then act as your route map to PR success!

You may already be aware that I used to be an entertainer, and back in the days when I used to book large venues (theatres and halls etc) for my shows, radio stations have often come to my rescue on occasions when advance ticket sales have not come in as expected. On such occasions I have called up the local radio station and given an interview, excerpts from which very often repeated throughout the day, which resulted in those particular evening shows being total sell outs.

The radio can be a very ***INFLUENTIAL*** medium and sometimes your interviews will be heard by a very large and responsive audience which could be responsible for swelling you bank balance; so be certain to give radio a try because in my opinion it will produce some of the ***BEST*** media exposure you will get.

Gaining TV exposure...

Now some topics just lend themselves to television news and you will immediately know if yours is one of them. If so, you should send your news release to the TV channels news room in exactly the same way as you would any other news room. We will be going into fine detail of dispatching your release later in the tutorial...

The ***BIG*** problem with TV is that even after confirming that they will cover your event, if another story, which they believe to be ***MORE INTERESTING,*** comes along, they will drop you faster than a ***HOT*** potato. Unfortunately, this is the nature of the media and this happened to me ***VERY*** recently when ***TWO*** news channels had promised to cover the same event and neither of them turned up; not even a phone call – ***VERY FRUSTRATING!***

However, on the positive side, the TV exposure which I have received in the past has led on to some interesting opportunities such as appearances on programs such as the 'Generation Game' and some considerably lucrative corporate contracts. So, although it can be frustrating, it is well worth the effort when it works.

Notes:
Please use this margin for writing your ideas thoughts, inspirations and personal plan of action.

This Tutorial will then act as your route map to PR success!

Online PR...

Now this section would not be complete without mentioning ***ONLINE*** PR because this offers you many additional benefits which I will mention in just a moment. First however, is that ***ONLINE*** PR is likely to attract a completely different audience to your traditional PR; a ***GLOBAL*** one, so it's not an 'either/ or situation' – ***DO BOTH!***

If you are creating a news release to gain more traditional media exposure, you will be able to ***VERY QUICKLY*** adapt your release for online use also; this is a good habit to develop and only takes a few minutes to do. *(I will be going in more depth in a later chapter.)*

The ***BIG*** benefit however, is that ***ONLINE*** PR websites will archive your news releases which go on providing traffic to your website for ***YEARS*** to come. Your release will get indexed in the search engines often ***VERY*** rapidly, and will provide, what are known as 'Back links' to your website, which from a respected PR news site, can be ***VERY VALUABLE.***

In a nut shell, 'back links' are likely to help your website pages appear higher in the SERPs *(Search Engine Results Pages)* which in turn means more traffic, generally, proving you are offering a quality product or service, more ***SALES***! ...and that's what getting PR is all about.

Notes:
Please use this margin for writing your ideas thoughts, inspirations and personal plan of action.

This Tutorial will then act as your route map to PR success!

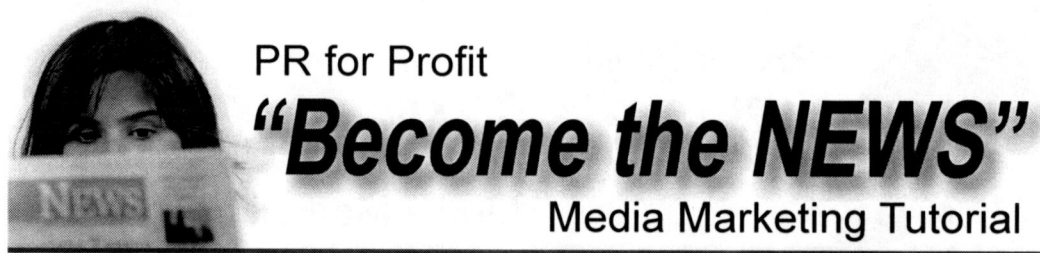

ONLINE PR could almost become a book on its own and is ***VERY*** closely related to ***SEO*** *(Search Engine Optimisation)* and a completely different subject to PR marketing, which I will talk more about later.

So which FORMAT of PR best suits you?

Whatever your answer, let me remind you that the ***ULTIMATE*** objective of this PR tutorial is about you making more ***PROFITS***, and we also like to think, it's about having fun in what you do. So for that reason we would like to encourage you to experiment with all the different ***MEDIA*** formats, so that you gain a better understanding of PR marketing in general.

Finding MEDIA contacts...

In the past we have used a variety of media directories, but have found the best to be 'Ben's Media Directory' which is presently being published by 'Hollis Publishing'; you can find a current link on our resource website pages. However, media directories do not come cheaply and the current cost is approximately £200 which is steep if you only require the names of a few of your more local publications, so let's look at cheaper alternatives.

You could use the internet and you will find a variety of different lists and sources, or if you know the publication name, search for it directly.

Or, may I suggest you may consider visiting: www.mediauk.com

At the time of writing this tutorial, 'Media UK' offer a free service, but I would imagine this may change in the future. They will show you ***MOST*** of the UK publications which you may consider using in the future and are a ***REALLY*** great source of inspiration.

Notes:
Please use this margin for writing your ideas thoughts, inspirations and personal plan of action.

This Tutorial will then act as your route map to PR success!

The British media industry is here.

Websites, addresses, telephone numbers, email and more for all areas of the online media, including 822 radio stations, 546 television channels, 1,600 newspapers, and 1,957 magazines - from 260 media owners - are all here. This website is continually updated with **47 updates** over the past week; it was last updated 14 hours, 26 minutes ago.

They list virtually every UK publication you will ever need unless you are aiming to set your sights on foreign PR. As you can see from the quick screen grab, their listings are ***VERY*** comprehensive.

A B C D E F G H I J K L M N O P Q R S T U V W X Y Z

Media UK ignores the leading 'Daily'
Looking for the Daily Telegraph? You'll find it under

Dagenham Express
Darlington & Stockton Times
Darlington Herald & Post
Darlington, Aycliffe anc
Dartford & Swanley Times
Dartford and Swanley Extra
Dartford Messenger
Daventry Express
Daventry Post
Dearne Valley Weekender
Deeside Piper
Denbighshire Free Press
Derby Evening Telegraph
Derbyshire Times
Dereham Times
Derry Journal
Derry News
Devon Diary
Devon Independent
Dewsbury Reporter

Notes:
Please use this margin for writing your ideas thoughts, inspirations and personal plan of action.

This Tutorial will then act as your route map to PR success!

Dewsbury Reporter

Coverage area: Dewsbury
Owner: Johnston Press

Contact details hide

Address: 17 Wellington Road Dewsbury West, Yorkshire WF13 1HQ
Map: See a map of Dewsbury Reporter's offices
Main - Tel: 01924 468282 **Fax:** 01924 457652 send a fax
Website: http://www.dewsburytoday.co.uk

News archive hide

See a full news archive for Dewsbury Reporter

Search the Dewsbury Reporter website hide

They give you all the main details such as general telephone number etc, but to find out more information such as their news room emails etc, you will need to visit their website. Put some time on one side to familiarise yourself with this useful website as it will highlight the ***TRUE*** potential of PR marketing.

Action Plan...

Before we move on to the next chapter I would like you to make some important preparations so when your first news release is ready for dispatch you will know precisely where to send it without delay.

As your first news releases are most likely to be local ones, invest a little of your time researching and finding the relevant details *(telephone numbers and email address)* for your local press and radio station news rooms.

From the directory at: www.mediauk.co.uk invest some of your time researching glossy and trade magazines, and which of them you feel your topic and line of business would be most suited. Make a list of these publications for future reference, be specific, find out who their readers are, and if they match the profile of your target buyer.

Think about the theme of articles you could write for the magazines you have just placed on your list; even start to write the title of your article to stimulate your creativity if you wish.

Now once again using: www.mediauk.co.uk go through the same process and create a list of ten radio stations on which you would like to be interviewed. This may require you to visit their websites to research the different programmes and find out the type of audiences they are aimed at.

> *It's common sense really, if the programme's audience consists of spinsters in their eighties they are not likely to respond too well to an interview on 'Harley Davidson's' and fun biking!*

If you see a particular program on which you would like to be interviewed, make a note of it, and also the producer's name, as you can often send your release ***DIRECTLY*** to them; they are likely to respond more favourably if they know you have spent a few minutes researching them and their programme in advance.

Okay, that list will keep you out of mischief for the next hour or so and will at the same time open your mind to other marketing and PR possibilities.

Notes:
Please use this margin for writing your ideas thoughts, inspirations and personal plan of action.

This Tutorial will then act as your route map to PR success!

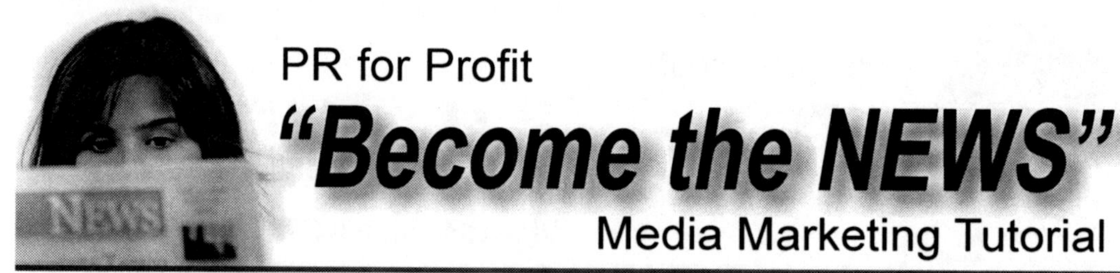

Notes:
Please use this margin for writing your ideas thoughts, inspirations and personal plan of action.

This Tutorial will then act as your route map to PR success!

Media Marketing Methodology

In an upcoming chapter we will be taking you through the precise step-by-step process on how to write news releases which will capture attention and get response. However, there is far more to PR marketing than just writing a news release as you will soon discover, and that is what this chapter entitled ***'Media Marketing Methodology'*** is all about.

We are now really getting into the meat of this PR tutorial and you are about to discover many of the main techniques that we use to develop powerful PR material that will qualify and highlight new prospects, and then entice them into taking the next step to becoming a paying client or customer.

As you are probably starting to understand, getting media exposure is one thing, but the real skill of PR marketing is in creating material which will convert into hard profits.

You don't have to use all of these ideas that are discussed; in fact some of them may be quite unsuitable for your particular line of business, or the way in which it works. However, you should know ***HOW*** to use them ***ALL*** as it is highly likely that many of these techniques, with just a little creativity, will easily adapt to your business. So please do not be afraid of experimenting to find out what works best for you.

Once set up and mastered, many of these techniques can be quickly duplicated and adapted for use in other news releases and PR campaigns, saving you ***TONS*** of time.

As you will have already read earlier in the tutorial, there are just two general types of news release. Those which require a 'Direct Response' of some sort from your prospect, and the second type with which you will be more familiar, that have been placed into a category we have called 'Profile Building'. Let's start to examine these techniques in far more depth.

Notes:
Please use this margin for writing your ideas thoughts, inspirations and personal plan of action.

This Tutorial will then act as your route map to PR success!

Profile Building PR techniques...

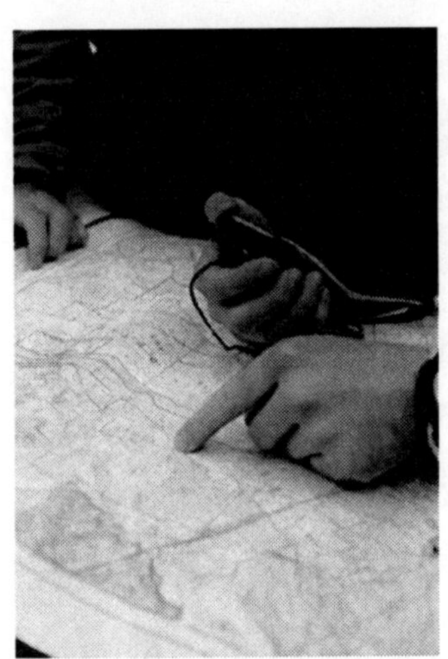

These would be best described as methods which do not require the reader, listener, or potential prospect to do anything. They do not contain an offer or call-to-action of any sort. Neither do they offer the reader any benefit other than entertaining and informing them. They are just used to ***POSITION YOU*** and your company in the minds of your prospects, so when the time comes, and when they need the type of product or service that you offer, it will be ***YOUR COMPANY*** they either call or visit first. You can have a lot of fun creating profile-building articles and events, and back in the chapter entitled 'Idea Mining' I gave you a whole bunch of quality ideas for use with this type of PR, for example by holding special fun days etc.

Used in isolation to gain media exposure, the profile-building PR techniques may be very unproductive, especially when it comes to adding profits to your bank balance. However, when they are used correctly, and as part of an ongoing PR campaign, the accumulative effect of gaining repeat and ongoing exposure will come into play and it becomes ***EXCEPTIONALLY*** valuable and effective.

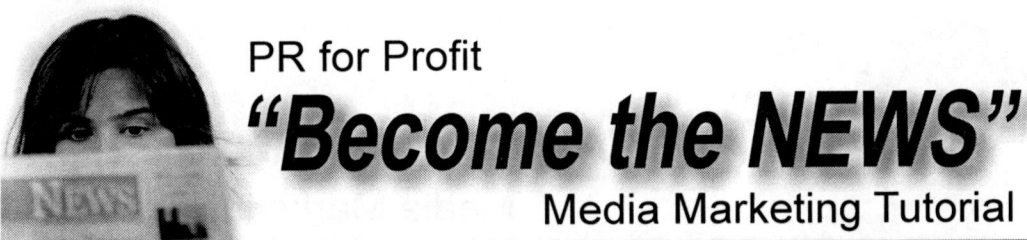

Notes:
Please use this margin for writing your ideas thoughts, inspirations and personal plan of action.

This Tutorial will then act as your route map to PR success!

By complete contrast...

Direct response PR techniques, all require your potential prospects to take an action of some sort; they contain trigger mechanisms, offers, and time-sensitive calls-to-action; for this important reason, 'Direct Response' PR techniques, should be your main area of interest and will be the central focus of this chapter.

So ***WHY*** is it so important to get your prospect moving, and take action?

There are many important answers to this question, the first being that by responding, the prospect is registering his or her interest with you, and you

may say that we are in fact separating the 'Men from the Boys' and the 'Wheat from the Chaff'! The simple objective is to ***IDENTIFY*** those who have a real interest, from those who are just curious, because they are the ones who will become our clients and customers of tomorrow.

By getting them to take an action, they are entering the start of our sales process!

An interesting analogy...

As a governor of my local primary school I often get asked into the classroom to work with the children. I suspect it is primarily because of my background as an entertainer. Perhaps it's my age, but I really enjoy it, and look forward to these FUN interactions, ESPECIALLY with the younger children of 5 or 6 years of age as they are so ENTHUSIASTIC!

Notes:
Please use this margin for writing your ideas thoughts, inspirations and personal plan of action.

This Tutorial will then act as your route map to PR success!

Recently, while working with such a group I asked for a volunteer to help me conduct a little magic trick. In immediate response to my request the hands of the whole group shot up in the air. However, what stuck in my mind was the HUGE difference in the levels of GUSTO which the children used to capture my attention and register their enthusiasm to be selected for this simple task.

Some of the obviously less keen or less confident children would hold up and waggle a limp hand at shoulder height to show their willingness to participate. While at the opposite end of the scale, there were a group of toothless boys who reached up so high, and with such energy, that they appeared to be in imminent peril of dislocating their shoulders. At the same time their pained mutterings and contorted facial expressions indicated their bladders could have been filled to capacity, and giving them severe pain.

The point of this story is this...

When someone takes action, they are in fact putting their hand in the air, and have offered us the opportunity to ***WOW*** and impress them. We now have to build their enthusiasm to the point where they, like the enthusiastic boys who wanted to be picked to help with the magic trick, raise their hand to full height indicating their readiness to purchase.

Another reason is that those who have become involved, feel more in control of the situation, and as a result then become more likely to purchase. Involvement often comes in the form of offering the opportunity to take advantage of a no-obligation trial of your service or product, which ***ALWAYS*** makes good marketing sense. So let's get straight into this interesting subject.

Notes:
Please use this margin for writing your ideas thoughts, inspirations and personal plan of action.

This Tutorial will then act as your route map to PR success!

The money is in the list...

You may have already heard the above saying, and for companies and

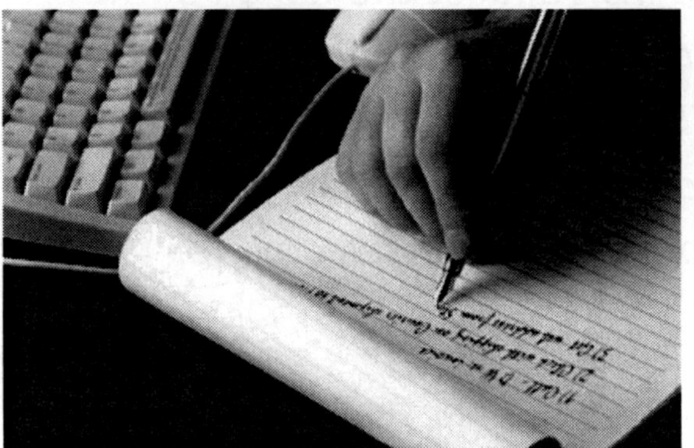

entrepreneurs who have worked at building their own mail lists will know this to be a ***VERY*** accurate statement. However, from years of hard experience, I think I am qualified to upgrade this statement to make it ***EVEN*** more precise and pertinent. It should read:

"The money is in the RELATIONSHIP you GENERATE with your list!"

Please remember that when someone subscribes to your list it is just the ***START*** of the relationship which could become a long and ***VERY*** financially profitable one for you, if you treat your new prospects well, and with the respect they deserve.

Now you may say that building a list is more to do with marketing than PR but I would disagree, because as far as I am concerned, the two are linked and share the same profit making objective.

What I do know for certain, and is applicable to almost ***EVERY BUSINESS,*** is that if you don't consider building a mail list of your own *(specifically an eMail list),* you are leaving a ***HUGE*** proportion of your potential profit behind, and for your competitors to claim! To highlight this fact let me remind you that your first sale will provide you with an income, but ***ONGOING*** and ***REPEAT CUSTOM*** from creating a relationship with your clients and customers, has the potential to make you very ***WEALTHY***!

Take EVERYTHING, but not my list!

To emphasise the value which most successful entrepreneurs place upon their lists, I just ***HAD*** to include the following. When asked, most modern Internet marketing gurus will often say that their most valuable of all possessions is their mail list. They claim they could lose everything, but armed with their list they can make it all back again in a very short space of time.

Now you may be ***SCEPTICAL*** at such a statement, and I can't blame you; however, I ***KNOW*** it is ***TRUE*** and I have had first hand experience and

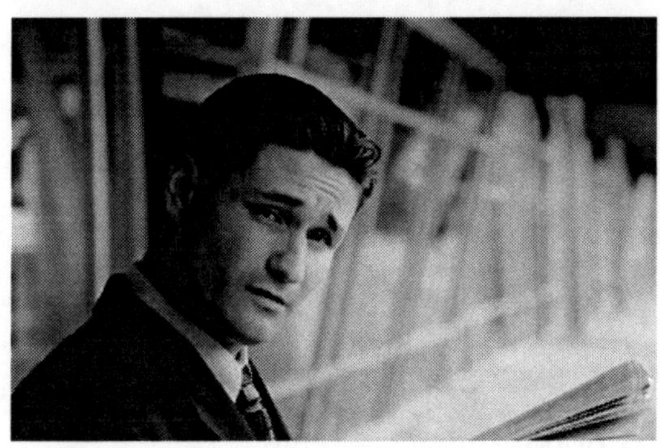

been privileged to watch this very scenario unfold. It all started when an acquaintance hit hard times, and as a result had the added misfortune of having his marriage breakdown at the same time; he walked out of his exceedingly comfortable lifestyle with ***JUST*** the clothes he stood up in, and his small mail-list.

He didn't waste any time in getting started rebuilding his life, and when I saw him a few months later he looked happy and well fed; he put his present position into perspective by stating that he was '***AHEAD*** of the game'. Approximately a year after this, his business was once again flourishing, and soon he moved into a ***NICER*** house than the one he had before his downfall. He was an inspiration to us all, and had elevated himself from debt to zero, and from nothing to prosperity in under 18 months thanks to long hours of focused ***HARD WORK***, and his small but effective email list.

It makes ***GOOD*** common sense...

Notes:
Please use this margin for writing your ideas thoughts, inspirations and personal plan of action.

This Tutorial will then act as your route map to PR success!

However good at marketing you ***ALREADY*** are, and however good you

become at PR, you will ***ALWAYS*** attract ***FAR MORE*** potential prospects than will take immediate action. For example, let's imagine that your news release leads your interested prospects back to one of your websites to discover more about the product or service you offer. If it's a good offer, and because the timing may be right, a percentage of your visitors may take immediate action.

However, the ***MAJORITY*** of them, who could be as high as **99.99%** of your visitors, do not! Some ***WILL*** 'bookmark your site' and may return after consideration, most ***WON'T,*** simply because they forget, or do not have the time, which means that when they leave your website, they will be leaving it ***FOREVER***, and you have just lost a ***BIG*** opportunity.

The solution is simple...

Use the techniques we are about to cover in the rest of this chapter to change your offer around so visitors have the opportunity to get some ***UP-FRONT*** and without obligation ***VALUE*** from you. Let them experience and enjoy what you have on offer as you have very little to lose, but a ***LOT*** to gain.

As you will soon discover there are many methods for doing this which will allow you to capture their email addresses in return for access to the value or incentive which you promised to provide in fair exchange. The very fact that this opportunity has been made available to them via the press or media will add considerable credibility, and as you gain experience you can look forward to some outstanding results.

This time, and because of your improved ***METHODOLOGY,*** and at the prospect of gaining some up-front value, you should attract a ***MUCH LARGER*** volume of prospects than otherwise. Best of all is that a good percentage of your visitors are likely to subscribe to your mail list as it promises them some value and hasn't cost them a penny. Now I know you are curious as to just how well this technique works, so I will let you into a secret, and that is, one of my websites consistently subscribes 35% - 40% of first- time-visitors to my list! ...however, this is ***EXCEPTIONAL*** and generally I would expect an opt-in rate of between 10% - 25% if you were offering a worthwhile benefit.

Your new mail list ***DRAMATICALLY*** and very positively changes the relationship with your prospects, and the way in which you conduct your business. Rather than waiting for custom to come to you, armed with your list you can now market to them at will and be in a position of generating some ***EXCEPTIONALLY*** lucrative paydays.

Notes:
Please use this margin for writing your ideas thoughts, inspirations and personal plan of action.

This Tutorial will then act as your route map to PR success!

Notes:
Please use this margin for writing your ideas thoughts, inspirations and personal plan of action.

This Tutorial will then act as your route map to PR success!

Building the relationship...

Now like most things in life, maintaining an email list does have some simple

rules that need to be followed to ***KEEP IT*** profitable. You may think this is the point at which we start aggressively trying to sell your 'opt-ins' something, and depending upon the list you maybe right. However, and from experience, I have learned that the smartest action is to keep on giving them value so they will stay subscribed.

The way I look at it, is that every time I contact my list subscribers, it's an opportunity for me to make our relationship a little stronger, and just a bit more trusting. You have probably heard it said that the prospect needs to have contact with you on an average of seven times before they become receptive enough to buy anything from you. I am not certain if this true, although I am certain that the more ***VALUE*** you provide your potential prospects, the ***MORE LIKELY*** they are to become customers.

Keeping your list warm...

What I find difficult to understand are the people who go to the effort of building a list, and then do nothing with it and let it go cold. This is ***MADNESS***! and a bit like working hard to earn an income, and then throwing it all away. Obviously, your list will only stay profitable and receptive if you keep speaking to them, and maintain your relationship.

Notes:
Please use this margin for writing your ideas thoughts, inspirations and personal plan of action.

This Tutorial will then act as your route map to PR success!

There are no hard or fast rules as to how often you should contact your list; as a rule of thumb I try to walk the fine line that runs between 'Pest and Persistence' while at the same time maintaining ***ONGOING VALUE*** for my subscribers; follow this advice and you will not go far wrong. A lot will come down to, and be determined by, the subject of your business and the relationship you would like to develop.

Learn from experts...

There is no better way of learning how to maintain a high quality relationship with your mail list subscribers than from the experts who are already doing it on a ***DAILY*** basis. You will find no shortage of ***BIG INCOME*** earners who will be glad to show you ***EXACTLY*** how they maintain there lists for ***NOTHING!***

All you have to do is sign up to their email lists, and their emails will start arriving in your mailbox almost immediately. All you have to do is study them and then imitate what they do. I have compiled and placed an example list of Internet ***ENTREPRENEURS*** on the resource website, which accompanies this tutorial.

Build it once - and go on profiting for years...

As you gain experience in using list building in conjunction with your PR marketing, you will become aware of the ***HUGE*** amount of benefits having your own list offers. One of the best, which I haven't yet mentioned, is that with a list, *(even a small one)* you can obtain some very ***VALUABLE*** feedback and ideas for future projects, and have a good idea just how profitable they are likely to be if you develop them.

Notes:
Please use this margin for writing your ideas thoughts, inspirations and personal plan of action.

This Tutorial will then act as your route map to PR success!

I regularly ask my subscribers about their main problems and challenges, and am ***AMAZED*** and at what comes back as they often furnish me with highly specific answers. Used from this perspective, your own mailing list can be compared to owning a crystal ball...

Auto responders...

If you are wondering about the software used to build and maintain an email list, even a ***LARGE*** one many thousand names strong, they are known as 'auto responders'. They are quite amazing, and will ***LITERALLY*** do the work which just a few years ago would have taken a whole office staff to complete. If you are thinking "this sounds expensive!" You will be happy to discover that they are not, and in fact, cost ***JUST*** a small monthly fee to maintain.

As usual, on the resource website I have provided you with details of the 'auto responder' which I feel offers the best value for you to explore further if you wish. This will give you a full 28 day free trial so you can play and experiment without cost...

List building resources

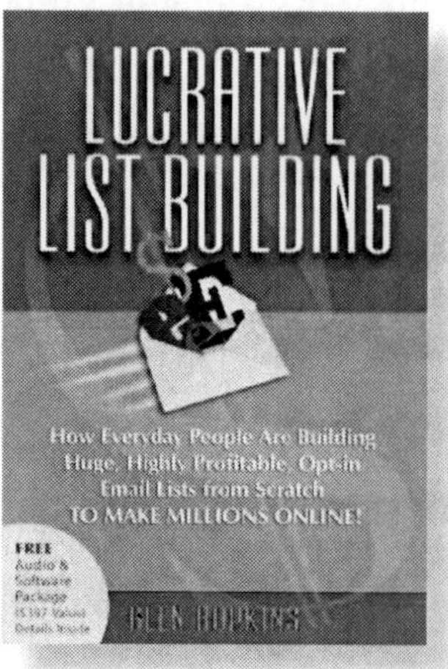

The following PR techniques will nearly all give you the opportunity to capture emails, so before we move on to them, I would like to recommend a little book on list building which, if you are interested, will broaden your understanding of this art. It's by: Glen Hopkins and is entitled: 'Lucrative List Building'. You will find it an easy and illuminating read.

Action Plan

Before moving on, visit the resource website and follow all the links next to the Internet marketing 'gurus' names and then subscribe to their news letters and email lists. This should only take you ten minutes or so, and as these people are ***VERY*** ethical marketeers you can unsubscribe and stop their emails at any time you wish.

I am suggesting you do it at this point because learning how to keep your list warm is so important and something you will thank us for encouraging you to learn as your list starts to generate an additional income for you.

While you are subscribing to these lists, examine the techniques that are used on the blogs and squeeze pages, and if you have started to use 'Snag it', capture images of the techniques you find most interesting for future use.

News release techniques

Okay let's now start to go through the methods that you can use to provide variety and make your 'Direct Response' news releases ***EXTRA*** interesting. At the moment these techniques are merely meant to give you ideas, and later as we start writing our news releases, we will give you working examples for you to follow and duplicate if you so wish.

Notes:
Please use this margin for writing your ideas thoughts, inspirations and personal plan of action.

This Tutorial will then act as your route map to PR success!

Notes:
Please use this margin for writing your ideas thoughts, inspirations and personal plan of action.

This Tutorial will then act as your route map to PR success!

The product launch...

Are you launching a new product or service in the near future? If so, it will turn

into an interesting news release if you include such details as to why the product has been created, and the advantage it gives to consumers, as well as fully explaining how it differs from other such products. It is possible for you to create and introduce an 'Early Bird Discount' of some sort. For example, if it were a book you could build interest by offering a 'Pre Publication Discount' and then you may get the opportunity of a second article by creating another release stating the 'Pre Publication Offer' was ***SO SUCCESSFUL*** that the order for a second edition had to be placed even before the first one came off the press! *("WOW, if it's that popular I had better place an order for my copy before it sells out again!").* You can see the opportunity for some creative PR engineering? ...the opportunities are endless!

So what if you don't have a new product or service? Well, with just a little creativity you could improve and revamp one of your older ones, and then ***RE-LAUNCH*** it; it will probably generate just as much interest as if it was a new product. This is a trick which many commercial brands use and no one ever seems to complain, so why shouldn't you benefit from it also?

Surveys...

You can come up with a multitude of interesting ideas as to why you are conducting a survey which will make a compelling article; but don't forget the ***REAL*** reason why you are doing it; that is primarily to capture email addresses; although it is possible that you may want to run a survey so that you can obtain some specific answers or feedback on a particular issue.

Notes:
Please use this margin for writing your ideas thoughts, inspirations and personal plan of action.

This Tutorial will then act as your route map to PR success!

Like most of the 'direct response' PR techniques, the best way to get good results is by offering something for free in return, and I will be giving you some ideas for creating simple and compelling free material at the end of this chapter; then, at the end of this tutorial, I will show you in detail how to produce them. Offering to share the results of the survey at its conclusion may in itself be an attractive incentive for many people to want to become involved.

Although you could offer to send an ***SAE*** *(Stamped Address Envelope)* by 'snail mail' along with the survey, the quickest way to get practical results would be to take participants to a website. There are loads of survey software packages available, although you should be aware that some of them can be ***REALLY*** difficult and time consuming to use. For that reason, on the resource website, I have given details of a very comprehensive and simple one which you may wish to consider using.

To capture their emails you can stipulate that the participants should include their details at the end of the survey before being given access to whatever ***FREE*** incentive you have promised. The biggest mistake I see people making again and again is to make the survey just too long or too complicated. As a simple guide line to follow, make sure that it can be completed inside just two minutes. For example, you should state the following fact in the body of the news release, *(that the survey comprises of just 7 multi-choice questions).*

Generating leads and appointments...

It would not be that difficult to generate leads and appointments in response to a good story. For instance, and this is a very quickly thrown together idea:

> Due to the economic recession, and to help local business owners over the ongoing credit crunch, PR marketing experts Kevin Martyn and Jeremy Fraser will be conducting a series of business clinics which will show forward looking entrepreneurs and companies how they can generate £20,000 of media exposure over the next 3 months ...
>
> ...30 minute appointment will be allocated on a first come first served basis

Notes:
Please use this margin for writing your ideas thoughts, inspirations and personal plan of action.

This Tutorial will then act as your route map to PR success!

Product testing...

A great way to gain publicity for a new project is to write a news article where you invite 'Beta' ***(new software release)*** testers, or individuals who would like to try out a product which is almost ready for production; for example:

Right now I am working on a new JV ***(Join Venture)*** product and website. Now, I know it is working perfectly well, but by generating a news release which includes the opportunity for a certain amount of individuals to try out this new software in advance of its imminent launch, I will catch the attention and generate an interest from many people who may in fact become customers. This would also be a ***REALLY*** great opportunity to gain testimonials for the product in advance of its launch.

Which is best?

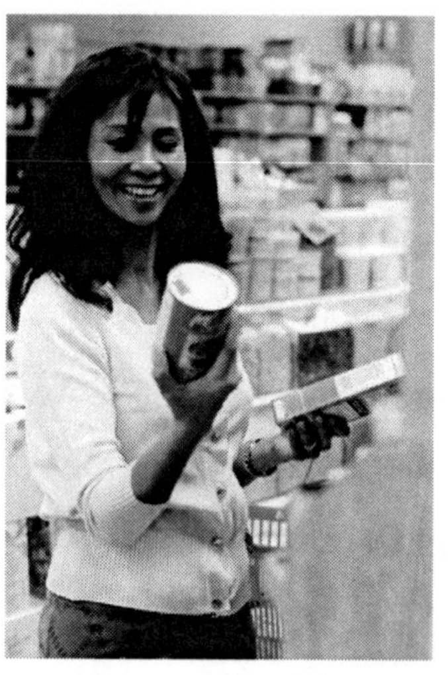

Now you may think that this technique should be listed under surveys, but I feel it is very much a stand-alone method as it can be used in a variety of different ways.

For this example, let's imagine you have written a new book which is almost ready for publication, all except for one thing - the book title. You have come up with three great examples, but you need help deciding which one to use. Again you could get participants to vote in return for access to the first chapter of the book and your survey software would help you to achieve this. Has your mind come alive with ideas at the ***HUGE*** amount of possibilities this technique offers?

Notes:
Please use this margin for writing your ideas thoughts, inspirations and personal plan of action.

This Tutorial will then act as your route map to PR success!

Run a competition...

Now this idea is just an alternative to the 'Which is best?' idea above. You would generate an almost identical news release but rather than asking for people to choose a title, you ask them to think up one of their own for which you could offer a prize.

Taking this idea a little further you could come up with a whole host of different ideas on this theme and find the only restriction you encounter will be your imagination. To capture the feedback from such competitions you could use a simple form where all of the information you required is sent to you and your auto responder by email.

Appeals...

Now this is another technique where you need to use a little artistic licence.

However, as a Nation, here in the UK I believe we are very charitable, and I say this as a result of some of the appeals in which I have been involved. I imagine you would get similar results wherever you live.

You will remember talking about how you will find no shortage of good and needy causes or charities which you or your company could help. In fact, there are far more which need help and support than you would ever have time for. Remember, you can create a news release which pitches your story in such a way that you gain tons of positive positioning and publicity, whilst generating the donations and funds it raises to the charity or good cause. Now that seems fair to me...

I recently became involved in such an appeal for a judo club which my children attend near Bristol.

Notes:
Please use this margin for writing your ideas thoughts, inspirations and personal plan of action.

This Tutorial will then act as your route map to PR success!

They really needed new mats for an upcoming championship. More than £3,500 was needed to purchase the mats, so I decided to combine this story with gaining some publicity for my daughter. The news release worked a treat and resulted in a series of articles being published and some valuable radio exposure, and I am glad to say we raised way in excess of the needed sum for the new mats without that much effort, basically because I set up a series of events that made for ***GREAT*** PR.

As I usually do, on this occasion I took the people who wanted to help and learn to a webpage; however, on this occasion, the page was not designed to squeeze their email out of them but rather a donation. So you can use this successful PR campaign as a working example as I have reproduced the exact webpage at: www.PR-forProfit.com/sponsorship/ By the way if you feel like making a donation while you are there please feel free as the PayPal buttons are all still live!

Seminars, talks and presentations...

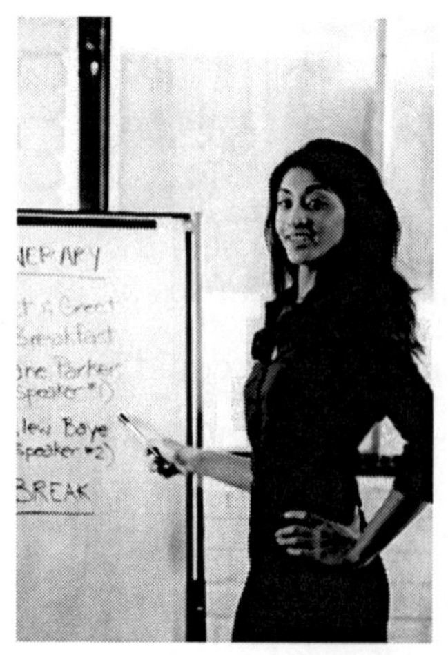

Always popular are news articles that offer their audience a live presentation for them to attend. Now hiring a venue to deliver your presentation can work out expensive, especially if you want to hold it in a local hotel or conference centre. However, if you consider using a local village or church hall as an alternative option, the cost then becomes ***VERY*** much less expensive, and may make staging such talks and presentations financially viable. You may also find a variety of business clubs and associations specifically run on your theme or topic which will be very ***HAPPY*** to invite you along to deliver your talk or give a presentation.

Notes:
Please use this margin for writing your ideas thoughts, inspirations and personal plan of action.

This Tutorial will then act as your route map to PR success!

Be aware in advance of just how many people your venue is licensed to accommodate. In the past I have enjoyed some ***MASSIVE*** responses to such invitations and have filled village halls to ***CAPACITY*** and then well beyond, which in today's atmosphere of ultra sensitive health and safety codes would definitely ***NOT*** be allowed.

So here is a *VERY FEASIBLE* alternative...

Rather than staging a face-to-face event why not consider running a 'Tele-seminar or Webinar'!

'Tele-seminars' are quick and easy to arrange and ***INEXPENSIVE*** for everyone involved. Although there are a number of ways in which you can hire a conference line, the ones I have run generally work like this: there is no charge for the facility they provide, but everyone involved pays a premium rate to attend the call and listen in, usually 8p per minute; this means a half an hour seminar costs the callers just £2.40 If you are giving value on your call this is a very small sum indeed for the privilege of listening in, and most people would find this to be very acceptable. Some 'tele-seminar', facilities will allow you to accommodate hundreds, perhaps even thousands of people, all phoning in at the same time.

As the seminar moderator you have a number of options available to you. Delegates can either be permitted to speak and ask questions, or just listen. Some of the 'tele-seminar' systems are very versatile and I have used ones which allow some of the delegates to speak some of the time, and give me full control of this facility.

Notes:
Please use this margin for writing your ideas thoughts, inspirations and personal plan of action.

This Tutorial will then act as your route map to PR success!

Some tele-conference facilities will 'for a small fee', record the whole of the call for you, which means you can use the recording as an additional incentive for list building, or it can be placed upon your website for those people who couldn't attend the 'Tele-seminar'.

The 'tele-seminars' which I have conducted, have usually been myself interviewing someone else, although I can easily conduct one alone. I have found the best length of call is between 20 and 40 minutes although this may be dictated by your subject.

I have also conducted 'Tele-seminars' where I have invited email questions in advance so that I can prepare answers for them. Then provided the people who have sent the questions a different call-in number so that I can switch them on to ask further questions and provide some interaction. On one occasion I also prepared a PowerPoint presentation, and seminar notes in advance and then gave the download location to delegates.

The other alternative is the 'Webinar'...

This adds in the missing visual element and 'Webinars' are ideally suited for live online training and presentations. You can hire the conference facility by the event, or by the month, and either option is generally ***VERY*** inexpensive and going down in price all the time as they become more popular.

The 'Webinar' interface is very simple to operate and allows you to see exactly who has logged in, and then enables you, with just a click of your mouse, to let them in on the conversation if you so wish.

Notes:
Please use this margin for writing your ideas thoughts, inspirations and personal plan of action.

This Tutorial will then act as your route map to PR success!

Generally, they see the presentation and slides which you want them to see ie; the ones which you see on your screen at that time. If you wish, you can also plug in your webcam and allow delegates to see you in a smaller window on their screen, presenting the seminar. You are in full control and can allow delegates to speak or interact with the presentation at will. A friend of mine swears by this facility and conducts one or two 'Webinars' every week for which he charges high fees. He also video records the event and packages them into tangible and ***VERY*** saleable products.

I just love presenting both 'Tele-seminars and Webinars' because they are so effective and productive. They give you the facility to deliver a powerful presentation to a World wide audience directly from the comfort of your own home, and when creatively combined with PR marketing, offer you a highly lucrative potential.

Stunts and events

Another PR technique you should unquestionably consider using are publicity

stunts or events as these can result in you getting heaps of media exposure, as well as attracting tons of potential new prospects. Probably the best way to clarify how you can capitalise on this method is to give you a working example, and then you can use a ***GENEROUS DOLLOP*** of creativity to come up with some compelling fun ideas of your own..

More recently I was consulting with a student who is a specialist in NLP *(Nero Linguistic Programming).* If you would like a simple explanation of this very confusing title it basically means 'programming your mind for successes or positive outcomes!'

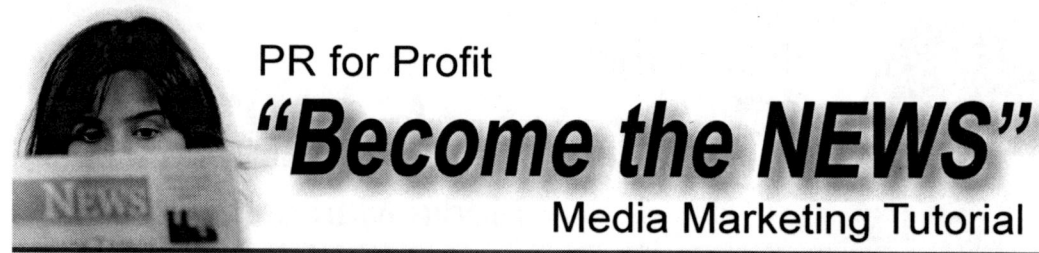

Notes:
Please use this margin for writing your ideas thoughts, inspirations and personal plan of action.

This Tutorial will then act as your route map to PR success!

The PR student wanted to find a way of generating some influential media exposure to use in his advertising, and he asked me to come up with some ideas, which I did. However, the spark for the ***BIG*** event idea came from watching a television program about airports. It seems that an ***ENORMOUS*** amount of potential travellers are ***PETRIFIED*** of flying, *(more likely - crashing!)* and for that reason are confined to the UK for their holidays unless they are prepared to go by boat.

The following day I asked our student if he could help such people and he replied that not only could he completely and ***PERMANENTLY*** remove their fear, he could do so in ***LESS THAN*** five minutes! I was impressed and he started to look for a victim to demonstrate his skills to me. I suppose it is 'sods' law, but try as we might, we could not find anyone who had a fear of flying; however, we soon found two people who were terrified of spiders! It seems that 'Arachnophobia' *(fear of spiders)* is a very common phobia which is shared by as many as 20% of our population.

True to his word, our student, in just minutes, and using a very non-invasive method, had ***TOTALLY*** removed any trace of the fear of spiders to a point where the two female volunteers where quite happy to allow a spider to walk across their hands without even flinching; it was ***AMAZING*** to witness. In fact, as they calmly handled the spider, it seemed that their fear had now turned to one of mild interest. This fascinating demonstration gave me another idea, so I presented my PR tactics to him.

I suggested that in conjunction with the major airports, which would provide the venues, we arrange for him to run a series of clinics throughout the day where nervous passengers, and those with the fear of flying, attend and he would cure them. I predicted that these events would lend themselves to a ***SUBSTANTIAL*** amount of media coverage, and could well lead to some interesting opportunities opening up for him.

The second idea was to do the same thing with spiders, and ask local zoos if they could provide a venue to promote better understanding of these and other small beasties.

I started to put both of these ideas into action by contacting the powers-that-be in a number of leading zoos and also at a couple of major airports; it immediately captured the attention of the people who mattered and I receive very positive feedback from those in the right positions who wanted to move forward with the proposal. However, the student contracted a severe case of cold feet and terminal stage fright, so totally backed out of the idea completely, which is sad.

I would like to bet if he had exploited this opportunity, he would as a result have generated ***HUNDREDS OF THOUSANDS*** of pounds worth of publicity, perhaps more! This would have been a really fantastic opportunity for him, and maybe he will come back to it one day.

To complete this chapter I would like to give you a few more ideas about the many different types of free gift and incentives you can develop to run along side, or even power your PR campaign and help you capture loads of email addresses and build your list. Remember that I will be taking you through the process of building some of them a little later on in the tutorial, so for the moment they are just to help you advance your creation process.

eBooks: I am not certain what exactly differentiates an eBook from a report other than the length of it. I have purchased so called eBooks which are just 12 pages long and have been sold for more than $100! You see, primarily, the cost comes down to the quality of the information it contained, and what it has the potential to generate for you.

Notes:
Please use this margin for writing your ideas thoughts, inspirations and personal plan of action.

This Tutorial will then act as your route map to PR success!

Notes:
Please use this margin for writing your ideas thoughts, inspirations and personal plan of action.

This Tutorial will then act as your route map to PR success!

This tutorial for instance easily has the potential to generate a £1,000,000 of publicity for ***ANYONE*** who follows the advice; ***SERIOUSLY***! and for that reason it is a ***BARGAIN*** when you consider what you have paid for it! My own definition of an ebook is something which exceeds 100 pages in length.

An Interesting Example:

The following story has been recalled to ***HIGHLIGHT*** just how valuable a short book or report can really be, and the volume of business it can help you to generate.

Many years ago I was primarily an entertainer and of course performed at a lot of children's parties and events.

Amongst the other entertainers in the area I ***ALWAY***S had the lion's share of the work. I was the '***KING***', but not because I was a better performer, but rather from the way in which I positioned and promoted myself in the eyes of potential paying prospects. You see I was ***CONSTANTLY*** in the media, gaining exposure, and then I would capitalise on this by ensuring that either I, or the smiling children with whom I was photographed, would be holding a copy of a little booklet which I wrote entitled "21 Winning Party Tip Ideas". Whenever possible, I would get the press to publish the fact that anyone who would like one of these books *(for nothing)* could have one by simply calling the telephone number provided, or by sending a letter to my address which they usually also published.

Over the years I gave away ***THOUSANDS*** of these little books and was glad to do so as they built me a ***LARGE*** and valuable mailing list of parents, who quite coincidently would have a letter sent to them reminding them of my services approximately six weeks before their child's birthday; I would also send a birthday card for them to give to their child from the magician on their birthday whether I was booked to perform at their party or not.

This little book, and the system that I developed around it was responsible for keeping me ***AT LEAST*** twice as busy as my closest competitor, for more than twice the average fee.

Over the years this little book was added to and improved upon, and eventually it became '101 Essential Tips and Ideas for the childrens Parties or Events!' The last copy of this book I updated on my computer, and when I finished entertaining as a career, I gave this little book to a good friend in the same line of business who I am glad to report, is still using it until this day. Over the years, he also attributes it to having generated him a considerable amount of business.

Reports: These can be as short as just 4 or 5 pages in length, just so long as they give the recipient value. Let me remind you that when someone accepts a free report from us it is our opportunity to **WOW** them, so let's do just that! I think the name 'Report' conjures up the image of information or a summary which will be concise and directly to the point.

Tip sheets: Your potential prospects will just love tip sheets! - well mine do anyway. Often these little gems will comprise of just 10 tips, each being a paragraph or two in length. They can take just 20 minutes or so to create, and go on giving value for years to come.

Action plans: These are very similar to tip sheets, in as much as they may just be a series of 8 or 10 bullet point actions that need to be taken to arrive at a predetermined outcome. I generally use action plans to tell someone ***WHAT*** they should do, and save the ***HOW*** they should do it for the accompanying product and after money has been exchanged.

Software: If you have the necessary skills you may be able to quickly develop software which is relevant to your specific line of business. I have created a number of calculation tools which give considerable value to the recipient which I have created in programs such as Microsoft Excel.

Notes:
Please use this margin for writing your ideas thoughts, inspirations and personal plan of action.

This Tutorial will then act as your route map to PR success!

Notes:
Please use this margin for writing your ideas thoughts, inspirations and personal plan of action.

This Tutorial will then act as your route map to PR success!

Audio: a great medium which can make an excellent incentive in exchange for your prospects' email addresses. For many years I have been providing audio files for my prospects to either download or stream *(Play on Line)*; the big benefit audio offers is that it allows prospects to put a voice to your name. Your voice plays a big part in building trust with your prospects so please consider using audio. Invest in a good quality condenser microphone and you will also find creating quality audio a simple task.

Video: I have recently become a big fan of Internet video because it is so easy to generate and put on line, and the short videos I create play well and start almost immediately. Again, and in the same way as audio gives your prospects the opportunity to put a voice to the name, video gives them the opportunity to put a face to the voice. As far as building trust is concerned you will find it hard to beat video.

Free memberships: Now here is another little gem you may want to capitalise upon, especially if you were already considering a membership website for your product or service. If you were already considering creating an incentive such as a report, give it as part of a free membership by doing this you are immediately setting yourself up for success.

In this way it is much easier to upsell your free members to a paying membership than it would be to get them to subscribe directly for a paying membership; can you see the benefit? There is loads of great membership software available which you can use to make this type of process work well.

£1 Trial memberships: Lets presume that you offer a 7 day,s trial membership for just £1 as I do at one of my websites; now the benefit of using this system is: when your prospects pay their £1 for trial membership access, they are informed that if they don't cancel their membership with PayPal *(our merchant providers),* after the seven day trial period is up, their card will automatically be charged for the full monthly fee; this continues every month from that point forward.

Notes:
Please use this margin for writing your ideas thoughts, inspirations and personal plan of action.

This Tutorial will then act as your route map to PR success!

Proper Planning Prevents Particularly Poor Performance

I have always known the title of this chapter as the '6 Ps' and it's a common

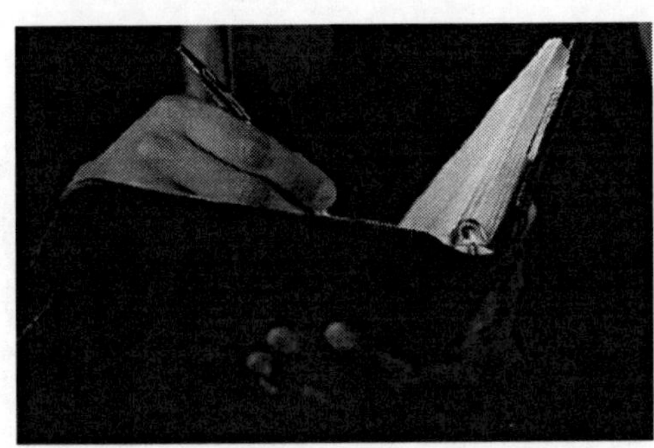

sense rule for which I have a lot of respect because hardly a day passes without meeting or speaking to someone who, a few months, or even ***YEARS*** earlier, told me that they were going to do this, or they were going to do that! They were going to write a book, start a website, take up a new hobby, lose weight, get fit; the list goes on and ***ON AND ON!***

When you ask the rhetorical question 'how is it going?' you are already fairly sure that you are going to hear that they were too busy, or they haven't yet being able to find the time, or will give some other ***TIME*** related excuse. The fact is we all have the same 24 hours a day available to us, and it is up to us to decide ***EXACTLY*** how we are going to invest them.

This fact leads nicely into and ***HIGHLIGHTS*** the following point:

"If you don't ***PLAN*** it, then it's ***VERY*** likely you ***WON'T*** to do it!"

The following saying is one of my favourites because it is ***SO VERY TRUE!***

"No one ***EVER*** plans to fail, but most people fail to plan!"

Now I am going to let you in to a little secret which may not surprise you. The people who are ***MOST LIKELY*** to succeed in life, at virtually ***ANYTHING!*** ...are all ***GREAT PLANNERS***.

These are the people who once they have made their decision to do something, ***FIND*** the time to sit down and start planning it, ***IN DETAIL***.

Notes:
Please use this margin for writing your ideas thoughts, inspirations and personal plan of action.

This Tutorial will then act as your route map to PR success!

They take time out of their diary and it ***GETS DONE***; the sooner they get started planning after making their decision, the more successful they are likely to be.

Planning is particularly important in PR marketing, and as this chapter progresses, you are going to discover the reasons why.

It's really quite easy to be successful at PR when you have organised yourself for success. None of what follows is anything more than common sense if you have the discipline to follow through and work well in advance and stay that way. The computer will make the job of getting organised simple, but it is you who has to maintain the system which we are about to develop.

PR Ideas...

From the earlier chapters of this tutorial you will already know many methods of generating ideas for your news releases, but if you don't write them down as you get them you will have wasted a lot of energy. If you plan on putting out regular news releases make sure you have a good stock pile of ideas which you can work with when you are ready. I used to use a book to write my ideas in, but I soon had so many that I found it easier to keep them stored in a computer file.

In this way I can visit them and update them as and when I have a little time available. Right now we could go to this file and you would see I have been playing with some ideas so much that they would only take a few minutes to finish off and have ready for dispatch to the media.

Notes:
Please use this margin for writing your ideas thoughts, inspirations and personal plan of action.

This Tutorial will then act as your route map to PR success!

Keep a flow chart or time line...

I create ongoing PR and news releases for a number of businesses and projects which I have running. There is nothing worse than the feeling of being snowed under, especially when you have a looming deadline; for this reason I am disciplined about staying ahead of myself and ***NOT*** getting into the position of falling behind. So I have set deadlines in my diary by when I must have certain tasks ready and completed.

Do something towards your next article EVERYDAY...

I usually spend the first half hour or so of my day working on PR, and because I have developed the habit of staying ahead, I always know what to do next and use my time well and wisely. I have found that I write my best articles and news releases by first playing with the idea and expanding upon it as much as possible, and this may go on for a number of days or sometimes weeks until it reaches the point where it must be written. However, at this point there is usually very little left to do, and it may just take 10 or 15 minutes to finish off completely. Then I like to leave it for a few days perhaps even a week and return to it where I always manage to improve it a little more.

Targets, goals and deadlines...

It's up to you what objectives you set for yourself and I am not going to impose my system on you because it will probably be a very poor fit. However, you are free to copy ideas which you feel would work for you.

I generally have my next news release ready for dispatch at least a week early and find it easy to stay ahead of myself in this way; however, there are one or two exceptions to this personal rule which I will cover next.

Notes:
Please use this margin for writing your ideas thoughts, inspirations and personal plan of action.

This Tutorial will then act as your route map to PR success!

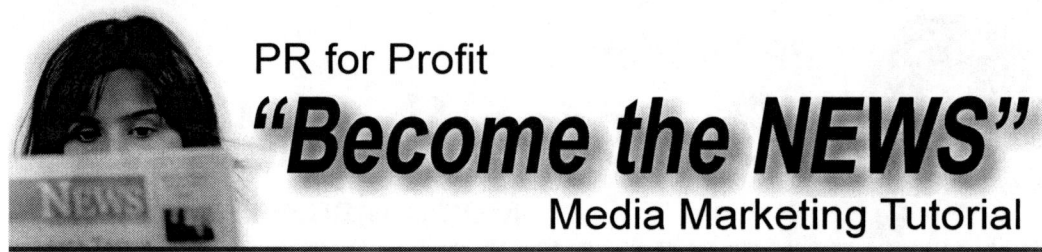

Breaking news...

Sometimes, changing circumstances and situations generate PR opportunities which need to be acted upon immediately. It may be a story in the news which I can bounce off or use to generate a news release of my own. When this happens I put everything on hold and start capitalising upon the situation before the opportunity is missed. You also will be presented with similar chances, and I advise you to take immediate action with them when they appear.

Seasonal opportunities...

Now I am sure all of the seasons, bank holidays and special days are flooding into your mind, and if you work far enough ahead you will think of some creative and compelling PR ideas and ways in which you can tie your business in with these. Right now its mid March and I am thinking about what season related tie-ins I can come up with for summer and the autumn periods, and have come up with some real gems for this year. Let's face it, if I had left it until a couple of weeks before the new releases were needed, I probably wouldn't have generated these ideas, nor had the time to prepare for them.

There is a retail clothing company from which I receive brochures who are champions of seasonal sales techniques, and every few weeks they come out with a new idea or approach which is related to the nearest holiday, special day, or time of the year. They are really creative and obviously have fun with the process and we in PR marketing should be also.

Quiet time opportunities...

Now I have already mentioned that there are a couple of times of the year when it is far easier to get your PR published than others, and these are the late summer, July and August, and then in December.
At these times the press and media are often quite hungry for stories or have just had too <u>many</u> seasonal stories, so if you offer something different, it stands a ***VERY*** good chance of being used.

Notes:
Please use this margin for writing your ideas thoughts, inspirations and personal plan of action.

This Tutorial will then act as your route map to PR success!

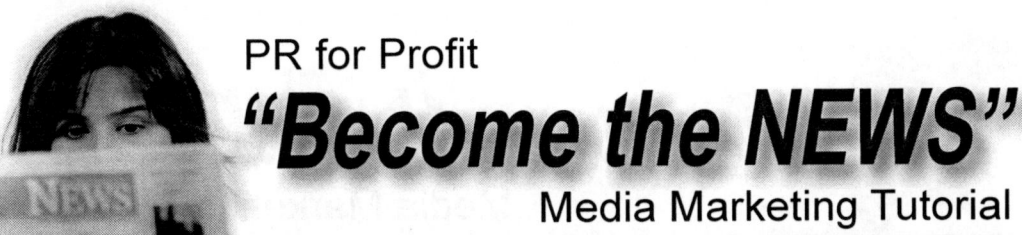

Now you are aware of these quiet times, you can take advantage of them by perhaps doubling your planned output for that month, which is simple to do if you work ***WELL IN ADVANCE.***

Start small and grow with experience...

I hope that this short chapter has put the importance of working well ahead into perspective for you. I suggest that you start by focusing on gaining one press or media story published a month until you feel confident with the process and then double your output of news releases, and eventually take them up to once a week. If you do this you will soon become very busy, but effective. In a later chapter I will show you how to simplify much of your PR delivery process.

Can you handle the response?

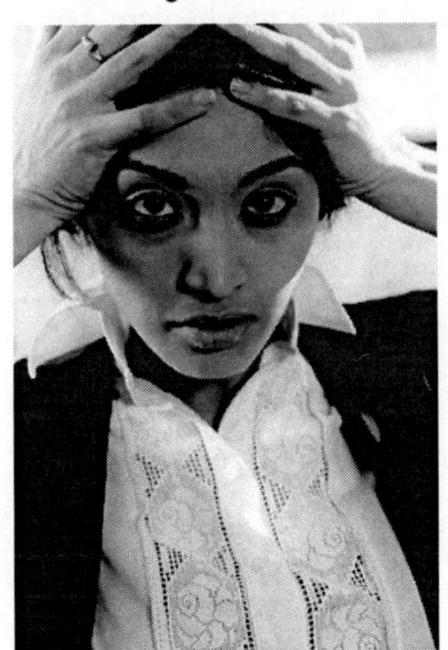

Now you may think that this is a rather strange chapter title, however, I can and will give you examples where I have had such ***OVERWHELMING*** response to my PR news articles that my business came to a ***HALT***; seriously, I am not joking, and I will go into detail by sharing a couple of my experiences in just a while.

Now I can almost hear some of you saying "You should be so lucky!" and I have to agree our aim is to achieve ***EXCEPTIONAL*** results and be just as busy as we possibly can, ***BUT***, without becoming overwhelmed and frustrated at being unable to handle the response, that's exactly what this section is dedicated to; preparing for success without becoming overwhelmed!

Notes:
Please use this margin for writing your ideas thoughts, inspirations and personal plan of action.

This Tutorial will then act as your route map to PR success!

Regardless of the content of your news release, there are just 4 ***MAIN*** methods and techniques for channelling your response which will enable you to benefit financially; in fact, more recently, ***ANOTHER*** practical method has became available which I am beginning to explore and will share with you. Here are those four ways...

- Telephone
- Mail
- Personal visits
- Internet

As I have no understanding of your business or the way in which you work I can't tell you that one of these methods is any better than the other. What I can do is go through the 'Pros and Cons' of each of them and then you can decide which one of them will suit your business, or direct response mechanism, best.

First, and as ***ENCOURAGEMENT*** for you to be properly prepared for all outcomes and unexpected responses, I would like to tell you about two personal experiences where I encountered a totally overwhelming response which was triggered by a secret and truly ***MAGICAL*** marketing ingredient, which should be used sparingly, and is known as - ***SCARCITY!***

Copywriters and marketeers have long known that when you add scarcity to the mix it will change the way in which people react. "***NOT ME!***" I can almost hear you saying; but sorry, yes, you also, and this is what happens. Closely examine human nature and you will discover that the fear of loss is usually ***FAR*** more of a powerful motivator than the potential of gain!

Scenario one:

If you can still find one in this age of charity shops, just take the opportunity to visit an old style 'Jumble Sale' and you will see ***EXACTLY*** what I mean. Such events often attract hoards of usually kind, caring and sweet little old ladies from miles around.

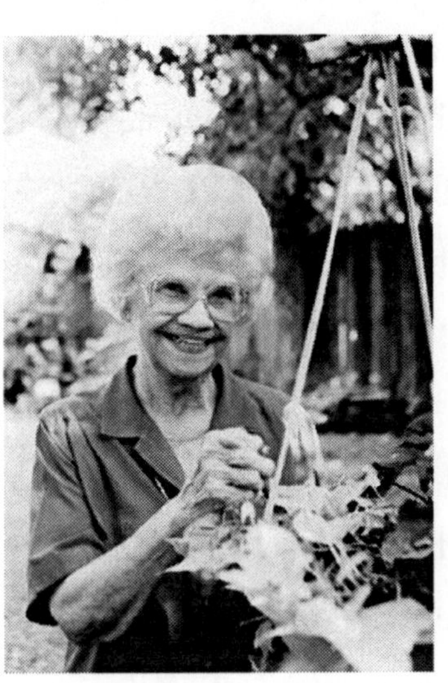

Motivated by the possibility of missing out on a potential ***BARGAIN***, frail 4'11" Grandma figures smelling of peppermints temporary change personalities and become ***FORMIDABLE*** and highly ***AGGRESSIVE,*** blue-rinse and silver-haired tigers! These 80lb senior-citizens come well armed with a pair of ***EXCEPTIONALLY*** pointed elbows, walking sticks and umbrellas which they are not afraid to use as weapons, whilst grappling to reach some discarded garment which they have spotted on the next table.

While in this transformed state, they can move at ***LIGHTENING SPEED*** over short distances, and can spot a bargain in a dimly lit corner of the scout hut at forty yards. Until they are satisfied that every last good deal has been ***GRABBED***, they will stay alert, and as mean as the local 'Scrap Yard Guard Dog' and should be given a ***VERY*** wide berth!

Scenario two:

If you need more proof that scarcity, as a marketing tool really works, see if you can find a traditional market where 'Pitchers' *(mock auction type salesmen)* still sell in this way. One particular 'Pitcher' I would go out of my way to watch working, used a whole range of clever trickery which nearly always involved the use of scarcity to part the often ***HUGE*** crowds he would draw in from their money.

Notes:
Please use this margin for writing your ideas thoughts, inspirations and personal plan of action.

This Tutorial will then act as your route map to PR success!

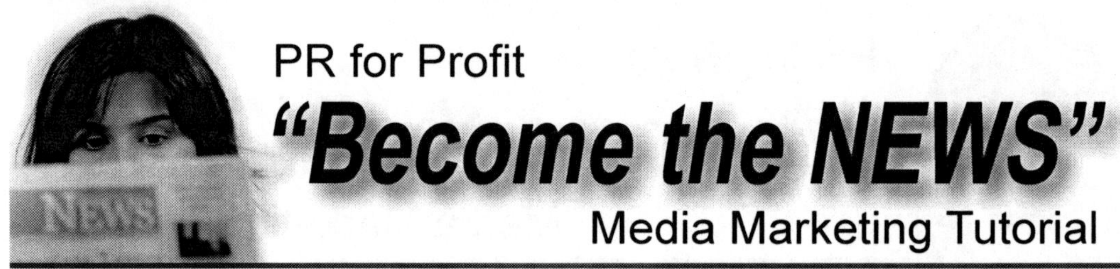

Notes:
Please use this margin for writing your ideas thoughts, inspirations and personal plan of action.

This Tutorial will then act as your route map to PR success!

Although many of these techniques are now ***VERY*** illegal, the one which sticks out in my mind most of all was one which also worked highly effectively on my wife.

The 'Pitcher' engaged the crowd, and cleverly sorted out the punters *(potential customers)* who had money, from those who did not. To do this he started offering bargains which were to become imminently available, and implied he would be giving certain items with high perceived value such as watches and jewellery away for just pennies. He was loud, colourful and ***HIGHLY ENTERTAINING***, and this teasing only subsided when the crowd watching him had grown to a size with which he was satisfied.

Focused on the ***SALES*** which he knew he was about to make, he told his keen audience that ***ONLY*** the people with bags could participate in this sale. ***OBVIOUSLY***, the bags to which he was referring were the ones which he was selling for £5 each! Apparently, the company he was representing, had stipulated that he could ***GIVE AWAY*** no more than just 20 of these ***AMAZING*** deals for introduction purchases, and ***ONLY*** to people with these bags.

He was a real expert and a true experience to watch as everyone in the crowd was made to feel that this man was doing them a favour by offering such a deal.

Once again I had the opportunity to see 'Scarcity' change the personality of usually moderate and considerate people. As the possibility of missing out on yet another ***BARGAIN*** reached the ears of this eager crowd, it triggered what could only be described as a small stampede of people who all leaped eagerly forward at the potential of this ***VERY LIMITED*** and ***NEVER TO BE REPEATED*** offer. It was a feeding frenzy of humanity racing forward and trampling underfoot without consideration anyone who got in their way.

Notes:
Please use this margin for writing your ideas thoughts, inspirations and personal plan of action.

This Tutorial will then act as your route map to PR success!

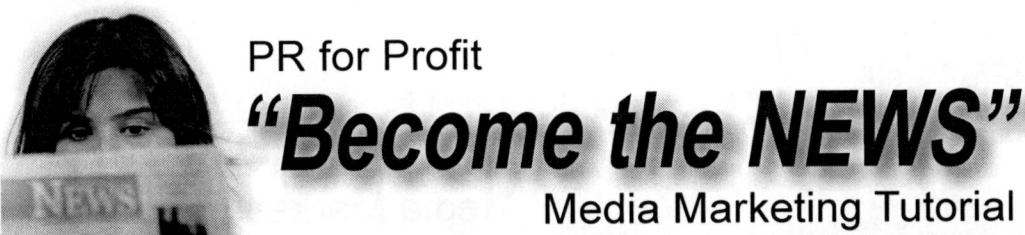

Unsurprisingly, the silver tongued 'Pitcher' didn't just sell twenty of his bags, but ***HUNDREDS!*** As I watched, as he turned an ***AMAZINGLY*** quick profit, I glanced over to my wife to acknowledge this amusing fact, only to discover that she had become one of the suckers who ended up paying £5 for a bag, which at that time probably cost him just 10p each to purchase in wholesale quantities. As I am certain you will have already guessed, the bargains which were to become available to the purchasers of these expensive ***BAGS*** suddenly became very much more ***UNATTRACTIVE*** than they had appeared to be just minutes before.

So will you consider using ***SCARCITY*** in some of your news releases?

You don't need to answer because I think it is fairly obvious that now you have a better understanding of the benefits it offers you, especially when used in a direct response news article. So let's re-focus on being prepared for success and what happened to overwhelm me.

Experience one:

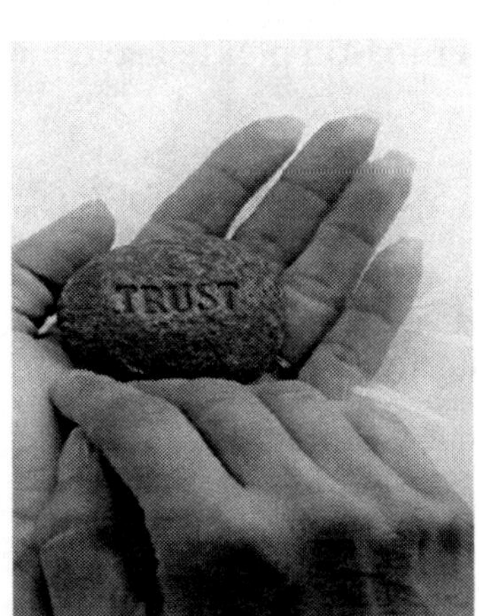

Unfortunately, and as many of you will know, marriage doesn't always last forever, and neither did mine. The decision that it was over, was made by my wife; and once made, she couldn't leave fast enough to start making someone else's life a misery. In her wake, and haste to leave, she abandoned three of her surrogate children named Thomas, Pip and Crumpet - a ***HUGE*** tabby cat and two cute Yorkshire terriers.

Notes:
Please use this margin for writing your ideas thoughts, inspirations and personal plan of action.

This Tutorial will then act as your route map to PR success!

This all happened while I was working abroad as entertainers often do. My father kindly stepped into the breach and took responsibility until I returned. As I was away working so much, I decided that the best course of action was to find new caring homes for the terriers, and my dad offered to provide Thomas, our aging 'Puma', a retirement home.

I was at home just for a week or so before having to go on tour again and felt the best and quickest way to find nice people who could offer a home to the pups, was by writing an amusing but attention grabbing - news release, which I did. ***BOY! DID IT WORK WELL!***

I knew that the article had been published because the very moment it appeared my phone started ringing with offers of homes. Then, every time I put the phone down, it rang again! This went on for the rest of the day and until late at night. With the sheer volume of offers I received I soon found nice people and good homes for my lovely little pets. However, the phone just ***KEPT ON RINGING***. In response I recorded a short answer machine message which said.

"Hi this is Kevin, if you are calling in regard to offering homes for the Yorkshire terriers, thank you for responding, but I am sorry, they have already been found good homes. If you are calling for any other reason please leave me a message!"

The phone carried on ringing ***NON STOP*** from 7.00am until approximatly10.00pm or 11.00pm at night, and this lasted for eight days! Probably much of this had to do with the fact that at that time pedigree Yorkshire terriers cost approximately £250 each! ...so two being offered to good homes for nothing was an opportunity just too good to miss.

Notes:
Please use this margin for writing your ideas thoughts, inspirations and personal plan of action.

This Tutorial will then act as your route map to PR success!

Here is the *POINT* of this story...

PR marketing and media exposure is an ***EXCEPTIONALLY*** powerful medium and can be responsible for ***MASSIVE*** responses such as the one I have just told you about. Imagine for a moment that the objective of this article was to generate leads. If this had been the case, my news article would have lost an ***ENORMOUS*** amount of its potential because I am certain that for ***EVERY*** call I received, there would have been at ***LEAST*** one other person who gave up trying to contact me in frustration, perhaps ***MANY*** more.

That's what motivated the title of this chapter of the tutorial...

Can you handle the response?

On this occasion I obviously couldn't!
I have experienced many powerful responses which would have ***TOTALLY*** overwhelmed me if I had not been prepared for them. I will tell you about another experience shortly, but for now, let's look more closely at the methods of response you could use.

Telephone responce...

Again a lot will depend heavily upon the type of business or service which you are offering. However, if you are going to use the phone, prepare yourself with either adequate staff, or a system which plays a courteous message, and then gives the caller the opportunity to leave their details for someone to call them when they are free.

Notes:
Please use this margin for writing your ideas thoughts, inspirations and personal plan of action.

This Tutorial will then act as your route map to PR success!

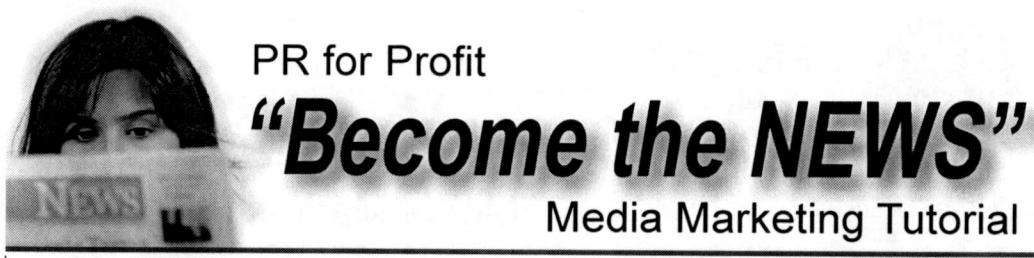

A colleague of mine works in the telecommunication business, and I am

fascinated at just how many practical, clever and useful systems there are now available, and even more amazed at just how inexpensive they have become; so be prepared to invest in your success. If you insist on using the telephone as your primary response mechanism, just like all good boy scouts, be prepared! ...because I can guarantee that as you get better at using PR to attract new customers, you will experience occasions where you will become overwhelmed by the sheer volume of response you receive, in exactly the same way as I did.

PROFIT TIP...

You may want to test the following technique for yourself, as for some companies it works like a dream. This is how; NEVER answer your phone and ALWAYS have your telephone system set up to play an outgoing message which may say something along the lines of:

"Thank you for calling: YOUR COMPANY NAME. At the present time we are receiving an EXCEPTIONALLY high volume of calls, and all of our staff are busy.

So, the best way to speak to us QUICKLY is by leaving your details at the end of this message, and then someone will contact you just as soon as they become available! Answering your call is our PRIORITY"

They may ring a number of times in the hope that they will be LUCKY enough to get through before becoming so frustrated that they leave their details for you to call them. This may lose a few potential prospects, but if they are serious, and a quality prospect for you, they will eventually follow your instructions.

I know of companies who have DRAMATICALLY improved their conversion rate by using this technique. It works because it offers first hand knowledge that you are BUSY, and presumably SUCCESSFUL. It also adds the perception of a MAGICAL ingredient you now know as ...SCARCITY!

You may also wish to consider the possibility of outsourcing your telephone response to a company that specialises in such work and will have professionally trained staff available to answer all calls.

Fax response...

While we are on the subject of telecommunications, and as it comes under the same ***GENERAL*** heading, I would like to mention faxes.

I have long abandoned the fax as a practical method of communicating information, especially for generating responses, as apart from businesses, so few people still use them.

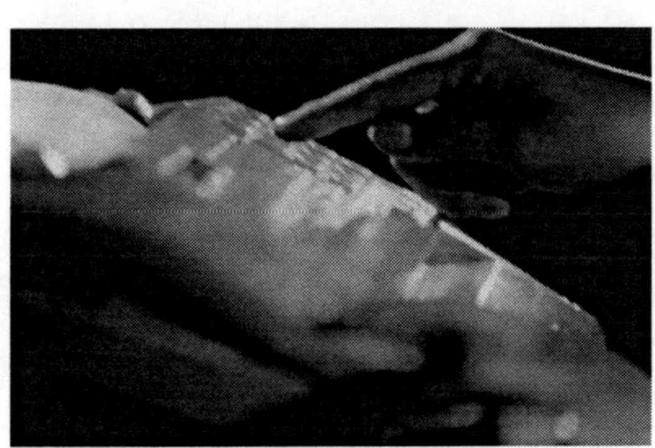

Mine was sent to the tip at least two or three years ago, after spending a further two or three years collecting dust as ***NOBODY*** ever sent me a fax. However, I was recently asked to fax a certain printed document to someone, so I simply scanned it, and then sent the image by email, which served exactly the same purpose.

Notes:
Please use this margin for writing your ideas thoughts, inspirations and personal plan of action.

This Tutorial will then act as your route map to PR success!

Notes:
Please use this margin for writing your ideas thoughts, inspirations and personal plan of action.

This Tutorial will then act as your route map to PR success!

I used to fax my news releases to news rooms and noticed that when I started emailing them instead, from that point forward they tended to get used almost word for word. I suppose that when they were sent by fax it required the journalist to retype them, and if they were going to have to go to that effort, they may just as well rewrite them in their own style. However, other than that I would not consider using fax as a means of response from your news release or published articles.

Personal visits...

It may be the case that your business is a shop or showroom or even has premises you work from and require the potential customer to visit personally; if this is the case it makes generating your PR very much easier and less complicated. Again you should give some thought to methods and ways of distributing the visiting times of this potential traffic across your day, or even week, rather than having an overwhelming crowd turn up which you can't service.

...let's imagine, a good example would be a restaurant, for which you gain

some good reviews and worthwhile media exposure. If the press are running your article anyway, just ask them to include two additional words: 'Reservations required' etc, which may go a long way towards avoiding disappointment if more diners turn up than you can handle.

Traditional SNAIL Mail...

As a method of response in your news release, using a traditional mailing address is very much outdated. In my opinion, an address generally takes up far too much space which would be better used to deliver an additional benefit of your product or service, or in engaging your potential prospect. However, exceptions to this rule are magazines, which seem keen on printing your postal address where a response is required: in such cases it adds to your authenticity.

In general I would encourage you to direct new and potential prospects who require further information back to a website for a whole ***HOST*** of ***HIGHLY*** beneficial reasons which we will come to in just a moment, and after I have related that other personal experience I promised, where I could have become overwhelmed.

Notes:
Please use this margin for writing your ideas thoughts, inspirations and personal plan of action.

This Tutorial will then act as your route map to PR success!

Let me set the scene for you...

A couple of years ago I was toying with the idea of writing a book, or generating a product on happiness; I still am, and it may be my very next project. Now, by reading this tutorial you have probably already guessed that I am quite ***FANATICAL*** about testing my ideas to see how strong the response is before I commit any of my most valuable commodity - which is my time.

On this occasion I felt that the best way to capture attention was by generating a compelling news article that offered a tangible solution. The press seem to really like news articles which offer their readers solutions, so I set about writing a short report.

The result took me just a few hours to write what I called: The Happiness Blueprint - "14 life changing steps which lead to lasting happiness!"

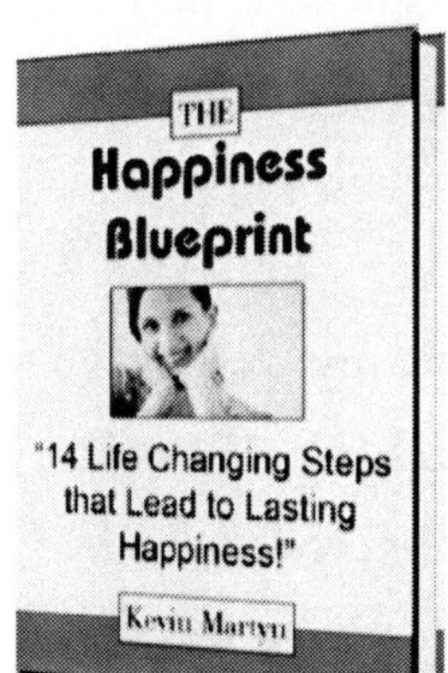

You can see the graphic I created to improve the perceived value of this report. To claim this free gift, interested parties would have to visit my website and submit their email address, and then the report would be emailed back to them.

Notes:
Please use this margin for writing your ideas thoughts, inspirations and personal plan of action.

This Tutorial will then act as your route map to PR success!

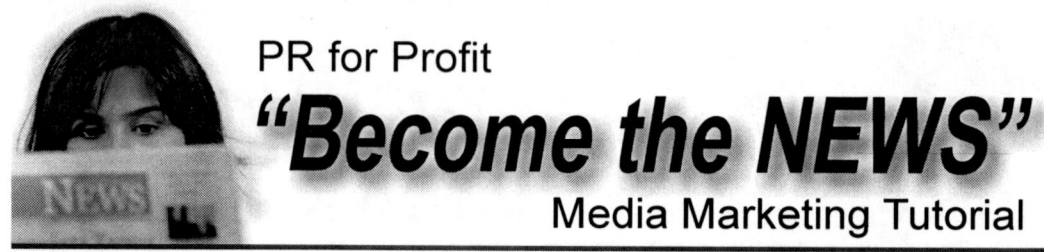

(Just to remind you, I will show you in fine detail how you can create such simple and free reports and tips sheets etc, including the graphics, in a later chapter.)

Next, and so I would know how many responses and the level of interest which this article was generating, I set up my auto responder *(this is the program which automates the email capture, maintains the list and delivers the email response for me)* to send me an email every time a new subscriber is added to my list.

On this occasion I was away during the day when the article was first published, and when I returned home I was unaware that I had been successful, or even that my article had been published. I started my computer, and then my email program, and clicked the send/receive email button to be told I had more than **6,000** emails to be downloaded!!!!!!

WHAT! – my first thought was that I was being aggressively ***SPAMMED*** which has happened to me on a couple of other occasions in the past, but never with as many as 6,000 emails before!
There was nothing I could do until the emails had been downloaded and this was when I first realised that these were confirmation emails, automatically generated by the people who were subscribing to download my new report!

I quickly turned off the command to notify me ***EVERY*** time someone new subscribed to download the report, and in the short time it took me to do this, I receive a further 150 email confirmations.

The next day I received notification from my website host that my websites bandwidth allowance for the entire month was ***NEARLY EXHAUSTED*** *(this is a hard one to explain simply, so lets just say I had run out of credits and a new coin needed to be put in the meter.)* In simple terms, my website was about to be shut down until the start of the next month, so I quickly contacted them and made the necessary arrangements for it to stay active.

Notes:
Please use this margin for writing your ideas thoughts, inspirations and personal plan of action.

This Tutorial will then act as your route map to PR success!

I am pleased I had the opportunity to relate these two personal stories in this chapter as they highlight just how IMPORTANT being prepared for BIG success really is. It's just like lightening; you are never quite sure where or when it will strike, and it happens quickly.

So just how successful was this particular ***NEWS RELEASE***?

My best result ever actually, and over a 4 day period I built an email list of 28,400 subscribers from just ***ONE*** news release! This story leads nicely into my favourite method for handling PR response:

The Internet put's you in control...

Over the past few years the public in general have become far more familiar with using the internet and most households in the UK have ***HIGH SPEED*** access to it. So unless your target market just happens to comprise of those who follow the 'Amish' way of life, you should be in luck.

The real beauty of the internet is its speed and versatility which is ***CONSIDERABLE!*** If you like to stay in control and get results quickly, you will have to be prepared to embrace the internet and set up squeeze pages and auto responders personally; but don't panic, once again it is ***NOT DIFFICULT***, and I will walk you though it, step by step. *(A squeeze page is a simple one page website with just one function, which is to **SQUEEZE** the visitors email out of them in return for an ethical bribe; in the above example it was a report)*

Notes:
Please use this margin for writing your ideas thoughts, inspirations and personal plan of action.

This Tutorial will then act as your route map to PR success!

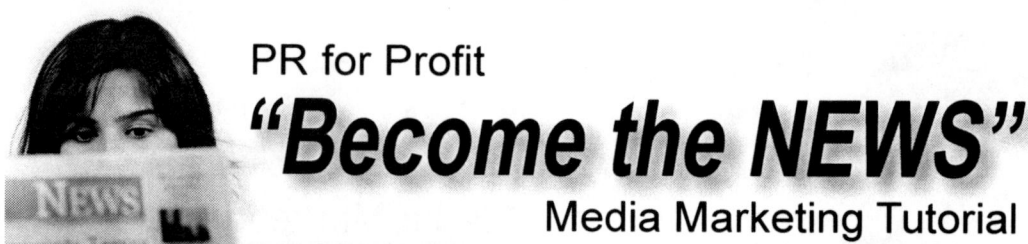

If you need to set up appointments to visit prospects, you will find that there are many programs now available which will easily install on your website. These will virtually automate the whole appointment making process. This means that in response to your news release, your new prospects could visit your website and book you in to visit them in their home and at a time of their choice, when you have indicated you will be available. The possibilities are ***AMAZING*** and will free you up for more financially productive pursuits such as creating your next news article to attract even more interest.

I enjoy playing with, and making video, and have found it to be a very effective method for me to give prospects who request further information they need. It is also an EXCELLENT opportunity to build rapport and the start of a healthy relationship with them.

Text messaging...

Now I mentioned that there was one final method of gaining response which I feel offers ***EXCELLENT*** potential, and is in fact a method I am personally experimenting with as we speak. It may work like this: In your news article you would offer further information and would be happy to send the download location by text to those who send a text to you on: 287463. *(Please note: this is a fictitious text number)* Your software would be set up to immediately respond with the location you have programmed into it.

Those who send you a text have just subscribed to your 'Text list' and now you can send them other offers as and when you wish. For added certainty you can also obtain their email address when they go to retrieve the information you promised, as you simply send them to your ***SQUEEZE*** page as mentioned earlier.

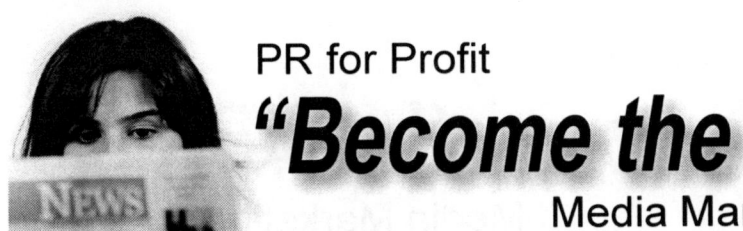

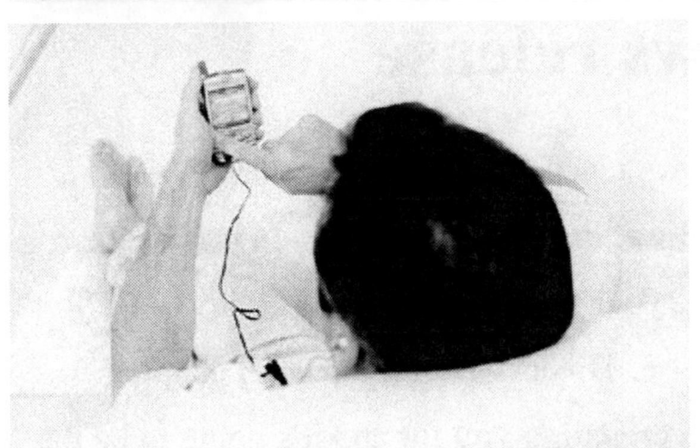

Now the software for this fairly new technology is ***UNBELIEVABLY*** simple to use and also ***EXCEPTIONALLY*** cost effective, as I have purchased my text messages in bulk at just 1p each!

I can't wait to see how well this works, but I believe, used in conjunction with a website, it will only increase my level of response.

You can find a link to the software on the resource website...

Notes:
Please use this margin for writing your ideas thoughts, inspirations and personal plan of action.

This Tutorial will then act as your route map to PR success!

Notes:
Please use this margin for writing your ideas thoughts, inspirations and personal plan of action.

This Tutorial will then act as your route map to PR success!

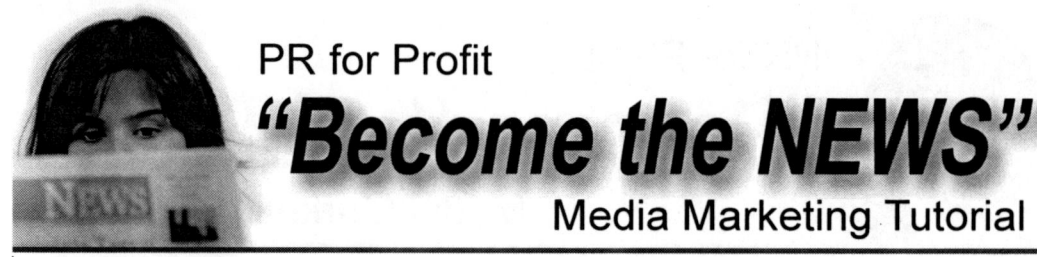

Writing your news release

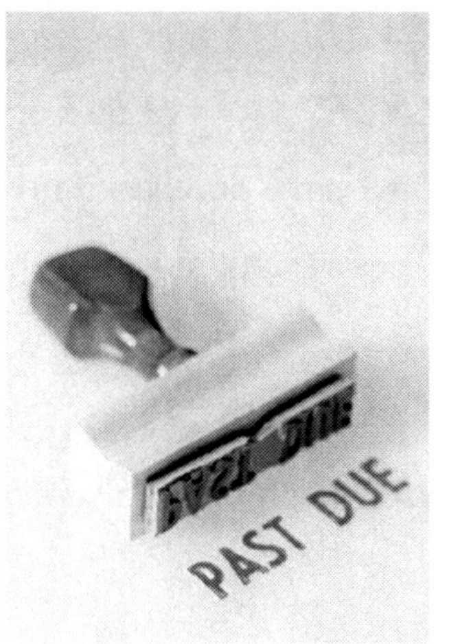

So at last we reach the chapter I know that you have been waiting for, and where you will begin generating your first tangible results with your PR news release. This is what all the other chapters have been preparing you for and it's going to be the most important chapter of all because your release is the most important component in the PR process, and without using them you are unlikely to get any PR results. However, as I promised, this is going to be quite a simple and fun chapter, as by this point you should already have a good understanding of the ***BIG*** PR picture, and be well armed with all the knowledge that you need to start creating compelling news articles that ***WILL*** get results.

If you have worked through the tutorial the way that is designed to be used, by this point, you will have many excellent PR story ideas ready for use in your first news release. Please remember, getting a quality idea is the real ***STARTING POINT*** in the PR process, and without one you will find writing your article a far more ***COMPLICATED*** task!

So to ***GUARANTEE*** you reach your full PR potential, please use this step by step tutorial as instructed, and thoroughly work your way through the preceding chapters before you begin writing. Starting work on your release ***WITHOUT*** having a good idea on which to build is likely to make the difference between writing the type of article which ***MAY*** get used, and one that immediately captures the attention of the news room, and is given priority consideration.

Notes:
Please use this margin for writing your ideas thoughts, inspirations and personal plan of action.

This Tutorial will then act as your route map to PR success!

Start by knowing *EXACTLY* what you are trying to achieve?

Before we go any further, I would like to introduce you to a term which may be new to some of you. MWO stands for 'Most Wanted Outcome' and the reason I am using this term is that as we progress we may develop more than one of them.

My number one MWO 'Most Wanted Outcome' is:

Every time I send a new news release out, my hope is that the media will pick it up in their news rooms and say "**WOW!** I am going to ***HAVE*** to use this! It's just what I have been waiting for, so I'll turn it into a ***FEATURE***!" As a result they may well get back to you to arrange an interview and set up a photo shoot. Not only this, but when the story is published, it 'catches fire' *(ie; reproduced by other publications),* is syndicated and used widely. One small news release can generate tons of quality media publicity, and make loads of ***MONEY!*** and the publicity this generates can be used again and ***AGAIN***, in promoting yourself and your business, and also as a means of creating an ***ONGOING*** stream of income.

Will this happen every time? No, it won't, but it ***WILL*** happen occasionally and when it does, it's wonderful. If you follow the formula I use and promote in this tutorial, you will be giving yourself the ***VERY BEST*** possibility of gaining the same outcome.

My number two MWO 'Most Wanted Outcome' is:

Again, the news room identify my news release as a quality news item and publish it verbatim along with the photograph I have provided. This is the most likely of the two scenarios and if you have created a well prepared 'Direct Response PR' release it will keep you busy with new business and prospects knocking on your door.

Notes:
Please use this margin for writing your ideas thoughts, inspirations and personal plan of action.

This Tutorial will then act as your route map to PR success!

The format is always the same...

Over the years we have made a lot of contacts around the globe who use PR in a similar way to us, and their news release format stays the same; the only very small exception to this is that in some countries, the people who send regular news releases out, place their ' for further information' contact details at the top of the page, rather than at the bottom.

CLARITY of purpose is fundamental...

Over the years I have learned that the most important ingredient in writing ***ANYTHING*** is ***CLARITY***. When you know ***PRECISELY*** what you are trying to achieve, the creation process becomes both simplified and very enjoyable.

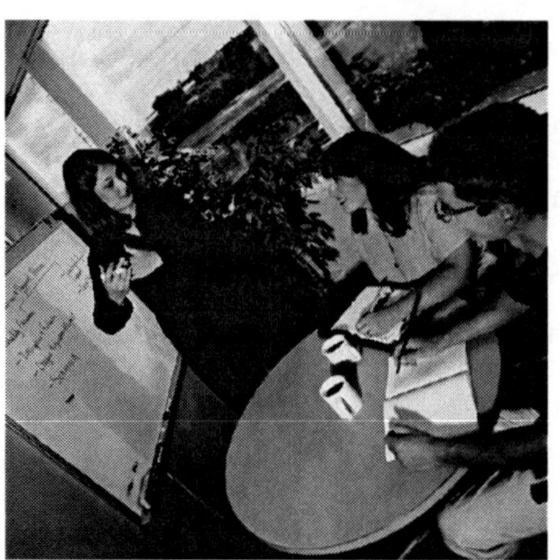

By contrast, you would not believe the amount of times I have started writing with enthusiasm, typing with speed and vigour, until I realised that I have written myself into a corner, rewriting the same words again and again without being able to find a conclusion to my objective. This is not only time wasting, but also highly ***FRUSTRATING!*** Don't laugh, because this may also happen to you, and when and if it does, I am ***CERTAIN*** the cause for this will come down to the fact that you are not clear in what you were trying to achieve at the time you started to write.

Having fallen victim to this frustrating pitfall a number of times I now ***CONSTANTLY*** take the precaution of writing a few sentences outlining my ***EXACT*** objective.

I clearly state ***SPECIFICALLY*** what I am trying to achieve, ie; "what is my story?" I not only apply this rule to news releases, but also when writing ***ANYTHING*** which is going to be read by others, eg: sales letters, blog posts, and even this tutorial etc.

I find spending a few minutes before I start writing making sure that I identify my aims, and the specific knowledge or information that I want to share with my readers usually results in the production of a quality release, in the minimum amount of time.

By starting with my article idea, I soon become ***VERY CLEAR*** about the type of news release I am going to write, and whether it is going to bring into play a direct response mechanism of some sort, or if it is going to be used to build my profile.

Then, in bullet point format I identify any ***UNIQUE*** features or benefits, differences, consequences or compelling points of information related to my products, service or event. This identification of objectives just takes a few minutes to complete, and I estimate that it saves me literally hours in frustrating and unnecessary rewrites. When my objective is clear and easy to refer to, it can be compared to a route map which leads directly to my desired destination, or to the outcome I am trying to achieve.

Stay focused on what the media want from you, and you will soon be turning out highly effective news releases which will make you ***MONEY!*** Keep in mind that the job of the media is first and foremost reporting the news; that is their primary interest, so give them what they want by keeping your information ***FACTUAL.***

Notes:
Please use this margin for writing your ideas thoughts, inspirations and personal plan of action.

This Tutorial will then act as your route map to PR success!

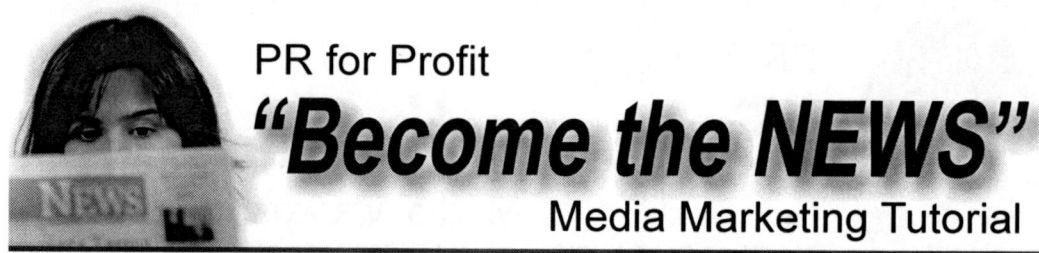

Notes:
Please use this margin for writing your ideas thoughts, inspirations and personal plan of action.

This Tutorial will then act as your route map to PR success!

To play the PR game with you, the media will expect you to be highly ***PROFESSIONAL*** by keeping your material relevant and believable. The last thing they want is a lawsuit on their hands so always be prepared to offer evidence and back up your claims. If you can do this whilst delivering quality news items you are onto a winner, which you can use to get an unlimited flow of new prospects knocking on your door.

Learning by example...

The best way for me to explain how to write a news release is to write one which we can then "reverse engineer", and take apart component by component. Although we will be giving you many examples for you to copy later in this chapter, I thought that the one I should use here would be relevant to this tutorial and the topic of PR. So I have chosen one that has proved to be highly successful in promoting the 'PR for Profits' tutorial which you are now reading. In fact, this could well be the very ***NEWS RELEASE*** that first captured your attention and from which you learned about this PR course.

So take a few minutes to read and study the following release which would have taken no longer than half an hour for me to write, and has generated an enormous amount of interest.

FOR IMMEDIATE RELEASE

Discover how to generate £20,000 worth of free publicity

As a practical method for businesses, clubs, good causes and charities etc, to stay ahead of the economic slump, two highly experienced West Country based entrepreneurs are offering local companies the opportunity to learn the basics of effective PR for nothing.

"Writing public interest news articles can be a win, win situation," explains Kevin Martyn who specialises in working with small enterprises. "The press and media are always interested in looking at attention-grabbing and compelling news and articles that are well written and presented correctly."

Their PR partnership formed after Kevin attended a local networking event where he met Bristol based Jeremy Fraser who specialises in helping charities with fund raising. A strong friendship was soon established, and it soon became apparent that between them they have been keeping the press and media well supplied with quality news material for more than fifty years, and have vast experience to offer local enterprises. Commenting Jeremy said "almost every small business or good cause had TONS of quality PR material and stories right in front of their very noses which are just waiting to be identified and used. When you know how to spot and present good news articles to the media, the rest is easy".

To enable forward looking entrepreneurial minded individuals who wish to learn the art of generating quality PR, Kevin and Jeremy are using cutting edge technology to present a series of mini seminars via the Internet *(webinars)*. These are being given totally free of charge and interested parties should visit: www.PR-forProfit.Com

[END]

For further information please contact Kevin Martyn on: 0800 675 xxxxx or you can email him at: info@PR-forProfit.Com

Notes:
Please use this margin for writing your ideas thoughts, inspirations and personal plan of action.

This Tutorial will then act as your route map to PR success!

Before we get into the specifics of creating the different sections of your release I would like to draw your attention to a few points relating to this one:

Appearance is EVERYTHING...

I hope you agree that it looks neat, which is ***VITAL***. As the name implies, a news release is first and foremost about the '***NEWS'*** which it is trying to impart. We don't want anything to detract from this, so anything which may complicate or compete such as highlighted or different coloured text etc, have purposely been left out as these are the very things which are most likely to have editors totally disregard it.

Length...

The release comfortably fits on just one page as the news room staff or journalists will not have time to read more than this. If your headline and first paragraph capture their attention they will read on and that is ***EXACTLY*** what it is designed to do. Ie; the whole purpose of course, is to get journalists to ***READ*** it from start to finish and then publish it!

The exception to this rule are the occasions where you need to provide brief 'Editors Notes' ***(please note: I said BRIEF!)*** or perhaps the download location to your accompanying photograph or attachment. However, whenever ***POSSIBLE*** do try to fit it ***ALL*** on to just ***ONE PAGE!***

A PR student recently commented that as we generally send our news releases by email, the page could be much longer! ***NICE TRY,*** but it doesn't work like that because if the news room staff feel that a release will be of interest to a particular journalist, they may want to print it out for them, and are unlikely to do so, if it is more than one page in length.

A friendly news room contact told me that any release longer than a page is routinely assigned to the 'round file' *(ie: THE BIN!)* Another said their publication followed a similar system to filter and reduce the huge volume of emails they receive. Obviously, they feel that if you are unable to communicate your news succinctly, then it probably isn't worth reading. To gain the maximum benefit from your PR efforts, stay safe and always follow the ***ONE PAGE*** rule!

The ***BIG*** benefit of this rule to us is the fact that once you get used to creating a release of this length, it doesn't take long to write.

- **Readability...**
  Did you notice how easy it is to read, with the very simple font, double spaced and with wide margins? This is so the editor or journalist can easily make notes as they read. As a matter of interest, focused and well written copy surrounded by loads of white space is ***ALWAYS*** a winning formula for getting your copy read.

- The complete news release is laid out in simple sections which we will be going through in just a moment; these will make it easy for you to master. It is simple and informative, and is ***NOT*** commercial in any way; it's interesting and offers the reader a direct benefit; it is in fact, ***EXACTLY*** what the news room and journalists want, ie; **'News'!**

Below are the nine main components which go into creating a good news release...

- Time Qualifier
- Headline
- Section 1 – Tells the most important facts
- Section 2 - Quotes and expand
- Section 3 - The call to action
- [END]
- Contact details
- Photograph *(attachment or website link)*
- Editor's notes *(which are not always necessary)*

Let's go through them now, one at a time, and in far more detail.

Notes:
Please use this margin for writing your ideas thoughts, inspirations and personal plan of action.

This Tutorial will then act as your route map to PR success!

Notes:
Please use this margin for writing your ideas thoughts, inspirations and personal plan of action.

This Tutorial will then act as your route map to PR success!

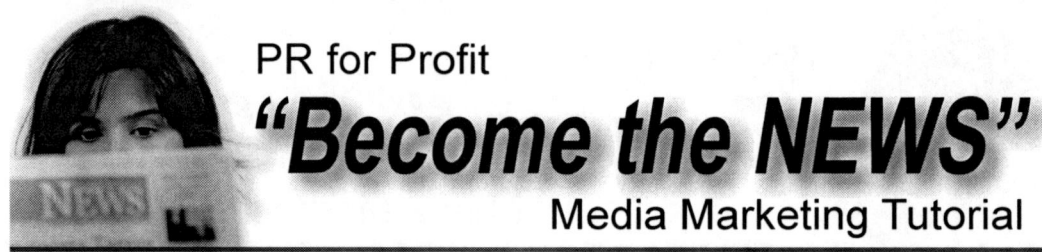

Time Qualifier...

Now this is fairly self explanatory as most of your news releases will carry the wording: ***'FOR IMMEDIATE RELEASE'***, and this is telling the journalist that they are free to publish your material just as soon as possible.

However, it may be the case that for what ever reason you do not want certain news to be released before a specific date. In this case, the heading on your release would carry an embargo, and for example may read: ***EMBARGO - NOT FOR RELEASE BEFORE 4th of July!***

In journalism and public relations, a news or press embargo is a request from whomever provided the information, for it not to be published until a certain date or until certain conditions have been met.

The HEADLINE...

Now without doubt, your headline is one of the most important aspects in writing ***ANYTHING*** as it is likely to be the first thing most readers see, and if it ***DOESN'T IMMEDIATELY*** capture their attention or interest they may not read any further, and the game is over; you have just lost a ***BIG*** opportunity.

For that reason I am going to be encouraging you to put a ***LOT*** of effort and energy into writing your headline. I have heard leading copy writers state that when they have written a good one, they are 90% finished, which really puts its importance into perspective for you.

Notes:
Please use this margin for writing your ideas thoughts, inspirations and personal plan of action.

This Tutorial will then act as your route map to PR success!

When I first started studying copywriting, one of the first things that I learned, was that ***EVERY*** line of text you write has just ***ONE PURPOSE***, and that is to get the reader to read the next line, and so on. This is really powerful and usable advice to follow. Let me ***REPEAT,*** your headline is the first thing that will be read, or registered in the minds of your reader. It can set the flavour for what follows, raise curiosity and sometimes excite controversy, so use it wisely.

SPIN can be a ***PARTICULARLY*** influential ingredient in PR and the headline is a good place to use it. Here is an example of how it ***COULD*** be misused...

I recently cancelled my subscription at a gym I used to attend because I originally joined to lose weight, and while I had been a member it had in fact increased considerably. However, this had nothing to do with the gym; they offer a great service and facility, it had not surprisingly, everything to with me, my lifestyle and what I ate. Time for a change, as I thought it would be far more effective, a good deal cheaper, and a lot more fun to go walking up and down the long sandy beach near where I live, accompanied by my two children.

Coincidentally, as my membership drew to a close I started to eat differently and began losing weight which was noticed by the gym manager, who also knows I am ***ALWAYS*** in the media and local press; so being a playful character, I decided to have a little fun with him. "I can just see the headlines six months from now" I said, as I played with the news possibilities in my head. How about this for a headline?

"23 stone man quits gym and loses 10 stone"

Upon hearing this the manager went white and very quiet; "I am only kidding I said" , and we parted friends.

Notes:
Please use this margin for writing your ideas thoughts, inspirations and personal plan of action.

This Tutorial will then act as your route map to PR success!

I hope this rather mischievous example highlights how you can use spin in a headline to capture attention? Obviously, such a headline would create huge interest, and if used as a standalone item could be quite wrong and misleading. However, if the article then went on to state that the weight loss was due to a new diet that had been strictly followed, etc, then this would be a good example of how you can ***POSITIVELY*** use spin in your PR headlines...

Learn to have fun with headlines, and the play on words that a little creative spin can produce, and you are going to come up with some interesting and very compelling results that will capture attention.

As we are experiencing a recession at the time of writing, which is generating much ongoing news, and I have also just being discussing weight loss, a connection between these two topics formed in my mind and generated the following headline which is a good example of just how easy it is to come up with something when you have the right inspiration.

"No better time to lose weight - recession encourages downsizing!"

The way to create a GOOD headline is to write lots...

I had considered creating an example headline swipe file for you to work from, and which would provide you with inspiration when creating your own. However, I also know that you will appreciate and value such examples ***FAR MORE*** if you harvest your own.

They are not difficult to find as you will see quality examples ***EVERYWHERE*** from which you can borrow, and in next to no time you will have built a valuable file of them for yourself, which you can refer to at will. So become a student of headlines and start your own collection today by using some of the techniques from the chapter entitled ***'IDEA MINING'***.

Notes:
Please use this margin for writing your ideas thoughts, inspirations and personal plan of action.

This Tutorial will then act as your route map to PR success!

When you find a new headline which you like, first add a copy to your growing swipe file, and experiment with it and adapt it to fit your subject; do this and you will soon discover some absolute gems, but don't stop until your headline is the very best you believe it can be. Creating compelling attention-grabbing headlines is a simple ***EQUATION*** - the more you write, the better you will become, and the closer you will also be to creating a headline which will be perfect for the news release on which you are working.

As they are so important I usually write ***AT LEAST 20*** headlines for every news release I create. It only takes me a few minutes and I believe it to be well worth the effort, however when a friend read this he felt I was being too hard by suggesting that you do the same, and perhaps I am a hard task master, so you decide how you best work. I have developed a very stylised system of writing, and a little like a butterfly as they drink from flowers, I will flit and hop between the different sections of my news release adding a few words there, or a paragraph here, or changing a word or two as the inspiration comes to me. In this way I do not become bored or stale in what I am writing and perhaps you could experiment if working in this way is a productive method for you too.

Sometimes...

You will write a really ***GREAT*** and ***DYNAMIC*** headline which you just know is the ***PERFECT*** one for your article, and it will immediately start driving your news release forward. When it does, you will find it hard to stop writing as your copy will flow quite naturally. This happens to me quite regularly, and is the reason why I put so much effort in to the headline.

By contrast, there will probably be occasions when you will create what at the time of writing, you think are really good headlines, only to revisit them a few days later *(depending upon the urgency!)* to come to the conclusion that they are not as good as you ***FIRST THOUGHT!*** When this happens, be philosophical about it as everything happens for a reason, and it also happens to all of us from time to time. So put a big smile on your face, and start afresh in good spirit, and you will probably find that this second time around, your headline is a ***STONKER*** (Colloquial English for ***FANTASTIC***!)

Notes:
Please use this margin for writing your ideas thoughts, inspirations and personal plan of action.

This Tutorial will then act as your route map to PR success!

The magic headline creation formula...

Many years ago I learned what a friend cruelly termed the 'Mentally Masochistic' creativity technique; you can call it what you like, but it has helped me come up with some of my very ***BEST*** and most ***PROFITABLE*** ideas. I wasn't too sure if this tutorial was the correct place to share this technique as I can tell you in advance that it ***WON'T BE*** for everyone. It is a little 'Off the wall' and requires a large amount of discipline and persistence to make it work. However, it works really well for me and I have loads of fun with it so please give it a go and see what results it produces for you.

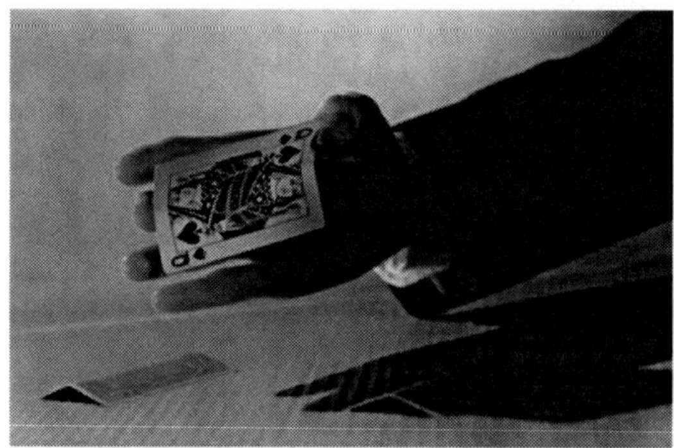

Although really ***PRODUCTIVE***, I can't remember for the life of me where I heard this method mentioned, but I am very appreciative to whoever gave it to me. I initially learned to use it for coming up with ideas, and soon realised it is really great for generating headlines; this is how it works...

Let's imagine that you are looking for headline ideas for your next release. Now you have to be really disciplined and set a ***SPECIFIC*** number of ideas which you intend to generate; say 29 - and then be prepared to give it 101% effort and determination until you have reached this total! I came up with that figure because I sincerely believe I can generate that number of headlines on most subjects, although it could be a really big challenge to do so. It may be this very belief that could make what you are about to learn work so well.

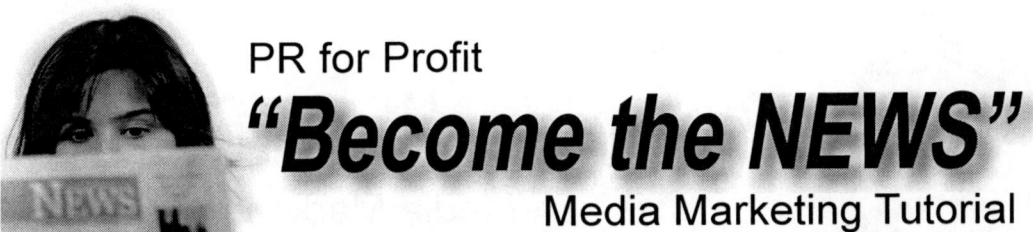

Notes:
Please use this margin for writing your ideas thoughts, inspirations and personal plan of action.

This Tutorial will then act as your route map to PR success!

So decide upon a number of headlines for yourself and whatever that number is you ***MUST NOT*** make it too easy for yourself to achieve; neither however, should you make it too difficult or impossible as this will dishearten you ...the idea is to ***STRETCH*** your creative process and belief system.
At this point I would start scribbling down the idea for my headlines just as quickly as I could and leave the elaboration or refinement for later. The first few headlines would come quickly, and then probably slow down as my target came into view. Remember these are just ideas, the spark of a headline I record as brief bullet points, and which I can return to and expand upon when I have finished. If you need further inspiration revisit the chapter on ***'IDEA MINING',*** where you will find many different methods you can use to power your creative process.

When you have reached your target number of headlines, refine them to make sure that they are all practical and not duplicated; be disciplined and delete any which are of a poor standard or don't sum up your story. Eventually you will hit your target and I am sure will feel pretty good about yourself for doing so; it's now when you can use this 'Magic Formula' to create what are likely to be the best headlines of the bunch. Reach deep into your mind and come up with another number; I have just done so and come up with the number five - and now I have to come up with five fresh headlines!

WHAT! Now hang on a moment before you start complaining and telling me that I am mad. What I have found is that these ***ADDITIONAL*** ideas, the ones which you are about to generate, are the ones with the real ***NUGGETS*** and ***GEMS*** hiding within them. ***SERIOUSLY!*** I have gone through this masochistic exercise ***HUNDREDS*** of times and found it to work ***EVERY*** single ***TIME!***

Notes:
Please use this margin for writing your ideas thoughts, inspirations and personal plan of action.

This Tutorial will then act as your route map to PR success!

Now I suspect the reason is quite obvious; by the time you have pushed yourself to find the entire first group of headlines, you have taken your thought process to the next level ...and now it is running on super unleaded ***HIGH OCTANE*** jet fuel, and working at maximum effectiveness, by providing you with quality headlines.

Remember that this ***VALUABLE*** method will work with virtually every creative process. So please give it a try!

Notes:
Please use this margin for writing your ideas thoughts, inspirations and personal plan of action.

This Tutorial will then act as your route map to PR success!

Which headline to use?

Sometime you will reach the situation where you have created two or even three quality headlines, and then become frustrated and confused about which one to use. I have been there on ***many*** occasions and although exasperating, having a choice is a good position to be in.

I am lucky enough to have a number of friends in related businesses who are at their computers for most of the day who I ask to play 'Devils Advocates' by giving their opinion on which one they think is the best, and you may be able to do the same. If so, I would like to bet that the one they choose, and the one which you feel is right, will be different. But listen to them, because often we get too close to our work, and they are likely to offer a good representation of the readership of the publication to which you are going to submit your news release.

Three headline killers...

Throughout this tutorial I have endeavoured to deliver the positive actions

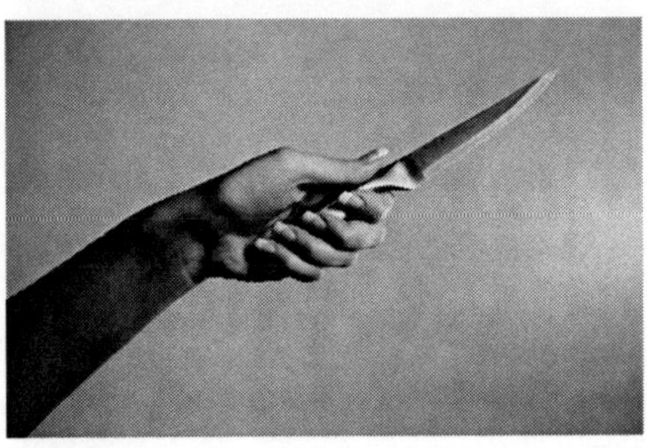

you need to take which will result in the creation of a quality news release. I really do not like being negative and telling you what you shouldn't do, but on this occasion it is ***REALLY*** necessary because what follows are three actions which are likely to get your news release rapidly rejected.

Notes:
Please use this margin for writing your ideas thoughts, inspirations and personal plan of action.

This Tutorial will then act as your route map to PR success!

Before we explore these headline criminals, I want to tell you that as a copywriter, and in the past, I was really guilty of using all three of them on a regular basis, but eventually a friend pointed out the errors I was making, and now I get a ***FAR HIGHER*** percentage of my news releases published.

Over sensationalising...

This is a very central part of the copywriter's tool kit, and I find it difficult ***NOT*** to add a generous dose of this to the mix. So ***BE WARNED***, if you do, like I did in the past, you must expect to pay the price of having a far lower proportion of your news releases published. Instead I suggest that you experiment with the English language by purchasing a Thesaurus as you may find combinations of words which will serve exactly the same purpose.

Forget the *SALES* hype...

There is really not much to add to the above paragraph. I just love creating copy using compelling words and superlatives, but a PR news articles is not the place to use them. I have to regularly remind myself that the advertisements which often appear on the very next page to my article use such copy, and they probably don't get a ***FRACTION*** of the returns or income that my articles generate, and the advertisers are paying a ***STACK*** of money for the privilege.

Don't write a 'Guinness Advert' headline...

I used to think that I was thick, and perhaps I am, because I found it difficult to understand those adverts which Guinness created to try and position themselves as the drink of the intellectual! Certainly, they were clever and entertaining, but whether they achieved their objective I am not sure; I do know that they spent a ***SMALL FORTUNE*** on producing them. As a rule of thumb, don't expect others, ***ESPECIALLY*** in something as valuable as your headline, to share your humour or level of intellect. Follow the ***KISS*** rule – Keep It Simple Stupid!

Notes:
Please use this margin for writing your ideas thoughts, inspirations and personal plan of action.

This Tutorial will then act as your route map to PR success!

Section 1 – Tells the most important facts...

Now the first section of your release only needs to be four or five lines long and

should tell your reader all about your release, and then you can elaborate in section 2. If you follow the 'famous five principle' of '***WHERE, WHEN, WHY, HOW*** and ***WHAT***', you should find it quite easy. The way I write my articles is to start broad, by writing as much as I can, and then ferociously ***PRUNE*** to the desired length. I may initially use half a page to write the first section so that I don't miss anything of value, and then I start pruning until I have condensed it so it reads well, and is just a few lines in length. As you can see from my first section, I have used this very process by starting with ***WHY***, I then gave details of ***WHO***, and finished the section with ***WHAT***.

> ***Section 1***
> "As a practical method for businesses, clubs, good causes and charities etc, to stay ahead of the economic slump, two highly experienced West Country based entrepreneurs are offering local companies the opportunity to learn the basics of effective PR for nothing."

Section 2 - Quotes and expand...

In section 2 of this release all I have done is elaborated on, and clarified the story further by first highlighting the credentials of Jeremy and myself by including a little about what we do which confirms our expertise in working with local businesses and using PR. I have planted the seeds of desire by telling people a little about PR and the fact that they already have good stories which the media would be interested in, and may well result in something they want, ie: more profits and an easier way of life.

Notes:
Please use this margin for writing your ideas thoughts, inspirations and personal plan of action.

This Tutorial will then act as your route map to PR success!

Section 2

"Writing public interest news articles can be a win, win situation" explains Kevin Martyn who specialises in working with small enterprises. "The press and media are always interested in looking at attention-grabbing and compelling news and articles that are well written and presented correctly."

Their PR partnership formed after Kevin attended a local networking event where he met Bristol based Jeremy Fraser who specialises in helping charities with fund raising. A strong friendship was soon established, and it soon became apparent that between them they have been keeping the press and media well supplied with quality news material for more than fifty years, and have vast experience to offer local enterprises. Commenting Jeremy said "almost every small business or good cause had ***TONS*** of quality PR material and stories right in front of their very noses which are just waiting to be identified and used. When you know how to spot and present good news articles to the media, the rest is easy".

Section 3 - The call to action...

The last section of the release is where you state your offer or call to action if your release is a direct response PR article such as this one. Although it is the shortest of the three sections it actually has the most to tell.

To stir up the audience into taking action I mildly provoke them by suggesting that they ***MAY NOT*** belong to my target audience. I specifically state who will benefit most from what's on offer by saying ***'forward looking entrepreneurial minded individuals'***.

I would like to bet that inside you have just said "that's me" because nearly everyone likes to think of themselves as ***'forward looking'***, as well as recognising that they are also ***'entrepreneurially minded'***. Finally, who doesn't think of themselves as an 'individual'? We ***ALL*** do! In fact, and although it may only register at a subliminal level, not identifying yourself as part of this group is a bit like admitting you are not that bright.

This is quickly followed up with the offer for them to learn more without cost, and the fact that they do not have to put themselves out much to gain benefit from this offer, other than visiting our website. The potential returns stated in this section are simple and uncomplicated, and at this point the reader is just one step, or website away from benefiting.

"Just in case you are wondering, this news release has worked ***WONDERFULLY*** for us and returns volumes of interested prospects!"

> ***Section 3***
> "To enable forward looking entrepreneurial minded individuals who wish to learn the art of generating quality PR, Kevin and Jeremy are using cutting edge technology to present a series of mini seminars via the Internet *(webinars)*. These are being given totally free of charge and interested parties should visit: www.PR-forProfit.Com"

[END] quotes...

You may wonder why I am making a point of telling you about the [END] quotes marks, but they serve a very important purpose which is to tell the journalist that we are at the end of the release and what follows is additional information to help them with their job. You may see releases which use a variety of different methods to indicate the release is ended such as -end-, ###, +++, etc, however, in my opinion there is no missing or mistaking [END] and is almost a statement of your level of confidence as much as anything else.

Notes:
Please use this margin for writing your ideas thoughts, inspirations and personal plan of action.

This Tutorial will then act as your route map to PR success!

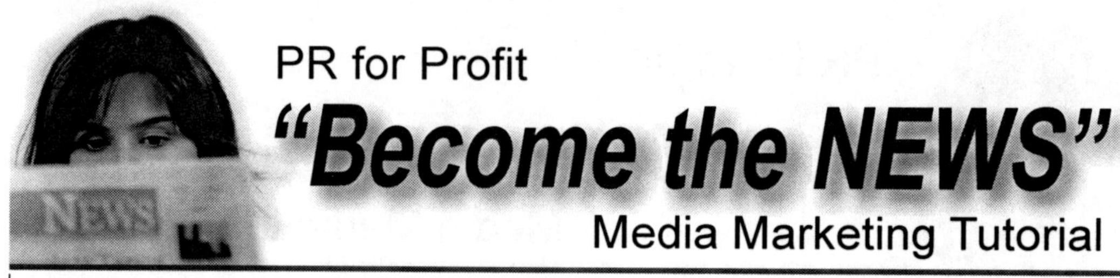

Notes:
Please use this margin for writing your ideas thoughts, inspirations and personal plan of action.

This Tutorial will then act as your route map to PR success!

Include your contact details...

Keep your contact details short and precise, who they should contact and where and how they can be contacted. I have found it best to provide both a telephone number and an email address. Usually a reporter will come straight back to me by phone, but sometimes they use email especially if their deadline is still a few days away.

As I mentioned, the World over the method of writing quality news releases stays the same, but in some countries they put the name and contact details above the release, although I don't really think it matters that much if you stick to putting it beneath the article because if your headline and body copy catches the journalist's attention they will not mind investing a few seconds more looking for your contact details.

The accompanying photograph...

Although this release doesn't have a photograph, most of mine do because

often a photograph makes the publication of your release more attractive, and likely to be used. *(Remember the old saying that a picture often says 1,000 words!)*

Now it costs the publication money to pay a photographer to come out and take a picture, and most of the ones I have come across are already very ***OVERWORKED*** and running around like a 'cat on a hot tin roof'. For this reason alone, you increase your chances of having your release published if you make it easy for the journalists by providing them with a quality photograph of your own, and in this day and age of digitised photography it is not difficult.

Notes:
Please use this margin for writing your ideas thoughts, inspirations and personal plan of action.

This Tutorial will then act as your route map to PR success!

However, it *MUST* be of good quality!

A lady I know who runs a local judo club is always amazed that the press never use her photographs which she has taken with her mobile phone camera. Although these cameras are becoming higher quality all the time, they do not take very large photographs or ones of the quality the media are looking for, these cannot in any way be compared with photographs produced by dedicated cameras. Let's face it, cameras in phones are a useful function to have for capturing that special *(surprise)* moment, or keeping a scrap book, but they are still a long way from capturing ***HIGH DEFINITION*** images.

So get serious...

If you are serious about making money from your PR, invest in a good quality digital camera. They have become so ***INEXPENSIVE*** and at the time of writing you can get a really good one which will provide the quality of picture you require for just £60 or £70. This is probably a half or even a third of the cost of hiring a professional photographer to take just one picture for you.

If you are providing a group photograph don't forget to include a thumbnail

sized picture with your release giving the names of the people in the image, for instance: "seen in the photograph from left to right, Nancy Hemming *(mum)*, 12 year old Lisa Hemming, and big sister Rebecca Hemming." The system I have been using for a number of years is to put a thumbnail copy on the release, and then underneath this state: A full resolution copy of this photograph can be downloaded from: www.yourwebsite.com/photo.jpg

Notes:
Please use this margin for writing your ideas thoughts, inspirations and personal plan of action.

This Tutorial will then act as your route map to PR success!

Placing your photograph onto the internet is a simple task which requires you to perform what is known as an FTP *(File Transfer Protocol)* of your image to your website. This process is really quite simple and can be performed by using a piece of ***FREE*** software called 'FileZilla'; just type this keyword into Google and it will return you the download position of this essential software. The software you see me using below is called "Cute2 and works in ***EXACTLY*** the same way by transferring your image file from your computer to your website.

As you can see it is a simple matter of opening up the location of your picture on your computer and then the target destination of your website image folder, and then dragging and dropping your desired file to the destination location, and the program will do the rest for you.

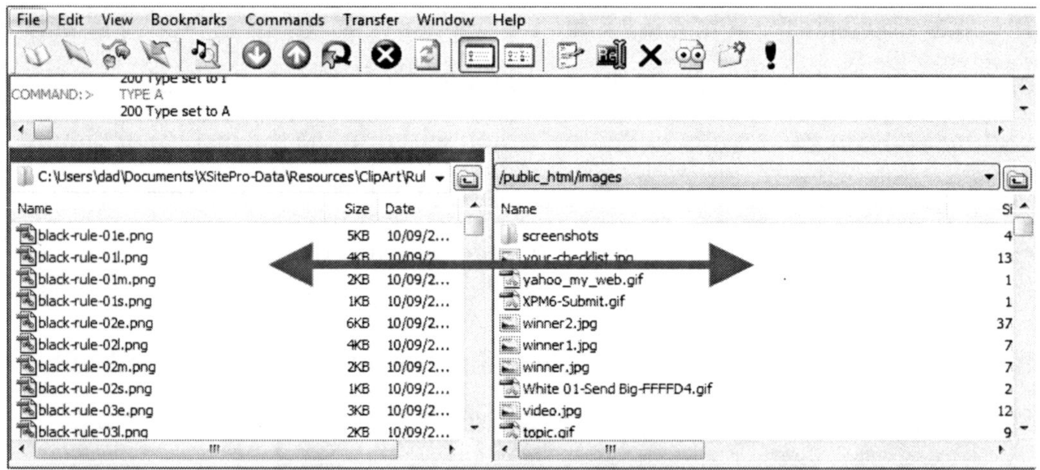

Visual layout Rules...

Keeping your article looking professional and readable is so important that I want to reiterate a few things before we move on to the action plan and the point where you write your first news release.

Notes:
Please use this margin for writing your ideas thoughts, inspirations and personal plan of action.

This Tutorial will then act as your route map to PR success!

Double or 1.5 line spacing...

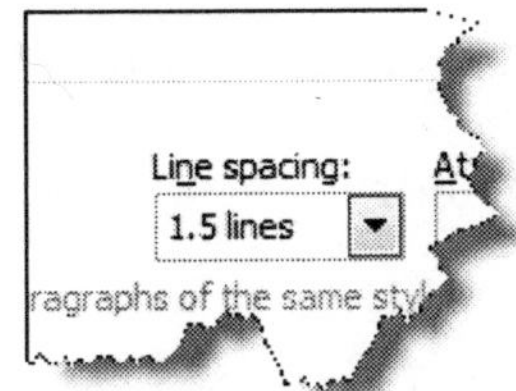

Remember that double spaced formatting makes it easy for journalists to both read and make notes on your copy, and is an essential component of generating a professionally presented PR release. Sometimes I use 1.5 line spacing which is what I have used on this tutorial because it makes it easy for you to read.

Use a SIMPLE to read type face...

I have just counted them, and my computer is stocked with 216 different types of text fonts and I probably use ***NO MORE*** than six in ***TOTAL***. Unless you happen to be a graphical designer, having this number of fonts simply isn't necessary. When you send the press or media an article make sure you are using a time tested and proven font such as **'Times Roman'**, or **'Courier'**; never use an unusual font as not only may it be off-putting, but if you send it by email, the news desk computer may not have that particular font installed, and by default, substitute a strange looking font instead, which could result in your news release being rejected.

Keep it to ONE PAGE...

Please remember the consequences of making your release more than a page in length! ...it may not make it as far as the reporters' desk and could be ***DESTROYED*** upon receipt. Don't risk this happening to you, it's not hard to keep your release under a page, and the more you practice, the easier it will become.

ALWAYS get it SPELL CHECKED before despatch!

I am not ashamed of telling you that at school I ***NEVER ONCE*** won a prize for spelling! ...I have a small arsenal of other talents, some of which are quite artistic, but I can't claim more than a 7 or 8 out of ten for spelling which is surprising for someone who generates most of their income from writing.

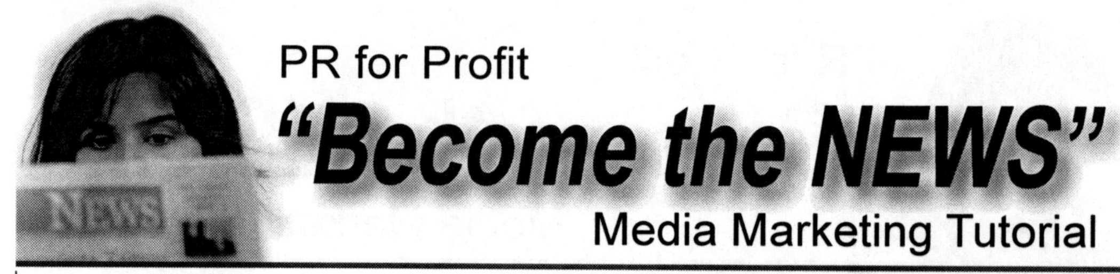

Notes:
Please use this margin for writing your ideas thoughts, inspirations and personal plan of action.

This Tutorial will then act as your route map to PR success!

Try as I might it has never developed into one of my strong points, but it has never stopped me writing either. Nowadays, I get a good friend called Carol, who is ***BRILLIANT*** at spotting and improving my mistakes to cast his eagle eye over everything I write before sending it out, ***EVEN*** this tutorial!

If your spelling, like mine, is suspect you need to find a Carol of your own, someone who is good at spotting such mistakes, to run through it for you. Although the occasional 'typo' or spelling error may well be forgiven and overlooked, if your material is riddled with them you will lower its perceived level of quality, and not make a good or professional impression with the media; in fact, you could run the risk of having your material ***REJECTED*** for this reason. ***POINT MADE?***

Action plan...

This is going to be the most important action plan in this tutorial because if you follow me through it, and take the actions as written, by the end of it you will have your first news release ready for despatch and also know where you are going to send it. So if you haven't already done so, now is the time to select one of your PR ideas from the stock pile of great ideas I hope you have created, and decide which one you want to use.

Identify where you are going to send your release when it is completed. I suggest a local publication so you can ***PERSONALLY*** check to see when it is published. If this is successful, and your release appears without problem, you can then consider '***ROLLING OUT***' *(ie: mass distribution)* your release to as many other publications as you wish. Or, you may save the '***ROLLING OUT***' for another occasion.

Notes:
Please use this margin for writing your ideas thoughts, inspirations and personal plan of action.

This Tutorial will then act as your route map to PR success!

Set a deadline...

Use some common sense here and don't make things either too easy or too difficult for yourself. However, I promise you that you will create a far better release if you set a ***DEADLINE*** to which you are prepared to work at your hardest to honour and fulfil. Also remember to allow a little standing time for your article to ferment and mature, because after a night or two of cooling off you will return to it with fresh eyes and probably add some significant improvements to your copy.

What is the objective of your article?

Now it goes without saying that you want it to generate some media exposure for you which will convert into a stream of revenue. However, to keep you focused, what I want you to do is write a couple of sentences which you can refer back to in case you get lost whilst creating. These need to be specific and relate to the information you want to share, or the action that you want the readers of your article to take, etc.

How are you going to write it?

What I mean by this is what type of article will it be? A profile builder? or a direct response PR article? Unless you feel confident I would advise you to make your first few news releases all profile builders, and then move on to direct response PR articles when you have gained a little experience and confidence. However, if you have decided on making it a direct response PR release, you will have to consider the feedback mechanism and getting that in place before you can despatch it.

The time qualifier...

Keep the first one simple and write the words: FOR IMMEDIATE RELEASE, across the top of your page.

Notes:
Please use this margin for writing your ideas thoughts, inspirations and personal plan of action.

This Tutorial will then act as your route map to PR success!

Headlines...

The next thing to do is start writing your headline. Write at least 20 of them and if you run out of inspiration visit some of the online news blogs and see the headlines they write. It is possible that some of them may easily adapt for your article, or provide you with further inspiration. Really push yourself in this task and remember that your headline is the single most important element of your article, so make them good.

Section 1

Now you may have been lucky enough to find a headline that drives the rest of the release, and if this is the case you will find writing this quite simple. Remember that you have to tell the entire story in just a few lines. However, in the writing process make it as long as it needs to be to contain all the facts of your story and then you can trim it down to size.

Section 2

Now you can expand and elaborate on your story, and if possible provide a quote from an expert source and that may be you. Aim to make the story interesting or even humorous. You can use more than one paragraph if you need to.

Section 3

If your article includes a call to action this is the time to write it and remember to keep it simple. If it is an event for the readers to attend be sure to provide an accurate address; if it is time sensitive, be certain to state this, and by when, and what actions must be taken! When you have finished, type [END] and centre it in your page.

Notes:
Please use this margin for writing your ideas thoughts, inspirations and personal plan of action.

This Tutorial will then act as your route map to PR success!

Remember to format your article to either 1.5 or double line spaceing for easy reading!

Read it out loud to yourself a few times and adjust if necessary. When you have got it to the point where you feel it is the best you can make it, put it away for a day or so, and then go through it again making improvements if necessary. If you are happy with it get someone who is good at spelling to check it for mistakes and then you have just reached the point where it is ready for despatch and publication. This we will come too shortly, but you have now just reached a really ***BIG*** milestone in your PR education.

Most important of all...

Please do not consider for a moment missing out this next ***VITALLY*** important action! Stand up straight, and away from all furniture, and then stretch your right hand high into the air. In an anticlockwise direction rotate your hand until it is pointing behind you, lower your arm and give yourself a good pat on the back. That is from Jeremy and I, and you sincerely ***DESERVE IT!*** Whatever the outcome of this particular news release doesn't matter, as from this point forward you can improve and refine what you have learned until you become an expert.

You have created your first news release and this is just the start of what will become a very ***ENJOYABLE*** and extremely ***PROFITABLE*** journey for you. From this point forward the PR process will become easier and much faster. It's up to you to be consistent because not far into the future you will be able to generate a considerable percentage of your income from PR marketing, probably saving you a small fortune in advertising and marketing costs.

Notes:
Please use this margin for writing your ideas thoughts, inspirations and personal plan of action.

This Tutorial will then act as your route map to PR success!

Writing articles for magazines, trade journals and other publications...

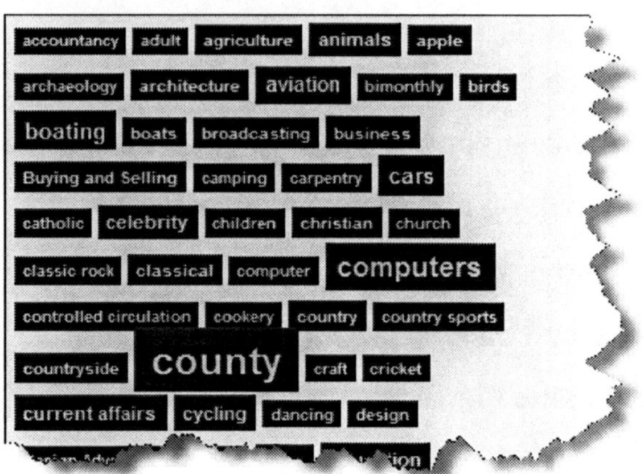

You may decide that you would like to get something published in a glossy magazine or a specialised trade journal, and I can't blame you as some of these publications have ***HUGE*** readerships. Not only this, but some magazine subscriptions are quite costly which qualifies their readers as an audience with a ***DISPOSABLE INCOME*** - the very market you are looking for.

However, getting them to accept articles from you is a completely different process to that of the usual consumer media, so let's cover this simple formula right now.

The easiest way to find what magazines maybe suitable for your line of business is to invest into a media director such as Ben's, which is the one I use. However, a great and ***FREE*** alternative is to search the listings at: www.mediauk.com which covers most UK publications.

If you live elsewhere in the World you will have to research at Google to find a relevant media directory for you to use; there is no shortage of them.

At the time of writing, mediauk.com list more than 2,000 magazines and specialist publications, so you can keep yourself ***EXCEPTIONALLY*** busy if you so desire.

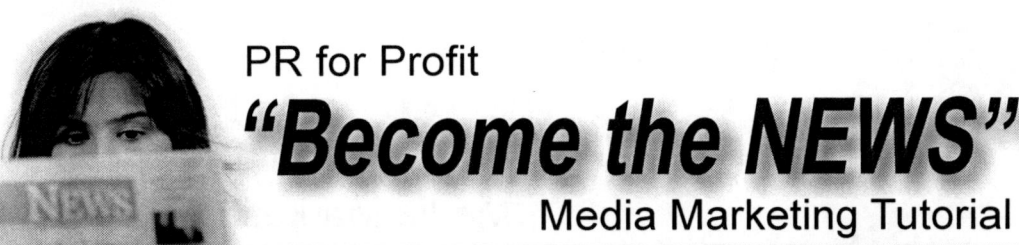

The screen grab to the left shows you just a small selection of the different publications which are listed under the letter G. This highlights the wide variety of specialised audiences available who you may be able to reach with a quality and relevant article. However, the best thing about providing articles for the eyes of a ***SPECIALISED*** and topic-focused audience is that your response rate is likely to be very much higher than for a general news publication such as your local paper.

- Game
- Gamemaker
- Games Master
- gamesTM
- The Garden
- Garden Answers
- Garden News
- Garden Rail
- BBC Gardeners' World Magazine
- Gardening Which?
- Gardens Monthly
- GAT: Girl About Town
- Gay Times
- Gay UK
- Generation
- Gibbons Stamp Monthly
- Girl talk
- Glamour
- Global
- Global Reinsurance
- Glory Glory Man United
- Go Girl!
- Go Healthy
- Go Mini
- Go Tenpin
- Golf & Travel
- Golf Course Architecture
- Golf International
- Golf Monthly
- Volkswagen Golf+
- Golf World
- GolfPunk

Whatever media directory you decide upon using, study the listed publications and write down the ones that are of immediate interest to you, as well as those whose readers are likely to have an interest in the topic of the article that you plan to write.

On this occasion and unlike newspapers there is no point in writing your article until ***AFTER*** you have contacted your target publications for a number of reasons, which we are coming to next.

Notes:
Please use this margin for writing your ideas thoughts, inspirations and personal plan of action.

This Tutorial will then act as your route map to PR success!

Notes:
Please use this margin for writing your ideas thoughts, inspirations and personal plan of action.

This Tutorial will then act as your route map to PR success!

Unlike newspapers, magazines generally work much further ahead, sometimes planning their features six or nine months in to the future, and this may well generate some interesting opportunities for you, as you are about to discover. Your first action in getting the ball rolling is to contact the publications you have identified and ask if they have a 'forward feature planning schedule' and if so, how you can obtain a copy? A number of outcomes ***COULD*** occur at this point and you should be prepared for all of them. They may tell you that they don't have one, or it is private, or pass you on to a journalist. We will deal with this also in just a moment.

Or, you may be asked why you want it, in which case you will have to say that you would like to submit an article for their consideration and their feature planner would help you create something which would be more focused, relevant and quite possibly useful to them. This may trigger them to direct you to a website page to either read or download this information, or they may offer to fax or email it to you directly. Again be prepared, as the media in general are ***VERY FOND*** of using the fax as a primary means of delivering information.

If they transfer you to speak to a journalist, make a note of his or her name, and the ***PRECISE*** spelling of it, if it is unusual. Introduce yourself, and be prepared to tell them about you, your business, product or service - specific skill, or expertise etc, and then ask them if they would be interested in receiving an article from you on whatever subject you feel would capture their interest.

Hopefully, and if you have made a good impression, they will say "yes" and this is where they may start to tell you about their forward feature schedule and how you and the article you are offering may fit into to it. Or, they may request an example of the type of article they would like from you: if this happens

Notes:
Please use this margin for writing your ideas thoughts, inspirations and personal plan of action.

This Tutorial will then act as your route map to PR success!

DON'T PANIC! Simply tell them that you haven't yet written anything and you are giving them the opportunity to benefit first. They will respect this, and probably ask you to submit something to them for approval.
You will then need to enquire what length of article they would like it to be. As this is the first time they have dealt with you they will probably request that you submit a fairly short one of just 300 - 500 words. You will also need to ask them when the deadline is for the issue in which they would like to use it. As already mentioned, they may be planning to use it months ahead, however, you should promise to deliver your article in the following week or so.

There are many reasons for this, and the first and most important is that you are trying to establish a relationship with them, and if you promise to deliver it on a certain date, and then do so, or even a little earlier, you will have taken the first ***BIG*** step in establishing what could become a very ***LONG*** and ***PROFITABLE*** association with that particular magazine. Just as important, is the fact that if you leave it too long, you may lose your enthusiasm, or even forget that you have promised to write an article at all. For this reason, in PR, it is ***ALWAYS*** best to strike while the iron is hot, and ***ALWAYS*** aim to do too much - ***TOO SOON***, rather than too little - ***TOO LATE***!

Remember that you are not the ***ONLY*** individual who will be offering them material for their magazine, and if you delay it is possible that your ***COMPETITION*** may slip in there before you, and steal what was going to be ***YOUR PROFIT***; you can already imagine how that would make you feel.

WARNING: If you ever let a publication down in this way they ***WILL*** remember your name for a very long time, and you can forget ***EVER*** going back to them again with another article in the future because you will have just ***DESTROYED*** your credibility completely and, at the same time, a valuable PR outlet that may well have generated a ***SIZABLE*** and ongoing profit for you! Not only this, but from experience, I can tell you that journalists often change positions faster than a game of 'Musical Chairs', or even work for a number of publications at the same time, so if you pick up a reputation for being ***UNRELIABLE***, like most ***BAD NEWS*** it travels at the speed of light.

Notes:
Please use this margin for writing your ideas thoughts, inspirations and personal plan of action.

This Tutorial will then act as your route map to PR success!

After sending your material call your new journalist contact to see if he or she has received it, and ask them if it is okay or if they would like anything improving or changed. This may sound like a time consuming business and I would agree it is! However, you are also trying to establish a relationship with them and little gestures such as this can make a big ***IMPRESSION*** in the mind of your new best friend! More importantly however is this; by asking this question they may open up to you and offer you some ***PRICELESS*** advice that could significantly help you improve aspects of your writing skills for future use and open up new possibilities.

Use the SAME writing formula...

As far as writing your article is concerned I would suggest that now your target publication has invited an article submission from you it would be a good idea to obtain a copy of their magazine for reference, and study their style of writing. However, if this is not possible, use the same formula as you have just learned in this chapter for writing your news release

Obviously, you won't need to include a time qualifier because they are already expecting something from you and they may have already given you a good idea of when it is likely to be published. Just write a great headline and then the three sections of the body copy as we have already covered and that will be all that is required. Stay aware of the finished number of words they have requested, start broad by writing lots so you don't miss anything and then prune to length and adjust for quality.

By the way, most word processors have a word count facility. If you are using Word 2003 or an earlier version you will find this under the tools dropdown menu, and if you are using 2007 or newer, it is on the bottom of the front page and it keeps an updated total of the number of words in your document as you type.

If the journalist requests for instance, a 500 word article, it is okay to go as many as 30 or 40 words either side of this number, but the closer you get to the exact request the better.

Notes:
Please use this margin for writing your ideas thoughts, inspirations and personal plan of action.

This eTutorial will then act as your route map to PR success!

What follows are 10 news release examples for you to gain inspiration:

Support

If you have a question please first check to see if you can find an answer by visiting our FAQ pages in the members resource section listed in the page footer.

If you can't find an answer send your question by email to: support@PR-forProfit.Com

HAPPIER LIVES FOR SUFFERERS IN CONTROL

A new publication written to help sufferers of any chronic or long term illness to cope more positively and gain a much improved quality of life by understanding their ailment and how to control it, is published on line this month.

Entitled 'The Feel Better Book' and written by renowned hypnotherapist and behavioral therapist Sharon Stiles, the eBook focuses on how sufferers from most mental and physical illnesses can significantly improve their health and outlook on life by fully researching their condition and determining to take control of their situations.

"Lack of control is a big cause of stress" says Sharon, "and stress can lead to a worsening of any existing health problem. Properly understanding what is wrong helps enormously to reduce anxiety and allows sufferers to rationally choosc thc best course of action to improve their wellbeing"

Packed full of easy-to-read, helpful, practical and sensitive advice, topics include, reducing anxiety, positive mindset and how to deal with a whole range of emotions. The eBook also features easy reference guides, end-of-chapter reminder summaries, links to many further advisory and charity websites, and an easy-to-navigate facility enabling the reader to instantly go from the index to any subject heading with just a click of a 'mouse'.

Available to download in digital format for immediate access at a special introductory price of just £14.99 (or as a printed hard copy at £19.99 + £3.00 p&p), 'The Feel Better Book' can be obtained by visiting www.thefeelbetterbook.com

[END]

For further information please contact Sharon Stiles on 0845 665 3024 or
Email: xxxxxxxxx

Note to editor: Sharon Stiles uses hypnosis, cognitive behaviour therapy, NLP and meridian energy techniques such as EFT and Chinosis to help people take control of their emotions and behaviour.

CANCER CARE CHARITY ART EXHIBITION TO AUCTION ROYAL WORK

Penny Brohn Cancer Care (formerly Bristol Cancer Help Centre) is to auction a signed artist's proof of a painting by HRH The Prince of Wales at an exhibition which is set to be one of the highlights of the art calendar in the South West of England.

Patron of the Charity, His Royal Highness's work depicts part of the organic herb gardens in the beautiful grounds of his country home near Tetbury, and is entitled **'The Thyme Walk, Highgrove House';** it is hoped that the picture will raise between £5-£10,000 towards the total target of £50,000 worth of sales, from over 400 pieces.

The exhibition which is to be held at the Charity's stunning new home in Pill, just outside Bristol during the weekend of October 4-5th 2008, will be the fifth it has staged over the past 8 years. 100 other artists will be showcasing their work in the house and grounds throughout the weekend, providing visitors the opportunity to view and buy unique pieces from established, influential and emerging new talent.

The prestigious event brings together artists who exhibit with Bristol Savages and The Royal West of England Academy ensuring an eclectic mix of traditional and contemporary expressions, including highly imaginative sculptural pieces.

Announcing the exhibition, fundraising manager Julian Withers, said "We are privileged to have His Royal Highness as our Patron and delighted that he has made this most generous donation. All profits raised will help us with our life-changing work caring for people with cancer and their families and friends."

For more information on the Charity and the exhibition visit: www……………or telephone:

[END]

BRISTOL EVENTS COMPANY KNOWS THE TRICKS OF THE TRADE

A Bristol based woman who came to the City just two years ago after a successful career in media and hospitality in London and Italy, is celebrating 2008 as the second profitable year for her events management company, due in no small part to a chance meeting with a local magician.

……………….of ………………….Events knew exactly where to start when she moved to Bristol being determined to put her corporate organisational expertise and experience to good use. After just one month she had the good fortune to meet ……………, one of the South West's leading magicians who quickly became one of the main attractions at many of the events ………..staged.

"Ever since I met ………..it's been magic!" Says ….:... "his table-side magic tricks and the mobile casinos he operates are always a big attraction at my events and it seems that ever since we met my business has increased dramatically"

Now ………is holding her own party this month to celebrate the second anniversary of her business and to thank her magician and growing list of clients for making 2008 a very good year, with the prospect of 2009 being – well, wizard!

2008 was no illusion for………. as her company now numbers amongst her clients such big names as …………..hotel, ……….consulting engineers, ……… the World's largest ……………….manufacturer, …………- the charity which carries out research into ……………and ………….. , and ………. magazine, as well as many private party givers. For more information visit:

Picture shows ………………of …………….Events with magician …………….casting the spell of success for 2009.

[END]

For more information please contact:

Salsa DVD Brings the Latin Beat to Cardiff

A new DVD to hot up these cold winter nights by learning how to Salsa, has been introduced by two top Salsa specialists from Cardiff.

Bringing the magic, passion and fun of this Latin dance to everyone who loves to 'let their hair down' and simply enjoy the infectious mix of vibrant rhythm and movement, the DVD takes the student through a series of easy-to-follow basic steps right up to being able to dance confidently in public.

Before linking up to form their own popular, Cardiff based, Salsa teaching club '....... ....', Cardiff born and bred ....and ....followed independent successful dancing careers having been taught by some of the World's leading tutors and subsequently winning many prestigious awards including ....Official ....Championship.

"Salsa dancing is enormous fun" says .... "not only that, it's a great way to keep fit and make new friends; After practicing the lessons at home, students should be ready to hit the dance floor quickly and easily, coming back to the DVD whenever they feel the need for a reminder; better still, they can perfect their new-found skills at our regular ....classes which we hold at some of the best venues in Cardiff".

The new 60 minute DVD which is supported by and features the music of the internationally renowned ....band costs just £......... and is available to order by visiting www..................where details of the ....dance classes can also be found.

[END]

For further information please contact:

TANTALISE YOUR WAY TO KEEPING FIT!

A new 'Dance School with a Difference' is attracting Bristol women from all walks of life, ages, shapes and sizes, as a highly effective and fun way to keep fit, build confidence - and boost up their sex lives!

Already enjoying great popularity with its innovative Pole Dancing classes, '............Dance School', is to now introduce workshops based on Burlesque – the erotic cabaret act that scandalised Parisian society between the two World wars and which is now enjoying a fashionable revival both here and in the US.

Capturing a mix of old Hollywood glamour and post modern fetishism, Burlesque is a sexy but subtle striptease routine with the emphasis on the 'tease' more than the strip, designed to tantalize and titillate whilst toning the whole body, improving firmness, posture and flexibility.

.............., proprietor and the primary dance teacher at '.......', is a highly acclaimed Burlesque striptease artist in her own right, performing regularly at high profile and prestigious events throughout the UK and overseas. With a circus performance background, she combines dramatic circus skills with her seductive routines.

Says ...."All the courses make exercising much more fun than going to the gym. There's always a great atmosphere with lots of laughs and you don't have to be fit or have dance experience to take part. There is no nudity and we find that our pupils relax and lose any inhibitions very quickly, often gaining life-changing confidence. We have many reports of great successes both in standards of fitness attained and new and exciting levels reached in 'home entertainment!'"

Held at a central ....venue, the new Burlesque workshops consist of two classes – the 'Show Girl Dance Routine' - seductive charm using various disrobing techniques including the removal of gloves and stockings, and the more vigorous ancient art of 'Tassle Twirling'! The next workshops are on Saturdays May 6th and June 3rd with the 'Show Girl' session from 1pm – 2.30pm and 'Tassle Twirling' from 2.40pm – 4.10pm. Prices are £20.00 each or £35.00 for the two.

To book and for full information on the school and both Burlesque and Pole Dancing classes telephone: ....or visit: www.................................

[END]

For more information please contact:

NEWS RELEASE

On Sunday August 27th on the bank holiday weekend, the first Polo match to come to Bristol will be played at the North Somerset Show Ground at Long Ashton.

Organised by the newly formed ....Club Ltd., the match will be the central activity of an action-packed, fun day out where families can bring their own picnics and enjoy a variety of support entertainment and planned attractions such as a falconry display, sheepdog demonstrations, champagne and beer tent, strawberries and cream and a trade 'village'.

The event also provides businesses in Bristol and the South West with a perfect opportunity to entertain their clients and other guests to first class hospitality within a corporate marquee and at an 'After Polo Party' which will be open to all in the evening with a bar, barbeque, live band or 'disco'.

Announcing the event, ...chairman and managing director of ....Club said: "Polo is a fast and skilful game – enormous fun to play and a tremendously exciting spectator sport. Our aim is to dispel some of the myths that surround Polo and make the game more accessible to everyone. We are delighted therefore to be able to offer the chance to introduce Polo to people in and around Bristol and the South West who perhaps may not have had the opportunity before to enjoy the sport at first hand."

The two teams, which include top International players, will be playing for the Isambard Kingdom Brunel Trophy in celebration of the 200th anniversary of one of Bristol's most significant contributors.

Supported by Star Radio Bristol and in aid of 'The Bristol Cancer Help Centre' the leading UK charity for cancer care of which ....is Patron, the event opens to the public at 12 noon; family entertainment is from 1.30pm-2.30pm and the match is from 3.30pm-4.30pm followed by presentations and the start of the 'After Polo Party' at 5pm with gates closing at 10pm.

Entry is £30 per car on the day or £25 per car for advanced bookings. To book now telephone:

For enquiries and bookings for corporate hospitality packages or for more information on sponsorship opportunities and trade village plot reservations telephone: ....or visit:...................................

[END]

Terrorism Related To Dramatic Increase In Health Related Problems

Stress related health problems are at an all time high. It is estimated that in the US the number of citizens who suffer with chronic pain ranges from 45 to 100 million people. And the figures are on a similar ratio for the UK.

Health experts agree that this wide spread reaction is clearly triggered by stress over terrorist and mugging attacks. Stress related problems are also intensified by the fear and uncertainty of what the future will bring to people's children.

"Stress affects the body in a variety of ways and what is most alarming is that people have no idea what to do to help themselves" says Richard Flook, the head of Meta-Medicine in the UK – an organization that specializes in accurately diagnosing all illnesses and diseases and provides advice on the correct therapeutic and medicinal treatments.

Flook says that there are 5 main categories which everyone must be aware of regarding their health and stress problems:

What are the 7 signs of stress and how they affect your overall health?
What your body is telling you when you are 'sick' and what it *really* means
What are the best ways to take control of stress in your life?
The 5 factors of good health and how to implement them into your life NOW
When taking some prescription medicines actually makes things worse.

Richard Flook is an expert in the field of health and healing. For over 5 years he has helped countless individuals and families with numerous health concerns ranging from ………… to all types of cancer.

For a lively and informative interview call Richard Flook on…………………………..

Meta-Medicine® UK

NEW INSIGHTS ON HOW STRESS CAUSES CANCER AND THE MOST EFFECTIVE TREATMENT THERAPIES, TO BE REVEALED IN BRISTOL.

One of the World's leading Naturopaths and CAM (Complementary Alternative Medicine) cancer treatment specialists will be coming to Bristol in September this year to lead an extraordinary 3 day seminar; for the first time in the UK German practitioner Christa Uricher will be teaching how she has successfully used a diagnostic system called Meta-Medicine® and related therapies to effectively assist cancer sufferers with their healing processes.

Together with Richard Flook, Managing Director Meta-Medicine UK Ltd who is establishing this approach in the UK, Christa Uricher will be discussing many of their cancer client cases to demonstrate how they have been significantly helped.

Brand new insights on how cancer originates and develops will be shared together with full explanations of a number of proven therapeutic methods that directly link to the root cause of cancers and combine to assist in recovery.

Commenting on the unique event, which is to be held in Clifton, Bristol. Richard Flook said: "This is the only seminar of its kind to be held in the World in 2007. We have traditionally seen cancer as a mistake of the body. However Meta-Medicine® can demonstrate that the body has NOT made a mistake, meaning that cancer needs to be treated by supporting the mind and body through the disease instead of fighting it. We look at *reversing* the emotional, environmental, social, spiritual and physical conditions that caused the disease to occur in the first place."

For more information on Meta-Medicine® and to reserve places at the seminar telephone: ……………………email: info@metamedicine.org.uk or visit: www.metamedicine.ogr.uk

[END]

Advanced Mind Body Diagnosis

Meta-Medicine ® UK

TAKING THE GUESS WORK OUT OF DISEASE DIAGNOSIS

A method by which sufferers of any illness or disease can help shortcut their way to renewed health, saving worry, time and money is being introduced to the UK.

Meta-Medicine dictates that every illness originates from an initial biological conflict or shock to the system which in turn triggers a stress phase resulting in physical symptoms that form a partial aspect of a comprehensive disease cycle.

Through scientifically mapping the symptoms via the brain, the root cause of a patient's illness and an exact diagnosis of the stage at which it has reached can be determined; As a result this allows the right treatment, whether medicinal or complementary therapy to be delivered at the right time.

Richard Flook, Managing Director of Bristol based, Open-Mind HR Limited, the company which is establishing the practice of Meta-Medicine in the UK, said: "Meta-Medicine takes away the current hypothesis of illness diagnosis. It ensures that by accurately recognising the symptoms, patients need no longer suffer the uncertainty of what is wrong with them and whether or not they are receiving the correct treatment for their future well being"

To find out more about how Meta-Medicine can help you and also how to train as a qualified practitioner call ………………or visit ………………………………

[END]

For further information please contact:

'30s FASHION FUN COMES TO BRISTOL

The spirit of the 1920s and '30s with all the style, fun and glamour of the between wars era comes to Bristol in August at a unique party filled with champagne, music, dance, exotic cabaret and a vintage fashion show featuring Bristol based couture designer Gilly Woo. A raffle is also to be held with proceeds going to 'The Prince's Trust'.

Called 'The First Fling' and staged by Bristol events company 'Impresario Presents', the event will be on Friday August 15th starting at 8.15pm at The Berkeley Square Hotel, Berkeley Square, Bristol. Tickets can be booked on line for just £13.00 at www...........................with a limited number available on the door at £15.00

Announcing the event, co-host James Breese said "some say nostalgia isn't what it used to be but a 1930s theme creates a great party atmosphere and this is a perfect opportunity to bring some fun and frivolity back into peoples lives".

The event is the prelude to a 1930s style, family and corporate event at Westonbirt House, Tetbury on the weekend of August 30/31st called 'The Spirit of The Age Jazz Age Garden Party'

For more information and to ensure places are reserved on the guest list for 'The First Fling', visit: ....and for information and tickets for 'The Spirit of the Age Jazz Age garden Party', visit: ....or telephone ....

[END]

For further information please contact:

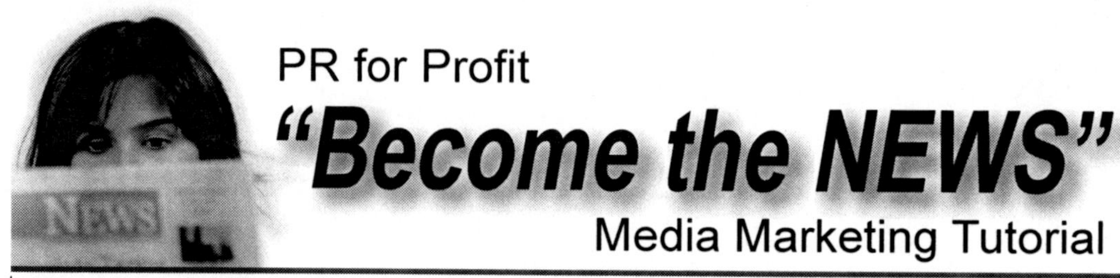

Notes:
Please use this margin for writing your ideas thoughts, inspirations and personal plan of action.

This Tutorial will then act as your route map to PR success!

Revenue from Radio Publicity

(The following examples have been provided as a template only so adapt accordingly depending on your own business and the products or services you provide.)

I could hardly wait to share this chapter on radio publicity with you as it is one of my favourite methods of gaining media coverage; it is so very easy to obtain and can be so highly ***FINANCIALLY PRODUCTIVE***. Now you don't need any special skills to conduct a radio interview and program presenters are not looking for an entertainer, just someone like you, with an interesting story to tell.

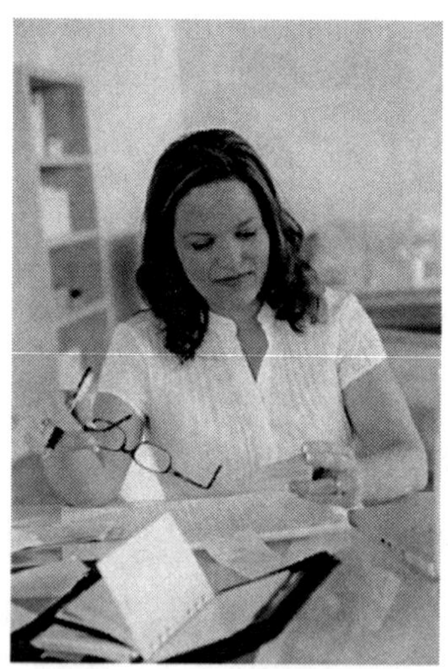

I have conducted as many as 17 short radio interviews across the country in just one day, and I could have done many more if I had pushed myself. There are hundreds of stations available, in fact I have just checked and mediauk.com has at present 827 commercial stations listed, most of whom are hungry for a good story such as the one you will soon have the skill to create, and more importantly, someone ***LIKE YOU*** who they can interview to tell it.

Best of all is the fact that some of these stations have ***HUGE*** audiences that, with the right product, service or story to talk about means you can gain massive and immediate response. To give you an indication of just how large they can be, I have built email lists which run into thousands from just ***ONE INTERVIEW*** and have filled 1,000 seat + venues from just one interview.

You will find that the presenters are generally very friendly and helpful; they will put you at ease and make it really simple for you.

Just follow their lead and they will make you look good and keep the interview flowing. Most interviews last just a few minutes in length, and are generally over before you know it. Neither will it be necessary for you to visit the radio stations' studios, unless you live really close to them and wish to do so, as the ***MAJORITY*** of the interviews can be conducted over the telephone and from the comfort of your own home or office; there have been occasions when I have been on the road when I have successfully used my mobile telephone.

Generally, after having arranged an interview time, someone from the station will call ***YOU*** so it is important to keep your line free and open or you will lose your opportunity. As a precaution I take my other phones off the hook before this time so I am not disturbed and the phone can not be heard ringing if someone else happens to call. Either the presenter or program producer will call just a few minutes before the set time and put you on hold, ready for your interview; you will hear the program going on in the background so listen carefully for your cue; you will hear them introduce you and then suddenly you are on!

What radio journalist wants from you...

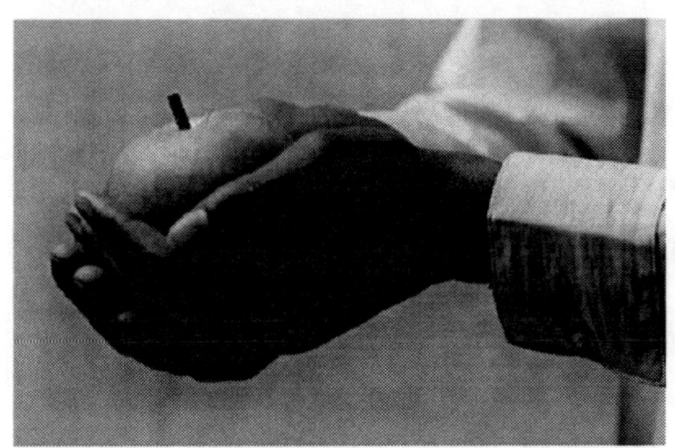

The job of the presenter is to provide quality, topical listening and entertainment for their programme audience, and like any other good journalist they sometimes just love a touch of controversy to put the interview into ***HIGH GEAR***; so if you can provide this for them you will be on to a winner. Presenters are generally very ***PROFESSIONAL***, and know why you are there and that this is a symbiotic relationship so they will play ball with you as much as possible. The best way to get them to do this is by providing them with a list of questions that you would like them to ask. We will be dealing with these in some depth in just a while. Providing them with questions seems almost too easy, although they may see it as you helping them to do their job more easily.

Notes:
Please use this margin for writing your ideas thoughts, inspirations and personal plan of action.

This Tutorial will then act as your route map to PR success!

Notes:
Please use this margin for writing your ideas thoughts, inspirations and personal plan of action.

This Tutorial will then act as your route map to PR success!

You may be asked in advance if you will take questions from listeners who phone in, and I would advise you to take ***FULL ADVANTAGE*** of this opportunity when it arises. Remember the presenter is there to help and keep control just in case you get a ***NUT*** on the line, which is possible; however, if things start to get out of hand, the presenter would ***QUICKLY*** take control of the situation, or switch the ***NUT*** off!

Now I have never yet had a ***NUT*** phone in, but I have managed to engineer situations that have made the radio stations switchboard light up like a Christmas tree before becoming totally jammed with other callers keen to ask a question. I have also had situations where the demand has been so great that a few days later I have been asked back to conduct a ***MUCH*** longer Q & A section *(question and answer)* with their listeners, which has generated ***MASSIVE*** demand for my services! Such fortunate happenings raise your perception as a valued ***EXPERT*** to an ***EXTRAORDINARY*** level and will almost certainly keep you on the Presenter's Christmas card list and get you asked back for other interviews in the future.

Summary or news release...

If the above heading is confusing, I apologise; let me explain it to you... PR expert Jeremy Fraser still sends the same format of news release to radio stations as he would to the press and of course they work perfectly well. However, I have a bad case of trying to fix things which are not broken and have experimented by creating something which was more specifically aimed at presenters and at obtaining radio interviews. So what you see on the next page is the result. I think it would be best described as a taster and summary of the subject on which I would like to be interviewed although I have left the foundation of a powerful PR story in it to capture the journalist's attention. I personally prefer using this method when generating radio PR exposure.

Notes:
Please use this margin for writing your ideas thoughts, inspirations and personal plan of action.

This Tutorial will then act as your route map to PR success!

You may remember me saying that I generated an ***EXTREMELY LARGE*** and surprise response and email list 28,400 strong, whilst testing the 'Happiness Market', and that I am now very seriously considering writing a book or creating a product on this subject. So I thought we could use this subject as an example for writing the PR related material as it is ideally suited to radio coverage.

So precisely what is different?

Actually, not a lot has changed; there are just a few subtle differences and refinements to make it more likely to accomplish the purpose of getting me an interview: let's go through it...

As you can see I have created a very descriptive headline which includes the fact I will be giving something of value away although journalists may not yet be familiar with the term 'eTutorial!' As we move into section one I give the ***WHY*** and ***WHAT*** of the story although I haven't said how the eTutorial can be obtained, which should keep the journalist reading.

In section 2 of the release I give specific details of a hypothetical situation which I believe all journalists will ***EASILY*** identify with and recognise as a quality ***PUBLIC INTEREST*** story. I finish the section by reiterating the fact that a solution to this common situation can be discovered in the eTutorial which I will be making available to ***THEIR LISTENERS***, although I ***STILL*** haven't specified how this can be obtained.

The last section of this release qualifies me as someone who is highly experienced in giving interviews and provides what for some presenters and radio stations may be seen as a distinct benefit by telling them I am also happy and prepared to take calls from their listeners.

Notes:
Please use this margin for writing your ideas thoughts, inspirations and personal plan of action.

This Tutorial will then act as your route map to PR success!

This adds 'meat' and value to the interview opportunity while indicating that I am experienced and confident in interview situations which should put a tick in the final box and get them to call me.

If they needed ***ANY MORE*** tempting, or proof that they should call me, I have left one last ***JUICY*** carrot dangling to attract them and that is the biographical data and fact sheet which is available for them to download from the Internet, without the need to call me first. I will come to the biographical data and fact sheet in just a moment as this, combined with the fact that I purposely still haven't told them how their listeners can obtain my free eTutorial, should hold their interest and get them to call me.

Putting money in your bank...

I am sure you have already realised that the way to generate income from such PR and media opportunities is to create, or have a 'backend' product in place. Although I have not yet designed it, I imagine my Happiness 'eTutorial', would be delivered over seven days with a couple of steps being delivered to subscribers each day. 'eTutorial' is just an attention-grabbing name for a short report which I have chopped up into bite-sized chunks and then used my auto responder to deliver by email over a period of my choosing.

Of course I would be telling subscribers ***WHAT*** they should do, rather than ***HOW*** they should do it, as that will be the content for my ***FULL*** course or much larger product which every email will be up-selling and promoting and of course a good percentage will purchase.

"14 Life-Changing Steps that Lead to Lasting Happiness!" - A Free eTutorial

To help combat the problem of deepening gloom, doom and general unhappiness during this time of economic uncertainty, West Country based "Happiness Guru" Kevin Martyn has written a short report entitled the 'Happiness Blueprint'. The eTutorial, which is being given away totally free, contains 14 highly effective and simple to use fun steps, which are guaranteed to deliver the simple formula for lasting happiness.

Commenting on the subject of 'Happiness', Kevin said: "Most people seem to think that happiness is 'Externally Referenced' and that they need 'Money, Romance, Success and Lifestyle' to make them happy; for instance, you will often hear others make statements such as: 'I will be happy when I lose weight', or, 'I will be happy when I have found a loving partner', etc. Unfortunately, these people have it the wrong way round! If they FIRST learned how to be happy, they would then automatically find it MUCH EASIER to lose weight or attract a loving partner, and so on. These people are putting their happiness on hold for another day, which unfortunately may never come – what a waste!" This fun eTutorial will help such individuals completely reverse such situations.

Kevin Martyn has spent many years as a professional magician and presenter. He is candid, highly entertaining and a powerful interviewee. He would be delighted to be interviewed and expand on this important subject, and would be happy to take calls from listeners or viewers. He can be reached direct during business hours on: 0870 737 1234

[ENDS]

NB: Biographical details and fact sheet available upon request, or:

Downloadable from: www.myhappinesswebsite.co.uk/facts.pdf

Notes:
Please use this margin for writing your ideas thoughts, inspirations and personal plan of action.

This Tutorial will then act as your route map to PR success!

Will you make a good interviewee?

You can sell yourself as I have in the last section of this news release and you may well really impress the journalist or program presenter; however, your news article alone ***WILL NOT*** guarantee that you gain an interview, as someone will call to speak with you and check that you are the real article, and as good as your self promotion claims you are.

So be prepared for this call, and ***ALWAYS REMEMBER***, you only have one opportunity to make a ***FIRST IMPRESSION!*** Even if you have been up half the night at you best friend's stag or hen party or are recovering from open heart surgery and a severe case of double pneumonia they are ***STILL*** going to expect you to be an enthusiastic and confident speaker who can communicate well and prove to them that you are going to be a good story for their programme. Be less than 100% and you may blow your chances out of the window and ***PERMANENTLY*** lose another profitable media outlet.

I am not trying to sound hard or scare you in any way, but rather prepare you!

These are easy people to deal with and you can be fairly certain that if your news release captures their attention they will call you back promptly. Now you are aware of this fact, don't go sending out your news releases last thing in the evening if you know that you are about to enjoy a ***BIG*** night out with your friends because they are likely to call first thing the following morning and it's hard to shine, or be at your best, if you are experiencing the after effects of one to many from the night before!

It's really just ***COMMON SENSE***. Why go to the trouble of writing and sending your release out in the first place if you know you are going to be ***ANYTHING LESS*** than your very best when they call?

Notes:
Please use this margin for writing your ideas thoughts, inspirations and personal plan of action.

This Tutorial will then act as your route map to PR success!

Make it easy for the interviewer...

As I already mentioned, the radio presenter will do everything they can to

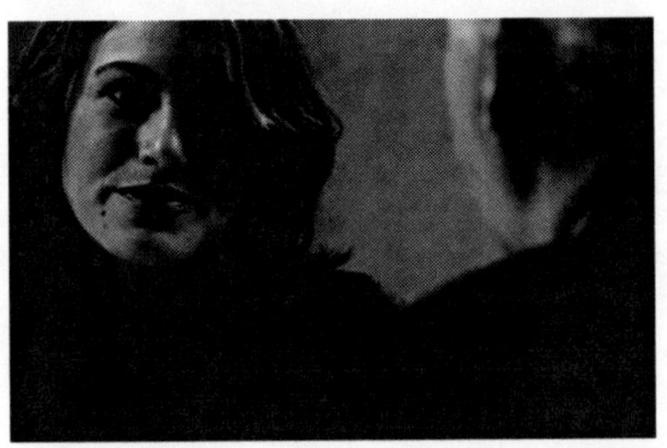

help you sound good and provide a quality interview; you can help them in a number of ways such as providing them with a biographical fact sheet, which we will come to next. Prepare an introduction for them to use, followed by a set of questions which you are prepared to answer. These will make you both look good, as well as generating ***HEAPS*** of listeners.

First the biographical fact sheet and we will deal with the one I have written to accompany the news release you have just read. The journalist who receives your news release may automatically download this to learn more about you and your subject. Obviously, to obtain ***MAXIMUM IMPACT***, your fact sheet should be written in conjunction with your release in the same way as mine. (see page 219)

As you can see, this is nothing more than a few facts about me, and how I became interested in helping people develop lasting happiness in their lives. It's a subject that I have a ***HUGE*** passion for, which I hope is communicated.

At the same time as I provide further evidence about my knowledge of this subject I am providing the presenter with some interesting background on it and a few interesting topic-related keywords which, when they interview me, will make ***THEM*** sound knowledgeable and ***PROFESSIONAL*** and as if they have done their homework in preparation for this interview just like every good presenter should.

The fact sheet is an ***ESSENTIAL*** tool for generating radio interviews...

When I have conducted interviews inside radio station studios I have provided the presenter with a biography and fact sheet a few days in advance. I have noticed that this is ***ALWAYS*** in front of them as they conduct the interview with the specific points they plan on using underlined, or highlighted, to pick out and easily read.

Kevin Martyn – "The Happiness Guru"

BIOGRAPHY AND FACT SHEET

For nearly thirty years Kevin Martyn has put ***BROAD*** smiles on the faces of audiences young and old, first as a professional magician, and later as a speaker and presenter.

The joy of his profession addicted Kevin to helping others find lasting happiness in their lives, so he qualified as a master practitioner in NLP *(Neuro Linguistic Programming)* as a way of helping more people; he then mastered other ***HIGHLY EFFECTIVE*** and ***NON-INVASIVE*** techniques such as EFT *(Emotional Freedom Technique).*

Unsurprisingly, the recipe for being just as happy as you wish is not such a secret as some would have you believe. ***EVERYONE*** already possesses all the tools they need to generate unlimited levels of happiness in their lives…

They just haven't learned how to use them yet…

Happiness starts on the inside, and then works its way out. It is the very ***KEY*** and starting point to success at virtually anything as the happy individual, is by definition, a success in life!
There is no one ***SINGLE*** secret to living a happy and fulfilling life, if only it was that easy! However, personal levels of happiness can be quickly developed and turned into daily habits. These techniques and actions are really simple and fun to master and ***ANYONE*** can start to practice and ***BENEFIT*** from them immediately.

For most people, being happy starts with the understanding of happiness - and then the rest is easy!

To arrange an interview with Kevin, please call him on: 0870 737 1234

Notes:
Please use this margin for writing your ideas thoughts, inspirations and personal plan of action.

This Tutorial will then act as your route map to PR success!

How to the get asked the QUESTIONS that you want to answer...

You now have everything you need to obtain loads of radio interviews. Next we need to turn our attention to creating a powerful introduction for the Presenter to use and a number of ***QUALITY*** questions for him or her to ask you. You would send these ***ONLY*** after the time and date for the interview has been arranged, which is usually the same or following day. To send them before this point would be seen as being presumptive and perhaps even manipulative!

Your introduction...

From years of experience as an entertainer I have discovered that there is one element that will make a ***VITALLY IMPORTANT*** difference to just how successful your interview/ show/presentation etc will be and that is the way in which you are introduced! A good introduction will set the scene and capture the attention of your audience ready for you to follow on. If the importance of your topic is well 'pre-framed' and the presenter can get the listeners' focused on the benefits or solutions you are about to deliver you will be starting well. However, if you just get a low-energy introduction, without a build up, you are starting at ground level and will have a much more difficult job.

Now most presenters will give you a good introduction regardless of you providing one for them to use, but to ensure that they position you in the way ***YOU DESIRE***, it's best to ***ALWAYS*** provide them with one of your own, which they will generally read verbatim.

As you can see from the short introduction I have written below it should raise the curiosity of the listeners, and make them think. It states the ***BIG*** benefits of listening and that they are about to discover tips and techniques on improving their levels of happiness.

Contact number for Kevin Martyn: 0870 737 1234

Suggested Introduction and Interview Questions

"The Happiness Guru"

Introduction

According to our next guest, 'Happiness Guru' Kevin Martyn, if you're not fulfilling your desires and expectations in life, it may have a lot to do with your levels of happiness, and the internal mental inhibitors you have developed, which could be stopping you from reaching them.

So stay tuned as we discover more about using happiness as the key to unlimited success and achievement at ***ANYTHING,*** and discover a few of the techniques you can use to become just as happy as you desire.

Questions:

1. So where is the starting point to attracting lasting happiness to your life?
2. Can you explain why being happy is the KEY to success at anything?
3. You claim we already have everything we need to make us happy?
4. How will becoming a student of happiness change peoples' lives?
5. I believe you have a method of instantly improving your levels of happiness?
6. Are happy people more likely to be more successful in their job or career?
7. Does the way people think affect their level of happiness?
8. Will your 'Happiness' techniques work for anyone?
9. What is the fastest route to happiness?
10. What is an 'eTutorial', and why did you choose this format?
11. If listeners just read your 'eTutorial' will it make them happy?
12. How can listeners obtain a copy of your 'eTutorial'?

To immediately begin benefiting from: "14 Life-Changing Steps that Lead to Lasting Happiness!" the 'eTutorial', interested listeners should visit www.mywebsite.co.uk

Questions which lead to sales...

As you know, on this occasion, my MWO *(Most Wanted Outcome)* is to get listeners to visit a website and opt-in to start receiving my eTutorial which will

be delivered over a seven day period, and will give me the maximum opportunity to build a relationship with them and upsell them on a ***LARGER*** paying product. By offering this eTutorial I already have reciprocity working on my side and this technique should build me a strong email list of subscribers to whom I can market at will.

However, I could just have easily been selling a seminar or promoting a book, or other product; this is just my preferred method as I have learned from experience that it is likely to be the most profitable.

So my objective is simple; to first get listeners to visit my website and then to subscribe to my auto responder list so I can start developing a relationship that will result in me making a sale. For this reason all the questions must be designed to start moving the listener towards this outcome; the answers I provide will be describing solutions and benefits which can be found in my eTutorial or related product.

The most logical way that I have found to design high quality questions that will get results is to start by writing down the answers that you want to give and then write the questions to get the response.

If you study the first eight questions you will see that they are progressive and move the interview towards a logical conclusion; however, from question 9 onwards we are providing information to build desire in preparation for the ultimate question which is the location of the website where listeners can learn more and obtain the eTutorial.

Notes:
Please use this margin for writing your ideas thoughts, inspirations and personal plan of action.

This Tutorial will then act as your route map to PR success!

Notes:
Please use this margin for writing your ideas thoughts, inspirations and personal plan of action.

This Tutorial will then act as your route map to PR success!

The answers I hope to provide...

Question 9: Will your 'Happiness' techniques work for anyone?
The reason for this question is that I was looking for the opportunity to tell the listeners that, ***REGARDLESS*** of present circumstances, ***ANYONE*** who isserious about attracting lasting happiness to their life could do so. Now this short statement should capture a lot of attention and leads nicely into the next question.

Question 10: What is the fastest route to happiness?
The answer I wanted to give here was that there is no single secret to lasting happiness, but rather there are many simple-to-implement actions all of which will give immediate and dramatic results. When used in conjunction with each other they are much more powerful and provide a lasting solution; this is the content provided in the eTutorial. Now by this point a lot of people will be saying to themselves, 'this is what I need', and when the Presenter reiterates the fact that is ***FREE,*** you should have hundreds, if not thousands of listeners racing for a pen to capture the details of how they can get their copy!

Question 11: If listeners just read your eTutorial will it make them happy?

This question is quite irrelevant; it just gives me the opportunity to make an important point, which is, many people are still very computer illiterate, so I wanted to let them know ***SPECIFICALLY*** what an eTutorial is, and the added benefit they will be getting by receiving this information delivered directly to their inbox ***EVERY DAY*** for 7 days.

Question 12: How can listeners obtain a copy of your eTutorial?
This is the one you have been waiting for and the one that will result in your pay off so make sure if you are taking listeners to a website page, that it is ***SIMPLE*** to spell and ***EASY*** to ***REMEMBER!*** ...otherwise you will lose many people in the attempt to find you and will have just wasted your energy as well as some credibility. I will be dealing more with this subject in the chapter on websites towards the end of this Tutorial.

Notes:
Please use this margin for writing your ideas thoughts, inspirations and personal plan of action.

This Tutorial will then act as your route map to PR success!

Apart from thanking you for the interview, the presenter may ask a few simple questions which tie it up, and a highly likely one, would be to ask if you have an alternative method for the delivery of your material for those people who do not have computers and I will that come to that point in just a moment.

So now you know how to have the right questions asked in order to monetise your radio exposure so experiment to see which ones give you the best returns...

You may also be wondering if the Presenter will use all of these questions and follow them in the order in which you have written them; The answer is yes ***USUALLY***, although he or she may deviate. I have also tried writing such questions in bullet-point format and have found that they then ask them in ***ANY ORDER*** so, as rule of thumb, Presenters stick to the ***NUMBERED*** order of questions, if they are leading towards an obvious conclusion.

Alternative forms of delivering your material...

Unlike printed media, radio interviews generally provide rapid results and the majority of your response will happen immediately afterward or within a few days, so you need to be prepared to capture it all. If you have a restaurant or have invited the listeners to visit you at a venue or physical address you will see your interview results walking through the door.

Notes:
Please use this margin for writing your ideas thoughts, inspirations and personal plan of action.

This Tutorial will then act as your route map to PR success!

However if, like me, you provide intangible products or decide to give a report, asking the listeners to send you a SAE ***(stamped addressed envelope)*** to a street address may generate a ***LOT*** of needless ***WORK*** for you. As I mentioned earlier it is not unusual to get ***THOUSANDS*** of responses from just one interview and for this reason, unless you have the staff to cope with this volume, you may consider surface mail is too much like hard work.

The telephone is not a good choice either as this also is unlikely to cater for the rush of eager listeners all trying to obtain their copy of your report at the same time; you will lose the majority of your potential responces.

My advice is to play it safe by using a website to handle your response which can serve ***THOUSANDS*** of visitors all at the same time without problem, whilst building you an emailing list for future use. Okay, if you are not computer literate, it sounds like a big job to initially set it up, but it isn't I promise you. And once you have done it you will be able to ***QUICKLY*** adapt or duplicate that page for a hundred other PR related uses.

Delivering your news release to the media

Unless your story happens to be breaking news or time sensitive material that can't be delayed don't be in a rush to deliver your news release to the press or media because letting it stand for a day or two before revisiting it for a final work through nearly always helps you to improve and fine-tune your work. If you work well in advance, as suggested, you will have the luxury of not being pressured and will be in a position to work on and improve your release until you are happy that you can't improve it anymore.

Notes:
Please use this margin for writing your ideas thoughts, inspirations and personal plan of action.

This Tutorial will then act as your route map to PR success!

Last chance safety check...

I am aware that repeating myself is probably starting to make me sound a little like your Dad. However, every day, an untold number of news releases which have had many hours of effort and work poured into their creation are totally disregarded as the result of a simple mistake that has been overlooked in the rush to send them out. Am I being too cautious? I don't think so; who wants to run the risk of having the article destroyed or deleted for a silly, unobserved mistake?

Giving your release a ***FINAL*** check over is just basic common sense and an exceedingly small price to pay for the knowledge that it is mistakes-free which may have prevented it from being published. Below are the four most obvious mistakes which could result in financial loss...

Has it been spell checked?

If you are confident that your spelling and grammar are ***EXCELLENT***, you will not need anyone to check your copy for you. However if, like me, you are not so hot at spotting typos and spelling mistakes, get someone to go over it for you and not your mum or sister unless they happen to be ***EXCELLENT*** at the task. In the past, and generally for a small and well worthwhile fee, I have used my old English teacher, a secretary-come-typist and a legal executive all who have done an excellent job in highlighting my mistakes for correction.

Notes:
Please use this margin for writing your ideas thoughts, inspirations and personal plan of action.

This Tutorial will then act as your route map to PR success!

Are your details correct?

Double check your URL...

In the chapter on websites I will be going into much more depth about URLs *(website address);* for now though, have you got yours correct? Don't reproduce the http:// bit of the address as this is confusing to those people who are less computer literate and it is not necessary; keep it simple: www.yoursite.com only.

Does your website process work?

If you are using a process of some type to capture your visitors' details such as a form or survey use your home computer to make sure ***EVERYTHING*** is working; then while you are out, check it again on another computer to make sure everything is still working well. Are your auto responders capturing your prospect's details correctly and delivering what you have promised in return? The more complicated your process the more opportunity there is to make a mistake, so check it all thoroughly.

Getting maximum results...

If you have just produced a new release that you intend to send to multiple media, the ***BIG*** temptation *(even for me)* is to send them ***ALL*** out at the same time. However, I would urge you to get into the habit of ***ALWAYS*** testing your release with just one or two local publications to make sure that it works. By working I mean that not only do the press publish it for you but that it also captures the attention of the target readership for whom you produced it for and that they respond to it. Then when you know for certain that it is producing good results for you send it out to every media outlet you had planned.

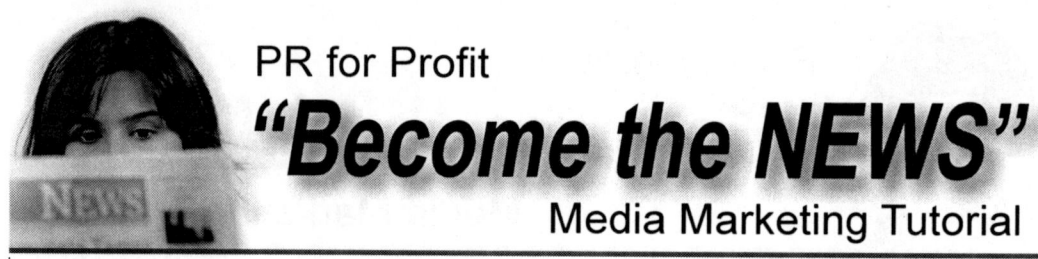

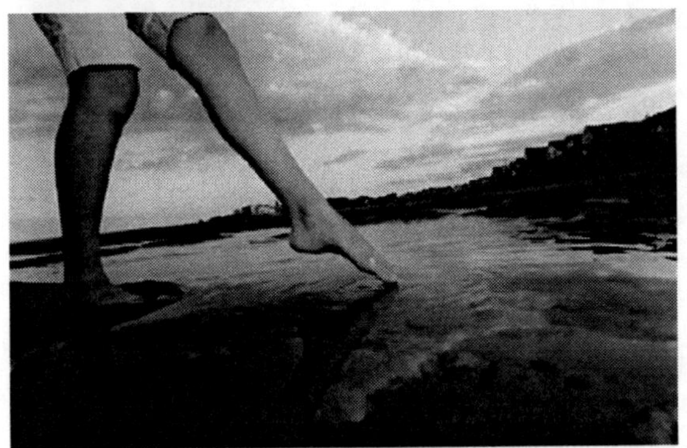

By testing your new release with your local press first you will easily be able to monitor when it is published. However if, for whatever reason they don't print it you may find it easier to discover the ***EXACT*** reasons why as the journalist or editor may be inclined to help someone who is likely to provide them with future material. If it gets printed but produces very little response, as sometimes happens to all of us, you will then have to consider the reasons why and decide exactly how you can improve upon it.

Once you have figured this out try it with another small local publication and see if the response improves. If it does so, the testing process has highlighted ***JUST*** how ***IMPORTANT*** this step really is and has saved you a fortune in lost revenue.

Monitoring your results...

This is an important aspect of PR marketing and nowadays many, if not most, publications have an online blog/ news site where they duplicate the articles they publish in their papers or magazines.

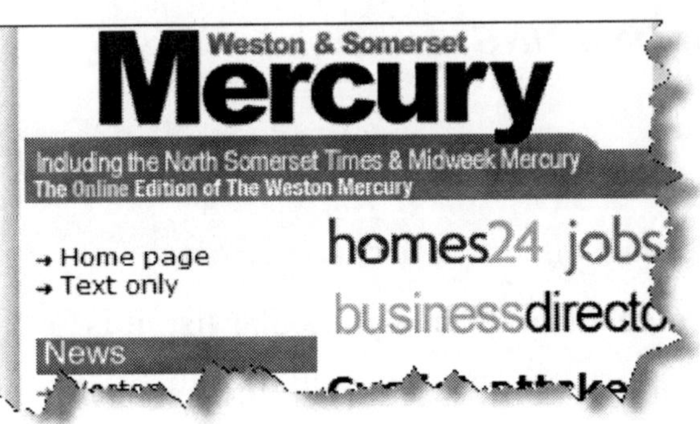

This makes monitoring your results easy as you can set up a few keywords in 'Google Alerts' to tell you when they have been published; I have written a lot about using 'Google Alerts' earlier in this tutorial to which you can refer.

Notes:
Please use this margin for writing your ideas thoughts, inspirations and personal plan of action.

This Tutorial will then act as your route map to PR success!

Notes:
Please use this margin for writing your ideas thoughts, inspirations and personal plan of action.

This Tutorial will then act as your route map to PR success!

Or, if you would like someone else to take care of this task, you should consider using a 'Press Clipping Service' to do the job for you. I have just used this precise phrase 'Press Clipping Service' as a search in Google and been returned 100s of results. The service these companies offer is generally fairly priced for the results they provide so I suggest you check them out to see what system of result monitoring best suits you.

The big benefit of using a 'Press Clipping Service' is not just knowing that your release ***HAS BEEN*** published but in getting the actual printed coverage you've generated sent to you from ***EVERY*** publication in which your release appears. Remember, the ***TRUE VALUE*** of PR marketing is not only in the direct results and customers that your coverage has generated for you, but also in the way in which you use this media exposure to promote yourself and gain ongoing results.

PR and media exposure can carry on generating profits for years to come...
My friend and PR expert Jeremy Fraser often gains literally ***HUNDREDS*** of ***THOUSANDS*** of pounds worth of publicity, sometimes much more for some of his clients, in a matter of ***JUST*** months! Maximising on this valuable publicity material his clients generate ***ONGOING*** revenue.

The Roll out...

This term is more often used in marketing when an offer has proved to produce a certain result with a small percentage from a particular list; it is then presumed that it will return the same level of results with the remainder. Generally the same can be said for news releases; if one gets a certain result with one publication then it should return similar results with another that has a similar readership. For this reason a 'Roll Out' does not necessarily have to happen all in one go; it can progress over a matter of weeks or months and at a speed that best suits and allows you to handle the results.

Who to send it to...

Now we already know that the way in which we deal with magazines and trade journals is different from the rest of the media and I have already gone into detail on this subject in a preceding chapter. However, the formula for every other form of media is exactly the same.

All you have to do now is decide who you are going to send it to. You have two choices; you can either send it directly to the news room and then leave it up to them to forward it on to a specific journalist or you can send it directly to the journalist who deals with your specific topic or subject if you can get his or her contact details!

Now you don't need to spend much time considering this question, but which do you think is likely to get the best results? - a news release which is sent directly to the news room? ...or one which is sent directly to the address of a specific journalist with:

For the attention of: Journalists Name – Publication, or news group name

You've got it! The one which is sent directly to the specific journalist is ***MUCH MORE*** likely to receive attention and get published and even turned into a feature because you have gone directly to the right person and used an ingredient which is ***PARTICULARLY VALUABLE*** in PR marketing known as – ***THEIR NAME!*** This may not seem particularly important but I promise you it is; when someone uses our name it really does make a ***BIG*** difference; if you disagree with me just take a moment to think how you feel and respond when someone calls you by the wrong name or pronunciation of it, or worse, misspells it! ...most of us are quick to correct such errors, showing that it ***DEFINITELY*** does matter.

Notes:
Please use this margin for writing your ideas thoughts, inspirations and personal plan of action.

This Tutorial will then act as your route map to PR success!

Notes:
Please use this margin for writing your ideas thoughts, inspirations and personal plan of action.

This Tutorial will then act as your route map to PR success!

The journalist receiving your news release will know that someone has gone to the trouble of finding out that he or she is the right person for this topic as well as obtaining their correct email address. For this reason you can be fairly sure that the news releases that are mailed directly to a specific journalist, with their ***'CORRECTLY SPELLED'*** name, will get more attention than those which have been passed on from the news room. Sending your release directly to a journalist also has another ***HUGE*** benefit which will give your future PR releases far more chance of publication. You now have a name to send your 'thank you' email to once your article is published and this starts building your relationship.

How do we find the right journalist?

Now we get to the part of PR marketing which requires a little initial ***GRUNT WORK*** *(manual labour)* as this is the point where you or one of your staff need to pick up the telephone and make a call. I am going to presume that you already know the specific publication to which you want to send your release. If you have purchased an annual media directory which gives the specific names of journalists I advise you to totally ignore them as journalists change positions faster than traffic lights at a busy junction.

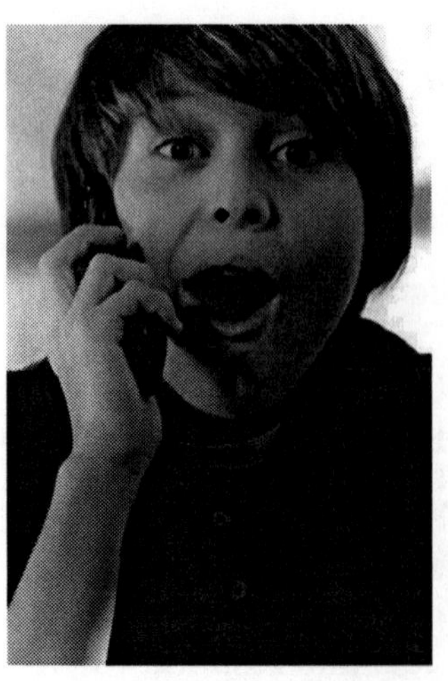

Call the publication and ask who deals with your subject; now they may tell you, and if they do, be sure to have a pen and paper ready to capture their name and the correct spelling; also ask for their email address. The receptionist may pass you on to the news room which may provide you with the details of the person you need, or on occasions put you directly through to them; if this happens be prepared and simply tell them you have a news release on a particular subject and believe that they are the person who deals with this topic. If they confirm that they are ask permission to send it to them; double check the spelling of their name and email address.

However, the news room may have a policy of deciding which journalist or correspondent they want to send your release to, which means you will have to rely upon their judgement; so to be on the safe side double check the news room's email address. By this point you should be in a position of knowing to whom and where to send your news release. Now you are almost ready to dispatch your first one.

Notes:
Please use this margin for writing your ideas thoughts, inspirations and personal plan of action.

This Tutorial will then act as your route map to PR success!

Which method of delivery should you use?

Now you already know that Jeremy and I use email for delivering our PR material and there are a number of ***VERY*** positive benefits for doing so, many of which we will be covering in the next chapter. However, this tutorial would not be complete without me mentioning the other two main methods which you could use to deliver your news release.

Snail Mail...

After many years using traditional methods of marketing and having spent two or three evenings a week stuffing envelopes with letters you can be fairly confident that the passing of snail mail as a practical means of marketing is not something I miss at all. It was costly, time consuming and compared to modern forms of communication ***SLOW***! ...it belongs in the last century! It does have its uses but, unless it's for sending legal documents by recorded delivery, I can't think of one.

Fax...

In its day fax was really big; it totally transformed the speeds of data transfer from overnight to a couple of minutes and, without doubt, the media for many years used this as a primary means of receiving and delivering information. Until more recently, fax had one ***GIANT*** advantage over email and that was, if it worked correctly, it would result in a printed copy of your news release popping out at the other end.

Notes:
Please use this margin for writing your ideas thoughts, inspirations and personal plan of action.

This Tutorial will then act as your route map to PR success!

That was of course if you had the right number, it wasn't already engaged, it was working correctly, had paper and toner, didn't jam or get scrunched up whilst printing, and was still legible enough to read. There was nothing attractive about even a well reproduced fax and I can see no benefit for still using them. Apart from being extremely time consuming the main problem with dispatching your news release with either of these methods was that you had to telephone to find out if they had received it and that in itself can generate many problems as you will discover in the next chapter.

*e*Mail...

In my opinion, if you are serious about getting PR and media exposure, you should use email as your primary means of delivery for the following reasons. It's fast, *(I have had call backs from interested journalists and presenters within a couple of minutes of dispatching my news release by email.)* It's a quick process and, towards the end of the tutorial, I will show you the tools we use which make the dispatch process simple and virtually automated. Emails are efficient and effective and have the power and ability to very much improve most businesses. In the next chapter I am going to introduce you to one ***HUGELY*** important benefit which email has over these other two possible forms of delivery.

When to follow up...

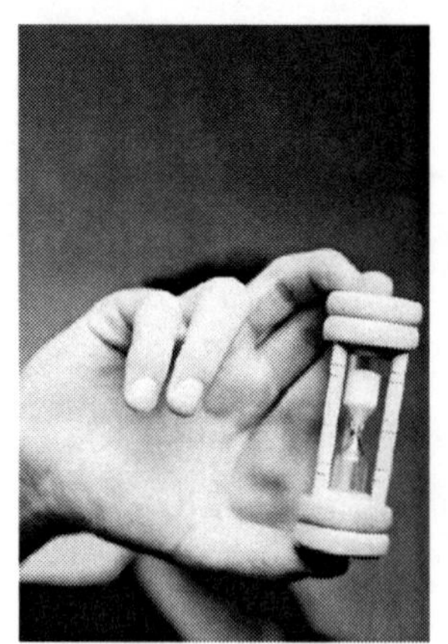

Let's imagine that you have written and dispatched your first news release and this is the point where it can become frustrating and you do need patience. Everyone who has ever sent a news release reaches this point and experiences the same feelings of impatience at having to wait. You don't know if your news release has been received, or forwarded on to the right journalist, and ***MOST FRUSTRATING*** of all is the fact that you don't know if it is going to be used.

Notes:
Please use this margin for writing your ideas thoughts, inspirations and personal plan of action.

This Tutorial will then act as your route map to PR success!

This is the bit of PR marketing that most students and practitioners dislike and we all share the same challenge.

The time it takes from delivery to actual publication ***VARIES*** greatly; just last week I sent a news release and photo on the Wednesday and it was out in print on the Thursday evening, which for my local press was surprisingly quick. Generally you should allow one or two weeks before expecting to see a result. However, if the media happen to have an abundance of news at that time, which also happens, they may sit on it for a few weeks. This is the only real downside of PR marketing you don't have control over when your material will be published. However, if you follow the advice in this tutorial and create plenty of stories, you should have something in a publication of some type ***MOST WEEKS!***

There are a number of solutions to this challenge, and I will go through most of them now so that you get the big picture and can decide which one is best for you. I am going to presume that you dispatch your news release by email as suggested because I can see no benefit in using the other methods.

How do we know our release was received?

Often the first indication we get that there is a delivery problem is the receipt of an automated mail master alert stating the following email couldn't be delivered! If you receive such a response it will give you the ***SPECIFIC*** reasons why not. In my time I have received ***HUNDREDS*** of these annoying messages and 95% of the time the problem will be the same; you have mistyped the email address!

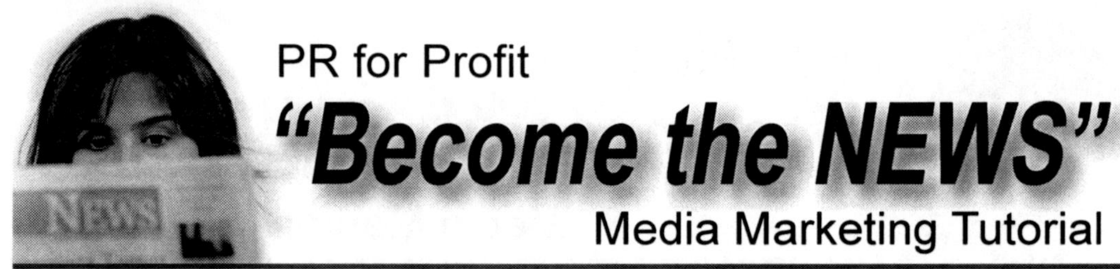

Notes:
Please use this margin for writing your ideas thoughts, inspirations and personal plan of action.

This Tutorial will then act as your route map to PR success!

More frustrating is that such mistakes can be difficult to spot and I have wasted ***LOADS*** of time over silly errors which later ***ALWAYS*** seem to be ***BLATANTLY OBVIOUS!***

If this happens to you, the best way to tackle the problem is 'Head On'; call back the news room to check the spelling of their email address and that, once altered, ***SHOULD*** correct your problem. If you can't spot the mistake, or you get a second mail master alert or 'bounce back', call again and ask if they have another email address; they normally do, and they will be as keen to receive your release as you are to send it.

If the problem persists, you could try sending your email again later. Now sometimes, and I have ***NO IDEA*** why, the next time you send it your email gets delivered and the problem has just solved itself! ...you will just have to put such happenings down to 'one of those things' that happen on the internet; they still happen to me ***REGULARLY!***

System auto responders...

Sometimes, and I am glad to say that this is happening more frequently all the time, the news room or publication's email system use an automated response that replies with an email stating: 'we are in receipt of your email', and 'no further action is required'. This is obviously to reduce the volume of telephone calls they receive! You could also get the very same message if you send your release directly to a journalist. Now you at least know they have it, but no more than that, and what we really ***WANT*** to ***KNOW*** is if it has been passed on to a journalist, who he or she is and if it is going to be used!

Notes:
Please use this margin for writing your ideas thoughts, inspirations and personal plan of action.

This Tutorial will then act as your route map to PR success!

The BIG temptation you must resist...

We have all done it, we become discouraged, impatient and in our frustration

call the newsroom looking for positive feedback or information concerning the publication of our article; what I want to tell you is that this action is a total ***WASTE*** of ***TIME***, for a number of different reasons.

If in response to your news release you are sent an auto responder message saying: 'no further action is necessary' you may get snapped at if you call because news rooms are generally very overworked and running to tight deadlines. However, at less busy times when they are feeling helpful, they may ask you to wait while they spend a number of minutes looking for it, often without success. This is hardly surprising as they are sent hundreds or even thousands of emails per day. If this happens, they will obviously request that you send your release again. Then, half an hour or so later, you call back a second time to wait a few minutes more while they search for it, to discover that "yes, it has indeed arrived" but they are not too sure who will deal with it. This was the ***REAL REASON*** why you called, and is an ***EXCEPTIONALLY*** time wasting and frustrating pursuit that I suggest you don't play or you will waste hours of your time ***WITHOUT*** result.

When this happens you will have to wait and then use a different strategy which we will come to later...

OCCASIONALLY, however, you may get lucky and a member of staff will tell you who you should be sending your release to and give you the email address for you to go directly to the ***RIGHT PERSON***. Why this wasn't offered in the first place and on your initial call is both confusing and annoying!

Notes:
Please use this margin for writing your ideas thoughts, inspirations and personal plan of action.

This Tutorial will then act as your route map to PR success!

The position we wanted to be in...

If the news room does happen to offer you the details of the right journalist

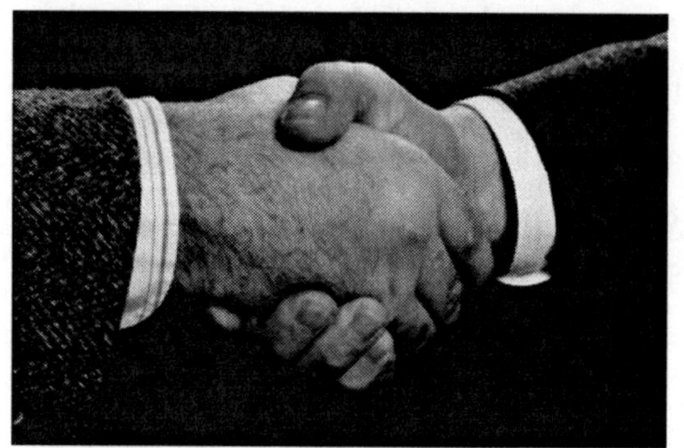

this is the outcome we wanted from the very beginning and one which we can now start to make work in our favour. In the future, and when you have developed a relationship with a journalist, you will be able to call him or her directly to inform them that you have a story available for their consideration.

This puts you in the position to call back to see if you can offer further help or information; however, what you are really doing is attempting to build this opportunity by encouraging them to turn your small release into a feature or something ***MUCH LARGER*** rather than just being reproduced verbatim.

However, until you have built up this relationship you will have to tread much more carefully. You may consider calling them to see if you can add anything, some journalists will appreciate this offer and you will have started to build a symbiotic relationship.

However, others who may just be having a ***BAD DAY*** may not appreciate your call at all and you run the risk of sharp words from an abrupt and busy journalist ***WORSE STILL*** putting them off publishing your release! I hate this with a passion so I have devised a system to avoid it ever happening which at the same time gives me the opportunity to build a healthy working PR relationship.

Notes:
Please use this margin for writing your ideas thoughts, inspirations and personal plan of action.

This Tutorial will then act as your route map to PR success!

How do we know if our release has been read?

Knowing that our release has been received is one thing, but the next and ***FAR MORE IMPORTANT*** step is knowing that it has been read and given consideration for publication. The perfect solution to this challenge is to have built up a relationship with the journalist dealing with it and then this matter is simple ...but until you reach that point here are a couple of solutions that will help.

If you use 'Microsoft Outlook' as your email program did you know that you have a built-in feature which allows you to request both a 'Delivery Receipt' and 'Read Receipt' from the recipient of your email? I am using 'Outlook 2007' and this function can be found under the options tab when you are composing an email or you could switch this facility on so that all the emails you send include these requests.

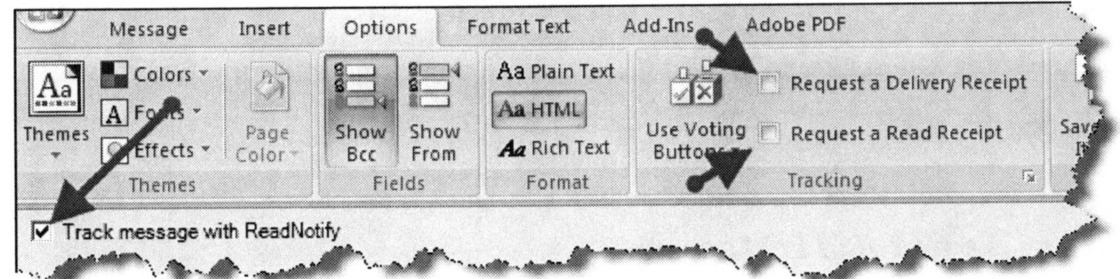

As you can see from the screen grab, all you have to do to use this function is to put a tick in the box or boxes of your choice and the system will do the rest; you will also notice that I have indicated another box which says: 'Track message with ReadNotify' and we will come to that in just a moment.
Here is a screen grab of an email 'Read Receipt'. As you can see I sent it at 9.05 and it was opened and read immediately. The system sent me the receipt at 9.06, which on this occasion was fast and reassuring evidence that my release was at least read.

Notes:
Please use this margin for writing your ideas thoughts, inspirations and personal plan of action.

This Tutorial will then act as your route map to PR success!

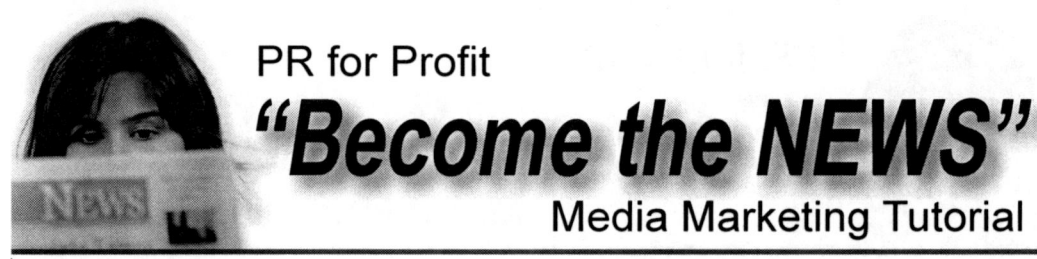

However, this system is not perfect!

Read: Here is the article as promised!
Kevin Martyn
Sent: Thu 26/03/2009 09:06
To:

Your message

To: marites@nairne.co.uk
Subject: Here is the article as promised!
Sent: 26/03/2009 09:05

was read on 26/03/2009 09:05.

The problem with using this system is that the recipient of your email is notified that you have requested a receipt, and is given the opportunity to say ***NO! DON'T*** notify them.

When I receive one of these notification requests it always makes me feel as if I am not trusted and being spied upon, which to some degree I suppose I am. So it would be far better if the recipient wasn't aware that the email was being monitored in this way! However, when you send a news release out why ***SHOULDN'T*** you know if it has been read? After all you are passing on information which can be beneficial to many people and knowing this is not harming anyone!

So here is a ***FAR BETTER*** system...

It's called 'Re@dNotify' and is available at: www.readnotify.com As far as PR marketing and contacting journalists is concerned this is a first rate bit of software as it is simple to use and ***REALLY INEXPENSIVE.*** At the time of writing it costs less than £3 per month!

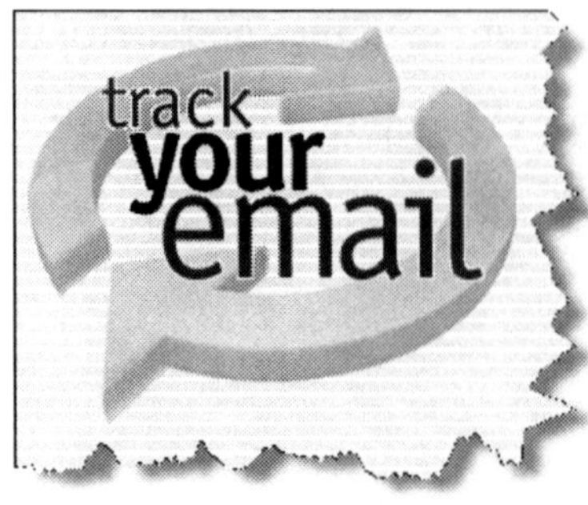

So what does it do?

Here is just a short list of the benefits it offers, and there are more...

It closely monitors your email and:

- Tells you when it has been delivered
- Tells you when it has been read
- Tells you how long after it was delivered it was opened
- How long it was open for
- How many times it has been opened and when
- If it has been forwarded to anyone

Now you can see all this information with just a couple of clicks of your mouse, or it will send you it by email. In fact, you can even make your emails ***SELF DESTRUCT*** if you wish! ...and by self destruct I mean the reader only has a few minutes to read and act on the information before it is PERMANENTLY deleted. Although, I can't see any benefit in using this function when dealing with journalists.

So what are the benefit?

- Firstly it tells us our news release has been opened and read
- How long it was read for - which gives us some indication of the level of interest

MORE IMPORTANTLY we know...

- If it was reopened - which means it is highly likely it has been given consideration
- If it has been forwarded - this tells us that it has been passed on, possibly to a journalist or correspondent; we can then see how many times they have opened and read it.

It's not a perfect system, but this knowledge does tell us that our news release is being passed around and read, and this is a ***MASSIVE IMPROVEMENT*** over not knowing if it has even arrived or wondering if it has been deleted!

Notes:
Please use this margin for writing your ideas thoughts, inspirations and personal plan of action.

This Tutorial will then act as your route map to PR success!

After your news release has been used or published

As soon as your 'Google Alerts', or 'Clipping Service' return you results confirming that your article has been published you are presented with the opportunity to build your relationship with the journalist a little further by sending them a "Thank You" email. However, if you really wanted to earn some Brownie points, and if you know them well do the same as Jeremy Fraser and give them a call.

Just imagine for a moment; most journalists probably get hundreds of work-related emails ***EVERY WEEK***; how many of those do you think are letters of gratitude? I can tell you with some certainty that it is ***NOT MANY***!

How long does it take to write a few words of thanks?

"Just had to drop you this short email to say a really **BIG** *thank you for your time and consideration in publishing my news release, which I sent to you last week. Lots of your readers have already downloaded the free report we provided and are getting great benefit from it. If there is any other information you need on this subject, or feel that I can be of further use to you or your publication in the future, please don't hesitate to give me a call..."*

These few lines, which should take no more than a couple of minutes to write and send, can really brighten the journalist's day and ***WILL*** get you remembered and your next call accepted. Remember to ***ALWAYS*** do this and you will soon be building powerful relationships which could be worth a ***SMALL FORTUNE*** to you in ongoing exposure and income in the coming years.

You will in fact have mastered the true meaning of PR – Press Relations!

Notes:
Please use this margin for writing your ideas thoughts, inspirations and personal plan of action.

This Tutorial will then act as your route map to PR success!

Dealing with rejection...

However good you become at PR marketing not all your news releases will get published and there could be a number of reasons why, which we will cover in just a moment. This is good motivation, as you gain experience in using these techniques you should step up your campaigns to ensure that every week you establish a new stream of interest and prospects heading in your direction. If you send just one news release and it gets rejected you are left with a total disaster and 100% failure; however, if you dispatch 30 – 40 news releases *(To a wide variety of publications.)* and as many as 10 of them fail to get published, you are still left with a 75% success rate and that is the essence of successful PR marketing.

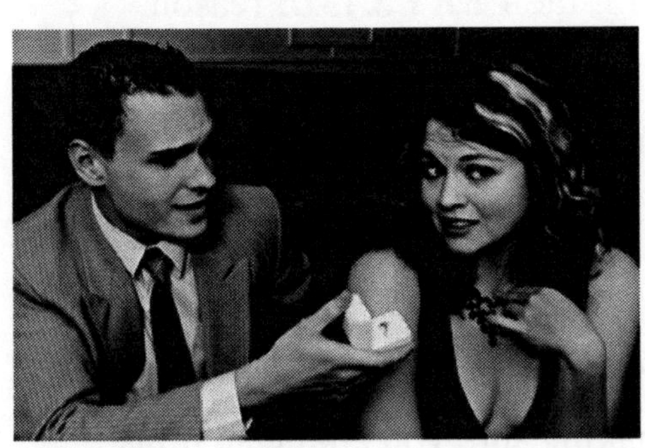

"NO" to your news release today, does not mean "NO" forever!

The fact is your release could be perfectly written and on any other occasion it would have been immediately accepted for publication but at that particular time the media outlet may have had too much time-sensitive news available, that ***MUST*** be given priority. If your news release will keep for later publication it may be put on the shelf for future consideration and use.

However, it could be that your release has been written with too much commercial spin for the liking of that particular journalist or it may not have a local focus which they require. These are just a few of the ***MANY POSSIBLE*** reasons why your release may not be used. If you find yourself in this position you could just cut your losses and simply write a new one, which may well be used without question. However, we would not advise this, as your new release could contain the same mistakes which prevented your previous one from being published in the first place, which you have now duplicated.

Notes:
Please use this margin for writing your ideas thoughts, inspirations and personal plan of action.

This Tutorial will then act as your route map to PR success!

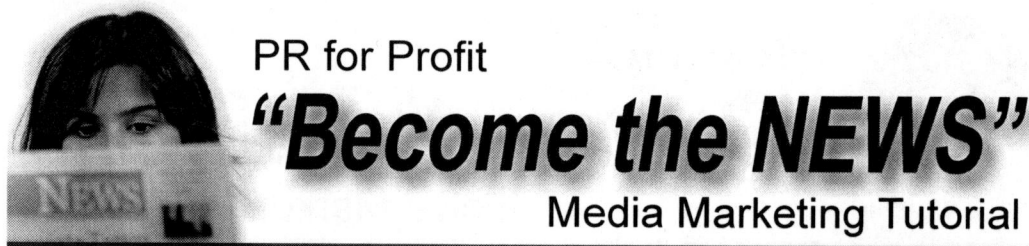

This action would mean you now have a second release with the same mistake which will probably also be rejected for the ***VERY SAME*** reason.

This makes your pathway forward quite simple and ***VERY OBVIOUS***; you will need to discover the reason behind this disappointment so if it is ***YOUR MISTAKE*** you can take action and learn from the experience by making sure you eradicate it just as soon as possible. If you have already established a relationship with the journalist this matter is easily overcome with a quick phone call.

However, if you have not yet had one of your news releases published in that particular paper, I would suggest that you write an email to the news room asking for their help and assistance; here is a short example of what you could write:

"Dear (NAME OF PUBLICATION) news room,

Approximately three weeks ago I sent a news release to this email address for your consideration, however, as yet it has not been published in your paper. Maybe I am being too impatient or presumptive by contacting you and please forgive me if I am. For this reason I wonder if you would be so kind as to look at the attached news release to perhaps identify the reason why it has not been used in order that I can learn from this experience and make the necessary improvements to make this and others acceptable to you"

...and of course ***ATTACH*** the original release for them to review. Now, this email may get your release published.

Notes:
Please use this margin for writing your ideas thoughts, inspirations and personal plan of action.

This Tutorial will then act as your route map to PR success!

Or, it's possible that the news room will pass your email on to a specific journalist for reply, and if they do, this action should achieve two things for you. First; it may result in some valuable constructive criticism and advice from an authoritative source which you can immediately turn to your advantage. Second; and more importantly, this response should be the start of a relationship with the journalist who writes to you as obviously you will have the courtesy to write an immediately reply thanking him or her for their help and assistance.

When this happens it is almost an invitation to refine your news release and send it to them again...

Please remember that journalists are tenacious by nature and will appreciate your resolve, so if you don't get a reply, send another email, or even another; stick with it or call them. Unless you are rude or offend someone your persistence will do ***NO HARM*** and should eventually gain you a positive result.

Online PR...

If you have an online presence, or use your website to take payment transactions, online PR has the potential to drive a ***MASSIVE*** amount of web traffic your way in an exceptionally short period of time. However, if you are serving a local market which may not be web based, it is probably not for you.

As online marketeers selling products to a global market, *(which includes this tutorial!),* online PR can generate a lot of sales for us and it does it in two ways. First are the individuals who read our news or product release and then decide to investigate further in what we have to offer them. They follow the link and arrive at our web site; hopefully they like what they see and then make their purchase.

Notes:
Please use this margin for writing your ideas thoughts, inspirations and personal plan of action.

This Tutorial will then act as your route map to PR success!

The second way that online PR article-publishing may help them to discover our web site is indirectly. It works like this: Your article will be published on a prominent news web site that publishes perhaps hundreds or even thousands of new news articles every week. As it publishes ***SO MUCH*** new content *(Gourmet Food for Search Engines)* their pages are searched and indexed regularly, sometimes several times ***PER DAY***, and for that reason new articles are likely to appear in the search engine listings quite quickly *(Sometimes within MINUTES!)*. So this means that visitors ***MAY*** find your article in the SERPs *(Search Engine Results Pages).*

However and far more likely, is this...

To rank well in the search engine listings your pages need a number of things; the most important being ***QUALITY BACK LINKS.*** By this I mean, other web sites which link to *your site*; that is exactly what the PR news site is doing when you publish an article through them as it will obviously carry one or even a number of links to your site for interested parties to investigate further. Your release may also be reproduced or even syndicated on a number of other websites, ***PERHAPS HUNDREDS***, all of which will be providing your web site with a back link which in turn is improving your web site SERPs and making it easier to find all the time.

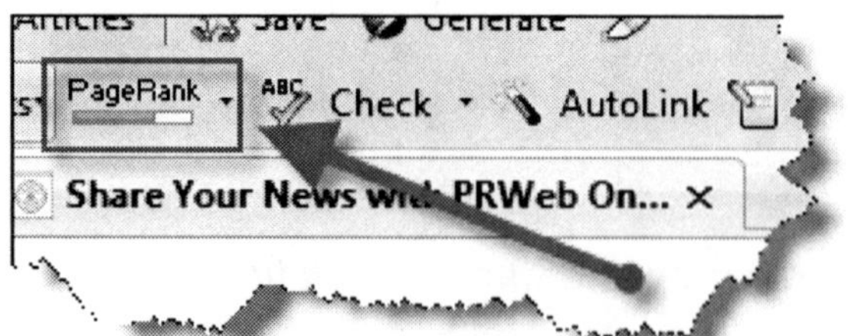

Now this is where, for the uninitiated to SEO *(Search Engine Optimisation),* it could become very complicated so I am going to provide just a ***VERY BASIC*** explanation of how this works. By quality back links I mean a link that has a high 'Page Rank' value and some of the news sites have ***EXTREMELY HIGH*** 'Page Rank' value indeed. Although you may not see the little green bar which I have highlighted in the illustration on your browser every web site and web page you visit is assigned a 'Page Rank' value of their own; the higher the value, generally the higher the SERP'S positioning they receive.

Therefore just having an online news release listed at a quality PR website can very quickly drive your website up the SERP'S for certain keyword or keyword-phrase searches. Are you starting to see the ***MAIN*** potential of online PR?

Notes:
Please use this margin for writing your ideas thoughts, inspirations and personal plan of action.

This Tutorial will then act as your route map to PR success!

Another possibility that online PR offers is that the traditional media may pick up on your article and want to run a story of their own, which is wonderful, although it seldom happens to me. In fact, I have only heard of it happening to people who live in the US and as yet, generally not in the UK, but this may change with time and the advancement of globalisation.

It's changing rapidly...

I was planning on giving you much more information on online PR than this meagre chapter has provided for you however it is changing ***SO RAPIDLY*** I fear that more than the basics are likely to become out of date very quickly. Online PR is very much ***MORE COMMERCIAL*** than what you have been taught in this tutorial. It is possible to turn ***BLATANT ADVERTS*** into so called articles.

Only you can decide if online PR will be for you and your company, but you will never know until you have tried. At the time of writing you can still get your articles published for free at my PR website of choice which is: www.PRweb.com However, that also may soon become something of the past.

There are ***DOZENS*** of quality PR sites about, but you only need to publish your article with a couple of them otherwise you will be wasting your time and perhaps money by duplication. As you become more familiar with PR and if your specific line of business is web-based I suggest you give it a try and see what happens as for you it may be the best thing since sliced bread and it could very possibly return you some amazing results. Please let us know if it does because we are always looking for success stories with which to update this tutorial.

Notes:
Please use this margin for writing your ideas thoughts, inspirations and personal plan of action.

This Tutorial will then act as your route map to PR success!

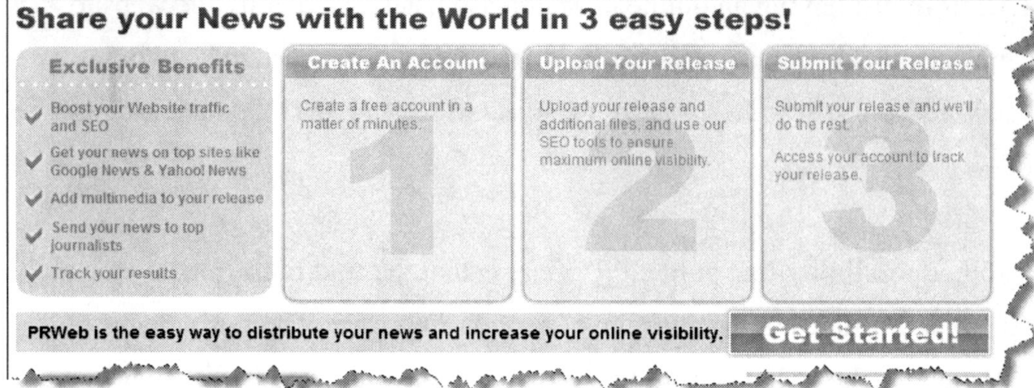

Making the most of your press cuttings...

One of the more powerful ongoing PR benefits is that your press clippings will go on paying you for years and years to come if you learn to use them ***CORRECTLY!*** If you keep them in a drawer or scrap book ***NO ONE*** will get to see them and you are simply wasting one of your most valuable resources. By contrast when you use them as supporting evidence of quality and popularity for your product or service they are ***FAR MORE*** powerful than a page full of happy customer testimonials, which by the way, prospects often believe are made up!

You don't have to take my word for this as you can easily test it for yourself. When you have enough clippings arrange a montage similar to the one you will see in the upcoming example. Then include a copy with every sales letter, brochure etc that you send out; then watch your conversion rate go through the roof! In fact you should use this powerful promotional tool with ***EVERY*** piece of your literature that could result in a sale.

The recipient is likely to quickly scan it and say **"WOW!"** They will see the powerful headlines and that your product has become a ***FEATURE*** story, as well as being used for prestigious glossy magazine covers. The perceived value of your product will rise considerably. If the independent ***MEDIA*** find this much to say about it then what you are offering must be ***GOOD!***

Notes:
Please use this margin for writing your ideas thoughts, inspirations and personal plan of action.

This Tutorial will then act as your route map to PR success!

The BEST WAY to use them...

Get into the habit of 'Scanning' your clippings into your computer just as soon as you get them otherwise I can predict what will happen to them. They will be shown to your mum, who will be so proud that she will want to show her neighbour's cousin's cat, they will get scrunched up, possibly fail to be returned and even lost. Even if you keep them in your office they are likely to get filed in books, drawers and folders which you will never find when you come to use them.

However, if you 'Scan' them the day they arrive, you can add them to your clippings file, and then, every-so-often, update the way in which you are using them by making new promotional montages of your PR or updating your website with them and in this way you are making your media exposure ***REALLY*** work for you. From mentoring our students, I know that you ***MAY*** be making mental excuses and saying to yourself; but I ***DON'T HAVE A SCANNER!*** ...my simple answer would be, well ***GET ONE!*** ...in fact ***ORDER IT TODAY!*** ...They are so inexpensive and failure to do so can only be compared to refusing an ongoing residual income.

You can use your clippings in a variety of different ways, but the one which is likely to have the most impact is a montage printed on an A4 or A5 sheet. If you lay them out well you can make them appear to be far more than they actually are. The clippings in the following example could have easily been rearranged to make another one or even two promotional montage sheets without the exposed material being seen twice.

Notes:
Please use this margin for writing your ideas thoughts, inspirations and personal plan of action.

This Tutorial will then act as your route map to PR success!

Once digitised clippings are easy to manipulate and move around until you get the appearance you want. I use 'Adobe Photoshop' to do this, however, there are many other graphic software packages which will easily achieve the same effect for you. Be creative with size and rotation of your clippings to make the more important aspects jump out at the reader. To stop them all blending in with each other put a light border around the edges. Experiment and have fun and I know you will soon create some interesting and effective results.

It is not necessary for your recipient to be able to read the clippings because they will be accompanied by your sales literature, which will sell your product or service far better than the media. Your montage is just to add weight and ***HIGHLIGHT*** the fact that the media are giving you their seal of approval - remember the ***HALO EFFECT!***

The example is one Jeremy asked me to create for the coverage he gained for a client who arranges polo events. As you can imagine this montage ***GENERATES HUGE*** interest and makes it far easier to attract supporters and sponsorship for his events.

We prove you don't have to be posh or privileged
By Kate Edser
THE new Cl
Club is gearin
inaugural m
August's bank
weekend by setti
unsuspecting m
including mys
exhibition game
main event.
POLO, ANYONE?
On 27th August the newly formed Clifton Polo Club is organising the first-ever Polo Match at the North Somerset Show Ground at Long Ashton in aid of Bristol Cancer Help Centre. The match will be the central activity of an action-packed fun day out where families can bring picnics and enjoy other attractions, including a falconry display, sheepdog demonstrations, strawberries and cream, and a champagne and beer tent. The two polo teams will include top international players who will compete for the Isambard Kingdom Brunel Trophy.
This is an opportunity for people in Bristol and the South-west to be introduced to polo. Businesses in the region will also have the perfect opportunity to entertain clients and guests with a corporate marquee and After Polo Party open to all in the evening with a bar, barbecue and music.
To help with fund-raising and for more details of the Polo Match please log on to www.bristolcancerhelp.org or contact the fund-raising team on ☎01275 370073.
FEATURE
BLAZING SADDLES
Fast, furious and not just for upper-class toffs...
Joanna Houseman can't wait for Bristol's first polo match
But the adage "Don't r
you can walk" is so true, a
glad we sat for half an h
watched the wonderful
Tomlinson, whose fam
Beaufort Polo Club near
show us how it should, a
not, be done.
When she moved effor
to the backhands we beg
gle and look wide-eyed at
er, all thinking there's r
would be able to conq
skills with just three pr
sions. After all, the
The Bristol Approach
Clare Benjamin tells us how one pioneering Bristol-based charity is providing holistic care for cancer patients
FEATURE
that surround polo and make
the game more accessible to everyone.
We're delighted to be able to introduce polo
makeover for
CHASING PACK: Action from the Isambard Kingdom Brunel Trophy match on Sunday.
www.clevedonmercury.co.uk
Polo stars trophy gam
BRISTOL, BATH AND CHELTENHAM FREE - TAKE ONE!
FOLIO
Polo Premiere
West Country
rich or posh to
Crowds flock as first polo match is crowned success
Clevedon Mercury 31 Aug 06
The Hunters team included Paul
founder and chairman of Clifton Po
organised the day.
The crowd supped beer, Pimms
browsed the trade stands, showe
the players and trod in the
Barrage for city's polo

Notes:
Please use this margin for writing your ideas thoughts, inspirations and personal plan of action.

This Tutorial will then act as your route map to PR success!

PR and Web Sites....

Whether you like it or not the Internet is here to stay and you can either embrace it and the many benefits it has to offer you. Or you can ignore it, and become increasingly left behind as it advances and develops, it's as simple as that!

The reason I am dealing with it in this tutorial is that the Internet offers PR marketeers an inexpensive and lightening fast solution to gaining response to their media exposure and at the same time building a valuable emailing list of interested prospects to whom you can then market your products and services to at will. In fact your web site or sites are the single ***MOST VALUABLE*** tools you have. Unfortunately not many people utilise even a small percentage of the ***HUGE*** power and potential they offer as just one computer has the ability to perform the combined work of a small, well trained office staff for you, if you only take the time to discover how.

Unlike human assistants, who have ***HIGH RUNNING*** and maintenance ***COSTS***, your website once set up can serve and assist ***THOUSANDS*** of prospects all at the very same time. It can be programmed to sell your products and services; answer questions; perform surveys; deliver interactive education. and handle your communications as well as a ***VARIETY*** of other tasks.

It's open 24 hours a day, 7 days a week, 365 days per year, and is ***ALWAYS*** willing and available to help your prospects at a time which suits them. It never arrives late for work; gets tired; needs coffee breaks; asks for a pay rise or takes holidays. Computers are amazingly effective marketing tools and by not taking the necessary time to discover the potential that your computer and the Internet has to offer you, and then taking ***FULL*** advantage of it, you are missing a big opportunity.

In this chapter we are going to discover just how simple it is to set up a one page website that will inform and educate your visitors, and ***EVEN*** capture their details in exchange for the report or tips sheet you have promised them.

You have two choices...

Employ others to do your web site development work for you,
Learn to do it yourself!

If you are on a tight budget, let me tell you, setting up a one page web site is ***REALLY EASY*** and I will show you a simple and ***FREE*** solution in just a moment which I had never used before but it took me ***UNDER*** 10 minutes to complete my one paged site and publish it to the Internet ready to start working for me. ***IMPRESSIVE STUFF!*** What we are going to build is known in the trade as...

The SQUEEZE page...

The software we are going to use to build our web site can be found at: www.weebly.com and at the time of writing you can develop a totally ***FREE*** website which they will even kindly host for you at no cost.

The first thing you need to do is visit their web site and sign up for a ***FREE*** account which is activated instantly. Just decide upon a user name and password and if they are available your account will be set up. Then make sure you keep a note of these details in a ***SAFE PLACE*** for future reference.

Notes:
Please use this margin for writing your ideas thoughts, inspirations and personal plan of action.

This Tutorial will then act as your route map to PR success!

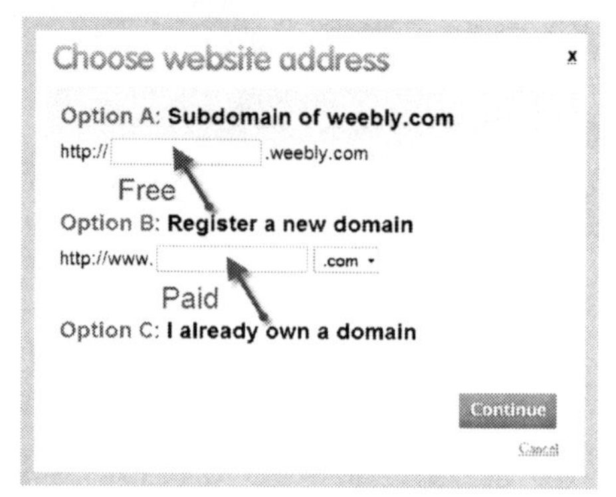

One of the first things that Weebly will ask you to do after opening your account is to choose a web site name and address, which you may have heard referred to as a URL. Now you basically have two choices, the first one being 'Option A' and that is the free selection we are going to use to build this example.

This will create what is known as a subdomain, which will serve ***EXACTLY*** the same purpose as a top level domain and we will come to this in just a moment. The only difference is the address or URL, and you only get to pick the first part of it. For instance I have decided to call mine pr-example, which means when it is published the address you would type to visit it would be www.pr-example.weebly.com.

This ***IS NOT*** a good address and could well put off many people from visiting it completely. It is obviously a ***FREE*** site which is not congruent with the professional image you will be portraying. So I would urge you to use 'Option B' when you come to build your site, which will mean you have to buy your address from Weebly, but your website address would be far simpler, such as: www.pr-example.com

Think out your URL carefully!

The following story will illustrate the reason you need to give your web site name and address much thought and consideration before you purchase it. When Jeremy and I made the decision to create this tutorial we soon came up with the name 'PR for Profit', and we both agreed it is a good descriptive name, so decided to stick with it. When I looked to see if: www.prforprofit.com was available I was disappointed to find it had already been taken. However, www.pr-forprofit.com was available so I purchased it.

And it has worked well for us and without problems, ***OR SO I THOUGHT***, until recently, this is what happened.

A close friend gave me a call on my mobile phone while I was watching my children at a Judo training session. For some reason the conversation turned to PR and I mentioned this tutorial which you are now reading to my friend and he immediately wanted to know more about it, so I told him the web site address: www.pr-forprofit.com

He typed it into his computer browser only to tell me that it didn't exist. I knew differently, so I patiently went through it with him a ***DOZEN*** times without success, only to eventually discover he was typing an underscore _ rather than a hyphen -. He tried again but he still couldn't locate the site; in ***FRUSTRATION*** I asked him to spell out loud what he was typing character by character only, to discover that he had typed www.pr-4profit,com ***HALLELUIAH!*** We had found the problem.

So what is the point of this story?

My friend highlighted to me how many different ways you could ***MIS-SPELL*** the address we had chosen and had thought was simple but with which he had experienced such a problem. How many ***OTHERS*** had experienced the same problem and failed in their attempt to reach our web site? ...how much lost revenue had this wide variety of ambiguous spellings generated? We will never know if he was the only one who had encountered such difficulties or if we have lost a small fortune and this is the ***POINT*** I would like you to learn from. It's a ***SIMPLE*** equation; if your web site address is easy to remember you will get far more visitors than one which is difficult or complicated and has many possible spelling variations. Simplicity is ***ESPECIALLY*** important if you plan to do radio PR where at the conclusion of your interview they give out your web address for those listeners who want to discover more.

Notes:
Please use this margin for writing your ideas thoughts, inspirations and personal plan of action.

This Tutorial will then act as your route map to PR success!

Notes:
Please use this margin for writing your ideas thoughts, inspirations and personal plan of action.

This Tutorial will then act as your route map to PR success!

In my humble opinion for most people: www.pr-forprofit.com would be far too difficult to remember even for a few seconds while they try to write it down. So for that reason, and if you are going to focus on radio PR you should consider using ones with a much simpler address such as: www.learningmore.co.uk which is why we use this and other such simple to remember URL's when giving radio interviews. You may be able to find a simple one which is linked to your line of business also.

Back to building your web site...

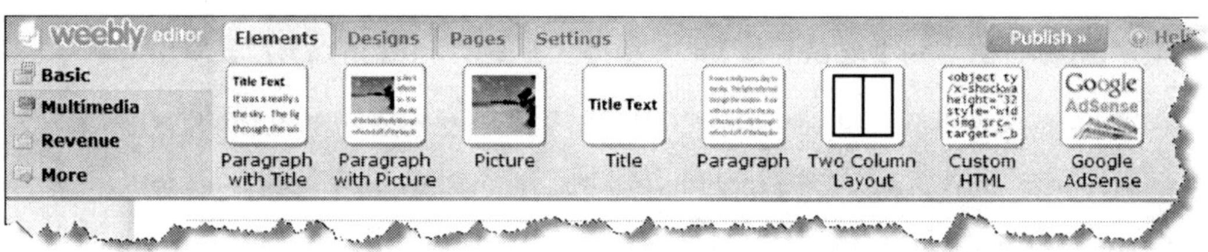

As you can see Weebly provides you with all the tools you need to create a ***VERY COMPREHENSIVE*** web site and most of this is achieved by simply dragging and dropping from the menu bar to your web page below.

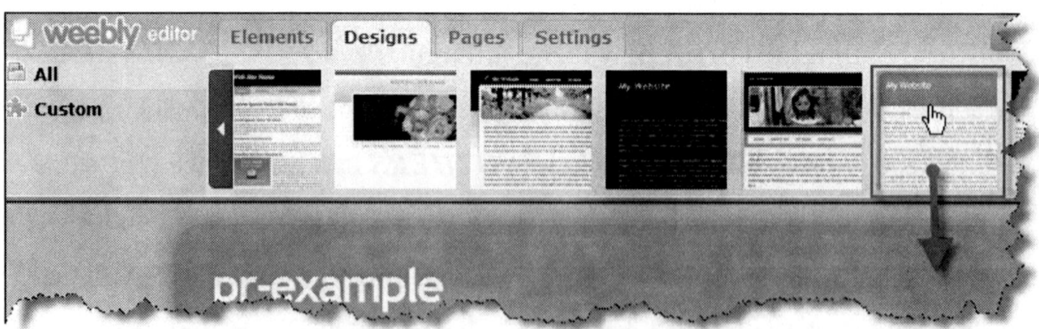

I have made a start by picking the design for my site and have just chosen something really simple, although you have ***DOZENS*** to pick from and some of the designs are really interesting. All you have to do to select the design of your choice is to place your mouse on the one you want and click on your left button and whilst holding it drag it to the page work area. And ***VOILA!*** the change is made.

Notes:
Please use this margin for writing your ideas thoughts, inspirations and personal plan of action.

This Tutorial will then act as your route map to PR success!

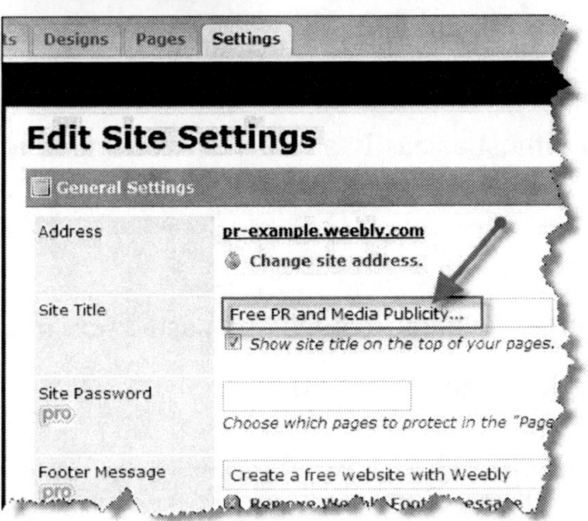

The next thing I want to change is the text on the page header and I do this by clicking on the 'Settings' tab and typing in the amendment into the 'Site Title' box and then click upon the 'Save' button.

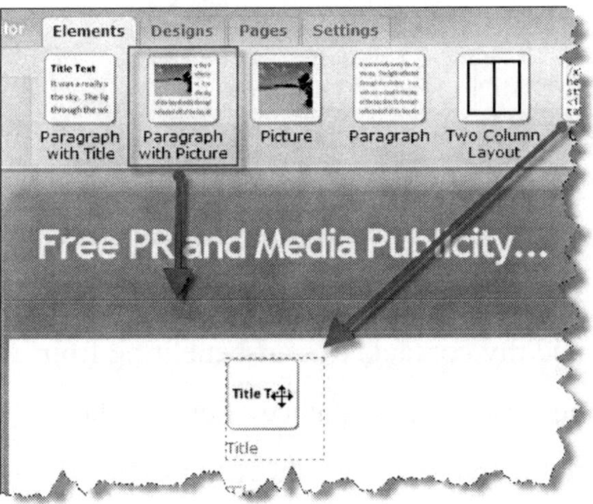

I also want a page headline, so I simply drag and drop the elements I want on to the top of the page and release; then I can edit and write the headline of my choice. To save time, I also want to place a picture below this with some paragraph text and I am going to drag this into place.

To place your picture or image you will have to upload it from your computer's hard drive which is an easy task to accomplish by just clicking on the 'Edit Picture' box and the upload link below will open.

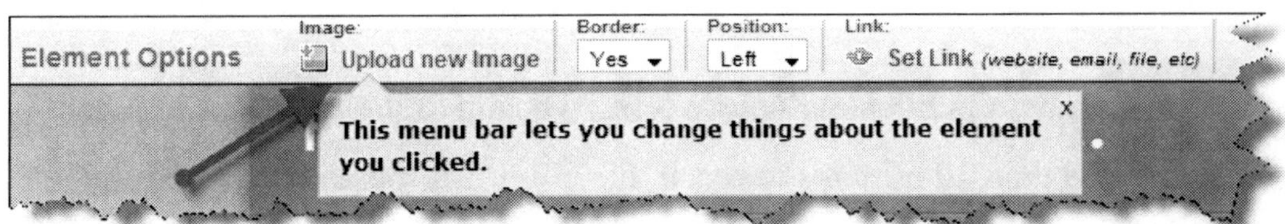

I simply locate the image I wish to use and upload it and when it has done so it will click into place automatically.

Notes:
Please use this margin for writing your ideas thoughts, inspirations and personal plan of action.

This Tutorial will then act as your route map to PR success!

To edit the paragraph text I simply click on it and I am allowed to amend it by either typing directly into the paragraph area or cutting and pasting from another source. I can also edit my text almost as easily as if I was working in a 'Word Processor'.

Under this I dragged another paragraph box which I copied and pasted text into before editing to keep it in the same style as the above text.

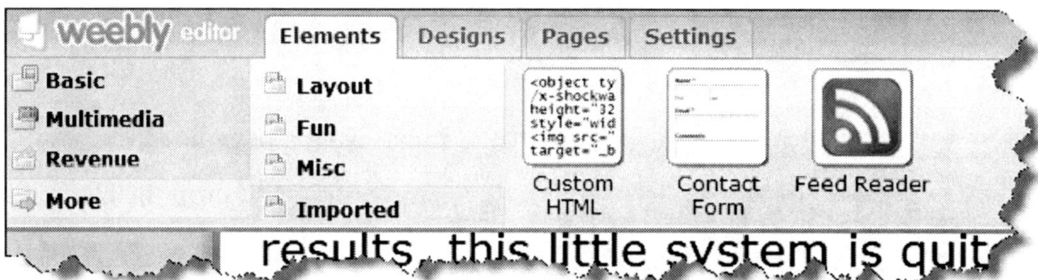

The final element for my squeeze page is a form to capture my visitors' email addresses. Now I could have used the contact form provided by Weebly but

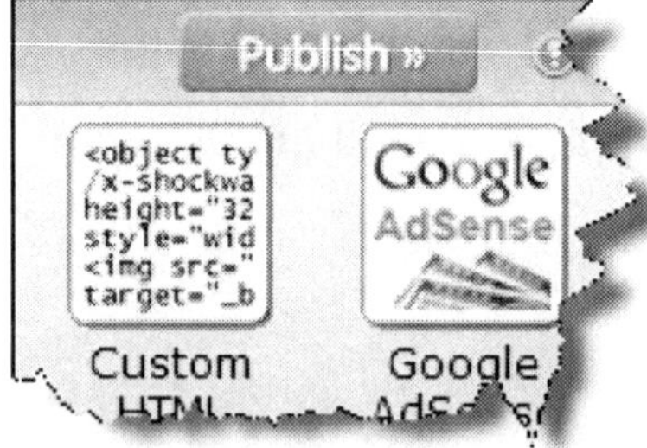

I wanted my contacts to start benefiting from my auto responder sequence of emails the very moment they subscribed, so I dragged the 'Custom HTML' into place and copied and pasted my auto responder form directly into this. If you would like to discover more about the auto responder you will need to go to the 'PR for Profit' web site resource page.

I am now ready to publish my new Weebly website to the Internet and it has taken me less than 10 minutes to reach this point. All that is left to do is hit the 'Publish' button and look at the results which you can see live at: http://pr.example.weebly.com

Not bad for a ***FREE*** web site! Now you don't have to complete *yours* in 10 minutes, take all the time you need and have fun experimenting. However, please buy an easy to remember web site name to make it easy for your potential prospects.

Free PR and Media Publicity...

Home

When it comes to achieving ***HIGHLY CREATIVE*** results, this little system is quite ***AMAZING*** - so you don't have to be!

"Inspiration Unlimited"

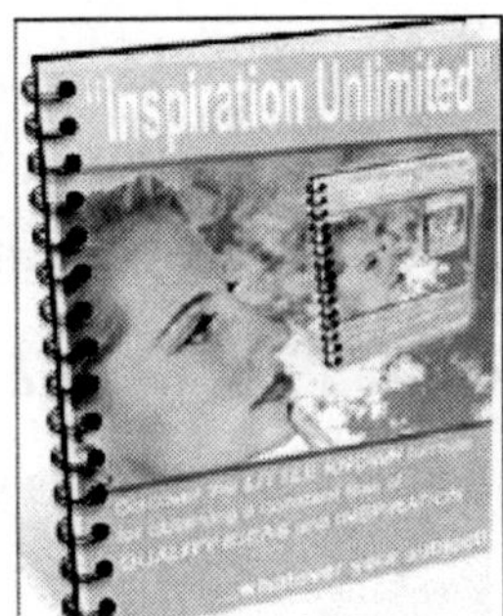

*You are just minutes away from discovering the simple formula which will positively **TURBO CHARGE** your creativity and provide you with an unlimited supply of inspiration and unique ideas...*

May I ask you a question?

Have you ever looked on, while others *(often in your own line of business)* come up with new ideas, products, services or improvements, etc, felt a little ***ENVIOUS*** and wish that you had come up with the idea instead of them?

This used to happen to me all the time!

Others would develop what seemed like a conveyor belt of ***QUALITY*** ideas and articles. Their ideas were always so simple, whilst at the same time ***HIGHLY*** creative, and often ***BRILLIANT*** .

How did they develop such ***GOOD*** ideas, and I didn't? I considered the possibility that creativity was inherent, or that I was a bit stupid. It was so ***FRUSTRATING*** watching others be so imaginative and continue to increase their income while I looked on in ***ENVY!***

Then one day ***EVERYTHING*** changed...

Amazingly, and almost ***OVERNIGHT*** I became just about the most ***CREATIVE*** person I know! You can ask anyone who knows me and they will tell you that Kevin Martyn is a ***GOLDMINE*** of ***VALUABLE*** information and ***VERY*** profitable ideas.

So ***WHAT*** happened?

I didn't learn my creativity from a book or at a ***HIGH*** ticket price seminar, although I have to tell you it would be worth ***EVERY*** penny in increased profits if that had been the case.

I had ***ACCIDENTALLY*** stumbled onto a source that provided an ***ENDLESS*** supply of ideas and inspiration, which was readily available on tap...

I quickly mastered how to use this source and it ***DRAMATICALLY*** improved my productivity and profitability. ***BEST*** of all, since I first discovered this method for myself it has improved by 1000% and has become a ***TOTALLY*** automated ***FORMULA*** which is completely ***FREE*** for anyone to use!

To help you get the most of this formula I have written a comprehensive 13 page report that will have you up and running in just five minutes at the very most.

And now it's my ***GIFT*** to you...

Simply complete your details below and I will instantly return you an email with the download details of this valuable PDF document so you can start benefiting from it today.

First Name:

Your Email:

Country:

Submit

PR for Profit
"Become the NEWS"
Media Marketing Tutorial

Notes:
Please use this margin for writing your ideas thoughts, inspirations and personal plan of action.

This Tutorial will then act as your route map to PR success!

Information products that attract new prospects like crazy

Spending a few hours creating a simple report, tips sheet, or similar

information product which has an attached high perceived value may be the most profitable investment of your time you ***EVER*** make! You can use your finished product as a method for building a valuable email list, or ***EVEN*** as a powerful stand-alone news story, and it could go on working for you for years to come.

There are a variety of ways in which you can use these types of simple information products in PR and for gaining media exposure. In fact your only restriction will be your ***IMAGINATION***. However you decide to use them, and whatever you decide to call them, there is one ***GOLDEN*** rule that ***SHOULD ALWAYS*** be followed and that is your product ***MUST*** give value! ...if it fails to do this you will immediately lose credibility and your potential prospects and customers of tomorrow.

When potential prospects subscribe, opt-in, or download your free product this is your opportunity to **WOW THEM**; it is the beginning of what can become a valuable and profitable relationship; if you mess this up, you may not get another chance, and you will have just lost another profit opportunity. However, when you get it right, your new prospects will be open, trusting and keen to learn more about your products and services. A simple tip sheet of just a page or two in length may result in them making their first cash purchases from you within just hours of receiving it.

Stay focused on delivering VALUE...

Certainly you ***SHOULD*** include a short sales pitch and links to your websites, products and services towards the end of your information for the reader to follow if they wish; in fact, they will probably expect you to do so. Above all else though make sure that you stay focused on delivering what you have promised them by giving your readers lots of value, and ***THEY WILL*** reward you for doing so.

No one likes having their time wasted...

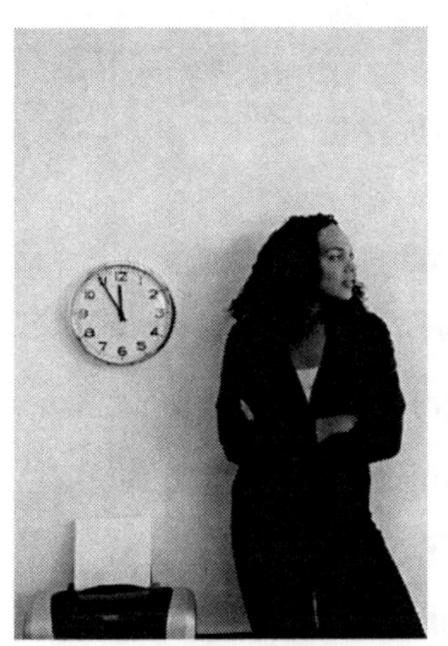

However, if like so many others, you simply trick your subscribers and opt-ins into downloading and reading your latest hype and sales literature, you will totally fail in gaining benefit from the ***HUGE*** potential which such relationship-building information tools offer you. Further more, those prospects will most likely immediately unsubscribe from your list and ***NEVER*** trust you again. Worse still, they may even tell others about you, ***LOTS*** of ***OTHERS***; remember that bad news travels ***REALLY*** quickly. For this reason make sure your report does everything that you claim and then a bit more ...if you aim to ***UNDERSELL*** and ***OVER DELIVER*** you shouldn't go far wrong.

How to create REPORTS...

The size of your report can be just a few pages in length just so long as you give the reader something of value that they can use, implement or duplicate to gain benefit from. Don't worry how your finished report will look at this stage; just concentrate on the quality of the content, and when you have got that to a high standard we can then make it look attractive.

Notes:
Please use this margin for writing your ideas thoughts, inspirations and personal plan of action.

This Tutorial will then act as your route map to PR success!

PR for Profit
"Become the NEWS"
Media Marketing Tutorial

Notes:
Please use this margin for writing your ideas thoughts, inspirations and personal plan of action.

This Tutorial will then act as your route map to PR success!

My reports usually show the reader how to do something or concentrate on solving a problem for them. After I have found a good idea on which to write, I jot down a brief outline to keep me focused on my objective. Then I start working on the headline and this is a subject to which I give a lot of ***EFFORT***, as your report title needs to be powerful and compelling for it to be successful and to attract prospects to subscribe. I record my headline ideas as they spring to mind and then visit my swipe file for further inspiration if needed. As I refine what I am writing, it usually triggers ideas which I can use in the report, so I jot them down, and make notes for expanding upon later.

Content...

I begin all the reports that I write by telling the reader why I have written it

(stating the problem or opportunity and how it will make their life easier or better) and exactly what they are about to learn, as doing this gives the report structure and focus. Right up front I inform them that the report will tell them ***WHAT*** they should do, but not necessary ***HOW*** they should do it, as that will be the focus of my ***PAID*** course or tutorial etc; I like to be honest with my readers and this is an ideal way of introducing my product or service to them. Creating a short report on the same subject as a full product you may be selling is a great sales technique and method of generating interest, as it gives you the opportunity to fully list all the features and benefits it offers. However, depending upon your product or service you can alter your content to suit.

Graphics...

If you have any good quality graphics, pictures or illustrations you should use them in your report as they add both variety and interest. As you will have noticed from this tutorial I use a lot of graphics to add a little interest and to break up the blocks of text up as you read. I purchased these quite inexpensively from: www.istockphoto.com although such quality photographs are also available from many other web sites and can be instantly downloaded. I nearly always place my own picture at the top of my reports because I know that some readers *(including me)* enjoy their read ***FAR*** more if they have a face to go with the words; having that picture helps me identify with the author and what they are attempting to convey.

When you have written the content of the report to your satisfaction be sure to include a quick commercial about you, your company, and how else they, the readers, can benefit and how they should contact you; when this is done you are almost ready to start making it look attractive.

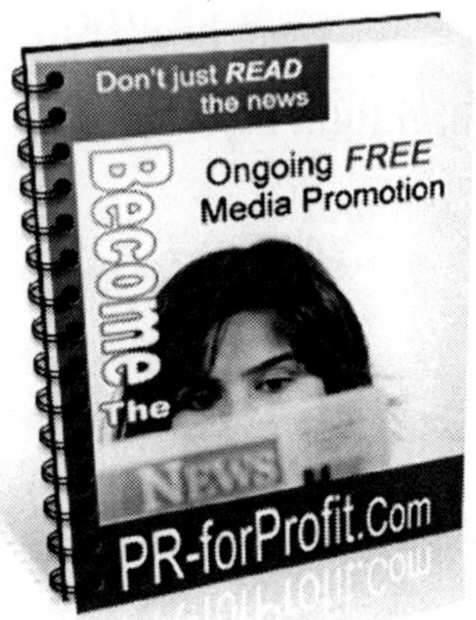

Two more things you should seriously consider creating to make your report look more professional are a front cover and a book-style graphical representation of it to use in your PR and on your website. This requires the skills of a graphical designer; if you are handy with 'Photoshop' you may be able to achieve this yourself. There are also many software packages around, which ***MAY*** achieve this for you, although they generally *(and in my opinion)* create ***POOR*** substitutes.

Notes:
Please use this margin for writing your ideas thoughts, inspirations and personal plan of action.

This Tutorial will then act as your route map to PR success!

Notes:
Please use this margin for writing your ideas thoughts, inspirations and personal plan of action.

This Tutorial will then act as your route map to PR success!

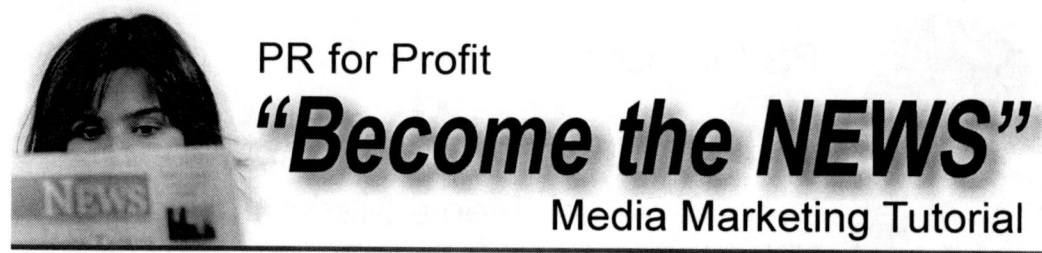

So my advice would be to check with your local Chamber of Commerce and see what local designer contacts they can provide you with. Or, and perhaps a much cheaper alternative, would be to go to: www.elance.com where you may find a foreign designer who will create you a wonderful design for just a ***QUARTER*** of the price.

Making it look sexy...

The look of your report will not only make it more attractive to read, but also add to its perceived value. I am sure that you agree, there is nothing worse than heavy blocks of solid text for putting a reader off and sending them to sleep, as solid text is quite difficult to read. For this reason, consider breaking up your report with lots of subhead lines and bullet point lists as they always draw the eye. If there is anything which you ***REALLY WANT*** to get your readers to look at place it in a box and this will ***ALMOST GUARANTEE*** that it will get read, but use this technique sparingly!

Remember to leave lots of white space around your report, and use the same 1.5 line spacing that you were encouraged to use when writing your press releases and as you can see I am using here. I like to use the page header to repeat my report title on every page and the footer to highlight my copyright notice and reproduce the link to my website or resource materials.

Delivering the finished article...

Once finished you have a variety of delivery formats available to you, so let's explore the most popular right now.

Option One – HTML

You could put your finished report on a web page which would probably be the simplest method of all. If you wanted to make it secure you could password the folder in which it is located and that is a really simple task to complete.

Then when a new prospect subscribes to your list your auto responder would send them the location where they can access it and the password to allow them in to do so ***SIMPLE!***

Option Two – Word

If you are using word to write and create your report you may consider distributing it in this same format, although it has three distinct disadvantages.

- **Security** – although this is not a major concern, anyone downloading your report could edit or copy your content to make it their own and there would be very little you could do about it as you have left it unsecured.
- **Size** – 'Word' and word processor files in general are not that streamlined and can be quite large, quickly using up your website bandwidth if you are planning to make it downloadable. This format has not been created with internet transportation in mind.
- **Version** – now this could be a really ***BIG*** problem as 'Word' seems to update every year or so and for this reason you would have to provide your report in a variety of version formats or run the risk of some subscribers not being able to read it.

Although 'Word' format initially seems a simple option providing your report in this way will generate many ***TIME CONSUMING*** problems for you to deal with.

Option Three – PDF

You have probably already seen the document extension .pdf ...and it stands for 'Portable Document Format'. PDF documents are simple to produce, generally small in size, can be made ***HIGHLY SECURE*** and can be read by cross platform operating systems; in other words, ***EVERYONE*** can read them without problem. If your report recipient ***DOES*** have a problem in opening it, they only need to upgrade their pdf reader to the latest version by downloading it for ***FREE*** from www.adobe.com

Notes:
Please use this margin for writing your ideas thoughts, inspirations and personal plan of action.

This Tutorial will then act as your route map to PR success!

Notes:
Please use this margin for writing your ideas thoughts, inspirations and personal plan of action.

This Tutorial will then act as your route map to PR success!

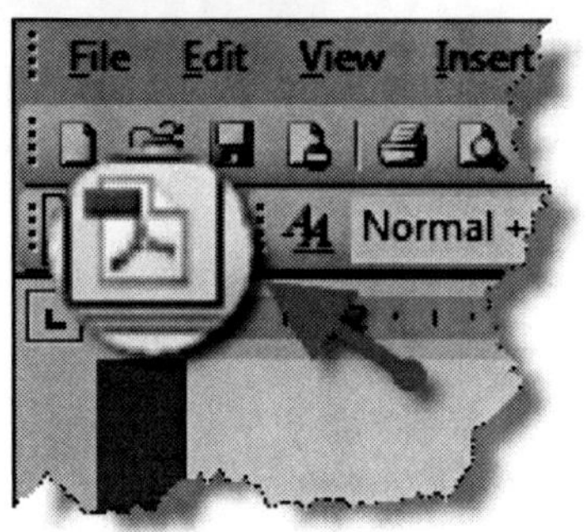

After your report is completed turning it into a pdf document is simple. If you have 'Adobe Acrobat' installed on your computer you will have a pdf button in your 'Word' tool bar and it is just a simple matter of clicking the 'Convert to PDF' button as seen in the illustration to the left.

However, if you don't have 'Acrobat' and don't feel you would use it enough to justify purchasing a copy of your own, there are alternatives. I have just typed the search term 'pdf creator' into Google and have been returned hundreds of results of web sites with practical solutions; in fact, one site will convert your document into a .pdf for nothing, and that is: www.primopdf.com When you come to making your .pdf documents I am sure you will find many other solutions.

Creating tip Sheets...

The great thing about these little gems is the ***HUGE*** interest which they can generate and the miniscule amount of time it takes to create them. I felt that the best way to show you how to write your own is by giving you a template which you can copy and duplicate. So below is a simple tip sheet which I may in fact use to promote this tutorial. It is under two pages long and took me less than an hour to write. Please note how I only tell readers ***WHAT*** they should do and then tell them where they can learn the step by step ***HOW TO*** process.

This short tip sheet does ***EVERYTHING*** it claims on the tin and after giving readers an overview of the PR process would hopefully build the prospect's desire to discover more.

"Obtain £20,000 or MORE of FREE publicity in just 3 months!"
- 11 Simple tips that tell you how -

With practice you could SOON be attracting 1,000's of qualified leads, customers and prospects to your business ***EVERY*** single day; ***SERIOUSLY!*** ...start by studying these tips, and then, if you would like to discover the step-by-step formula for using them to your advantage; at the bottom of this short report, I will tell you where to find it.

1. Make a commitment to get a 'News Release' out and in print in the next week; the sooner you get started, the sooner you can expect to begin harvesting the results.
2. Make a list of story ideas which you feel the press and the public would be interested in; please remember those two words 'Public Interest' as they are the ones that will get your story published!
3. Study newspaper articles every day to see what story ideas and techniques you can extract and perhaps even adapt for your own topic; pay particular attention to the headlines and how they are formed.
4. Start a swipe or reference file of ideas; these are basically cuttings of stories which have captured your attention and you feel have the qualities that you could use or adapt.
5. Be controversial – the press and media just love a good story, or you could hold an event of some type as these are generally very easy to write about as well as providing you with some interesting photo opportunities.
6. Try to discover the correct journalist to whom to send your 'News Release'; if you have a reporter's name, send it to him or her directly; you will stand a far better chance of getting it published.

7. Monitor your results carefully; if you live in the same publication area you could personally look through the paper to see if your story has been printed; if you are not in the area, you could employ a press cutting service to monitor this for you.

8. When you have confirmation that your story has been published, send a thank-you note to the reporter or even call directly. Establishing a relationship with media personnel can make a big difference to your future outcome.

9. Now you know your story is a success, if applicable, send it out to the hundreds of other newspapers across the country as what has worked in one publication is likely to work in another.

10. Study the tried and tested methods and techniques of monetising your PR; when you know how to turn your results into cash you will have just discovered the method for turning on a new stream of income at will.

11. Turn up the heat! When you have mastered the above steps you only need to multiply your PR output to generate an ongoing flow of new and ***QUALIFIED*** prospects knocking on your door to give you money!

The tips you have just read are the actual, (but very ***MUCH SIMPLIFIED***) recipe for attracting as much new business to you as you can handle; the process will work for ***ANYONE*** who knows how to apply it correctly. Just imagine, within weeks from now you could have developed many new highly ***LUCRATIVE*** streams of income and have the knowledge to repeat the process just as often as you wish. If you would like to discover more about the PR for Profit process I have just outlined visit: www.PR-forProfit.Com today - you will be glad you did!

As I was writing this page I remembered Jeremy telling me about a tips sheet he wrote 30 years ago for one of his clients which was a ***HUGE*** success for them year after year and a great example of how valuable and profitable tips sheets could be. Unfortunately, he did not have a copy of the original, but said he could quickly recreate it for today's market, so here it is:

Client: Major tyre distributor

Brief: To make the general motoring public far more aware of the company's name and the services they provide – and to sell more tyres!

Method:

Winter was fast approaching and with it the prospects of many more road accidents, a very inexpensive leaflet was printed featuring '10 top tyre tips for safe winter driving'. This was issued with a community-spirited message from the Managing Director saying that the company was trying to do something positive to help reduce the accident statistics by pointing out, amongst other essential car safety maintenance, the importance of making sure tyres are in top condition. ***FREE*** tyre checks and this ***FREE*** check list were of course available at all its outlets. Whether or not people came to have their tyres checked and to collect their free leaflets (in fact many did and as a result many more tyres were sold!) was almost not important…………..

Result:

What the exercise did was to massively raise the profile of a responsible and respected individual and his company resulting in National radio, newspaper and trade media coverage, reminding motorists that when it came to tyres, THIS company would be the one to choose.

Testimonial:

"Such a simple idea which resulted in a big increase in sales for us and a significant boost to our public image. We were delighted with the work"
Chief Executive

Notes:
Please use this margin for writing your ideas thoughts, inspirations and personal plan of action.

This Tutorial will then act as your route map to PR success!

NEWS
PR for Profit
"Become the NEWS"
Media Marketing Tutorial

Notes:
Please use this margin for writing your ideas thoughts, inspirations and personal plan of action.

This Tutorial will then act as your route map to PR success!

Part of the press release:

Company name is advising all motorists to pay close attention to their tyres as winter driving conditions start to increase the possibility of unnecessary accidents due to tyre neglect.

The company is offering a free tyre safety check at all its outlets and a printed or downloadable 10 point reminder as a free download from their website:

"With snow and icy driving conditions nearly upon us we want to make sure that drivers know about the importance of correct tyre safety maintenance in an effort to help reduce the appalling number of road traffic accidents during the winter months..."

TEN TOP TYRE SAFETY TIPS

Before starting a journey please note the following advice:

- Check and adjust as necessary the pressure of each tyre *including* the spare, to the level as stated in the manufacturers handbook
- Clean dirt from around the valves and fit dust caps to all tyres
- Remove foreign objects from the tread
- Check that tyres have at least 1.6mm tread across three quarters of the width of the tyre although it is recommended that motorists consider changing tyres when the tread falls below 3mm
- Check for uneven tyre wear which might mean steering misalignment or out of balance wheels
- Check tyres for cuts and bulges which could render the tyre defective and potentially dangerous
- ....recommends that any tyres which are replaced are done so in two's or all four
- If you are aware of having impacted a kerb with some force you should have the tyre(s) inspected for any damage and the vehicle alignment checked by a tyre dealer.
- Tyre sidewall damage cannot be repaired and may lead to possible failure because of the leaking of air.
- Current penalties for driving with illegal tyres is: Up to a £2,500 fine or 3 Penalty Points for EACH tyre!

Automating your PR delivery process

Welcome to the final chapter of this tutorial, which is meant to make the job of communicating with news rooms and journalists quick and simple. As you gain experience in PR marketing you will come to appreciate the true value of building strong relationships with media personnel. Whilst dealing with media publications you are likely to come into contact with many members of staff, all of whom can help you achieve your objective of gaining valuable media coverage, so the following advice should always be strictly followed to achieve maximum exposure.

Developing a ***STRONG*** relationship and rapport with valuable ***KEY*** personnel is not difficult if you follow the simple time-tested and proven strategy for success - which is; become ***GENUINELY*** interested in the person with whom you are dealing. Address them in a warm and friendly manner and whenever possible use their names – remember ***EVERYONE*** likes to hear their name used by someone else. If you can then instantly engage them on their favourite subject, or even recall a few snippets of personal and relevant information which ***HIGHLIGHTS*** your interest in them, you will be onto a winner and should not be surprised if they go beyond the call of duty to help you achieve your objective. Taking the little extra time to build such relationships, will generate a ***TREMENDOUS*** and profitable advantage for you.

Being extra polite and engaging doesn't have to take more than a ***LITTLE*** longer to achieve, but it is likely to make a ***MASSIVE*** difference to the way you are treated and your outcome!

If you think keeping track of such information is going to be difficult, you will really like the software I am about to introduce to you; this will also make the task of delivering your news releases and follow up information ***SIMPLE***, and often only requiring a couple of mouse clicks to complete.

Notes:
Please use this margin for writing your ideas thoughts, inspirations and personal plan of action.

This Tutorial will then act as your route map to PR success!

Notes:
Please use this margin for writing your ideas thoughts, inspirations and personal plan of action.

This Tutorial will then act as your route map to PR success!

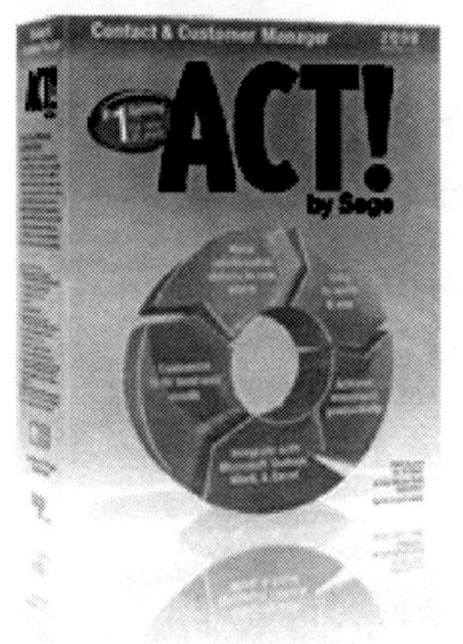

It's called ACT, by Sage Software, and the price you will be asked to pay varies depending upon where you purchase it. I obtained my first copy on eBay and paid just £15 for an older version 6 copy, which was a bargain as I used it for a number of years without considering an upgrade because it did everything I needed and a lot more. However, when I upgraded my computer it was fitted with the 'Vista' operating system, and I had to in turn, upgrade to version 10 of ACT to get it to function correctly. Unfortunately, but hardly surprisingly, this was a lot more expensive, but when I consider what it does for me, and the ***SHEER NUMBER*** of man hours it saves, the cost is ***WELL WORTH*** every penny.

Now there could be ***DOZENS*** of other systems out there that will do the same thing for you, I really do not know. What I am certain of, is that this simple and adaptable bit of software makes PR marketing a ***LOT*** easier and faster for us to achieve. This next chapter is ***NOT*** an in-depth study of how to use it, but rather an overview of its functionality and has been written to make you aware that it has some ***AWE-INSPIRING*** relation-building potential built in to it.

PLEASE NOTE: the screen grabs you are about to see are from the ACT demo database, as it would not be fair or ethical for me to expose contacts or information from my PR database! Mine looks similar, but has been adapted to suit.

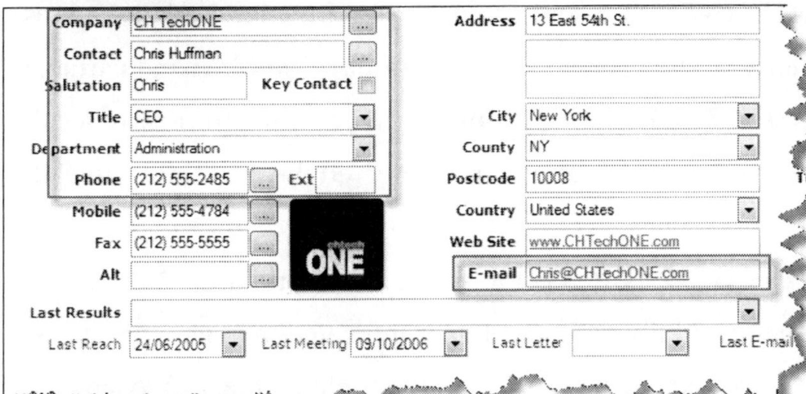

Notes:
Please use this margin for writing your ideas thoughts, inspirations and personal plan of action.

This Tutorial will then act as your route map to PR success!

Enter your contact's details once, then use them a 1000 times...

The above screen grab shows the main fields we would need to use when communicating with news rooms and journalists and as you can see they are very basic as you may expect from any database; I have highlighted the only ones I use in red, however, this program is versatile enough to be adapted to suit your own particular requirements.

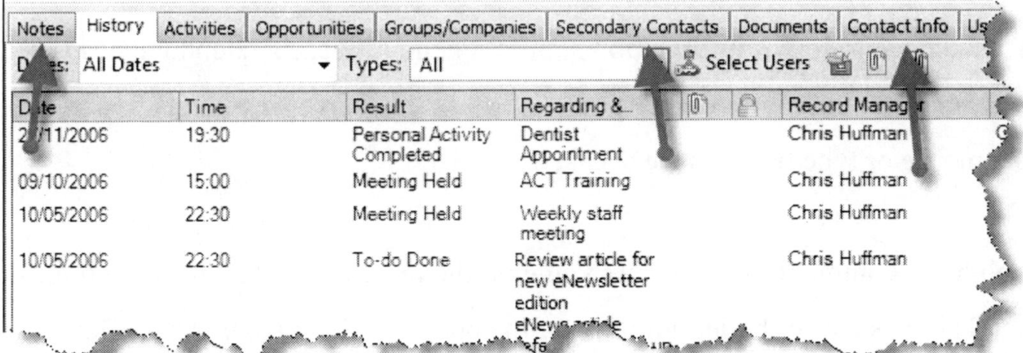

However just below this area is a ***MULTIPLE*** tab bar which we will come to shortly; at the moment the ***HISTORY*** tab is highlighted and will display all the activity between you and this contact. I have drawn arrows pointing to the other tabs which I regularly use, those being ***NOTES***, which allow me to instantly record anything of interest I hear or discover whilst speaking to media personnel, plus the PR results I receive.

Notes:
Please use this margin for writing your ideas thoughts, inspirations and personal plan of action.

This Tutorial will then act as your route map to PR success!

I open the ***CONTACT INFO*** to record any useful information I might later use to highlight my interest in this person such as birthdays, children and partners names, etc. It ***ABSOLUTELY*** amazes people when you can effortlessly recall such precise details and ***IT WILL*** get you remembered the next time you call.

SECONDARY CONTACTS. I often get to speak to receptionists, PAs and news room personnel, and I always record their information in case we speak again. Just asking, for instance: "am I speaking to Stefani" breaks the ice, and shows that you have already had contact with someone there before.
This can make the difference between getting the "Cold Shoulder" and speaking to or discovering the details of the journalist with whom you wish to build a working relationship. Often the people you speak to first are the most important and useful to you, as they are less guarded and will often tell you ***EVERYTHING*** you need to know about the key personnel with whom you should be dealing. They may well put you straight through to them or even put your press release under their very noses.

To make recording of information simple, I generally use a telephone headset whilst contacting news rooms or journalists as this leaves my hands free to use the mouse or type notes as we speak.

I highly recommend ACT to help you gain the most from you PR marketing, and below is a brief bullet point list of the benefits which using ACT offers us.

- It allows us to create an easy to search data base of all our PR contacts, and related information which we can view as individual files, or in list format.

- We can sort this data into groups for easy reference and rollout emailing, and update individual files or information as we progress.

- At the click of the mouse we can see the last time we called or sent an email and what was the outcome of this interaction.

Notes:
Please use this margin for writing your ideas thoughts, inspirations and personal plan of action.

This Tutorial will then act as your route map to PR success!

- We can also set tasks and alarms to remind us that we have to perform a certain action on a specific date.

However, the BIGGEST benefit...

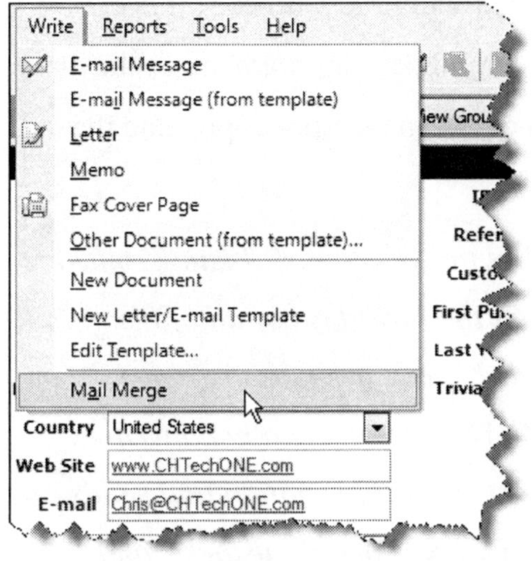

ACT also integrates with a variety of 'Microsoft' software products such as "Word", which is my 'Word Processor' of choice and allows me to ***MAIL MERGE*** information directly from the database with documents before emailing them out.
This means I can quickly integrate highly personalised information directly into my news releases and follow up information. This personalisation can make a ***HUGE*** difference to your results.

I often use this ***MAIL MERGE*** facility to add information to news releases which have been written for general distribution, but by form-feeding local area detail into the body copy, have made them appear to have been written specifically for the newspaper's local readership; by so doing, I have dramatically increased their chances of publication.

ACT also allows me to email directly through my "Outlook Software". As you can see it is really convenient and comfortably fits in with the way I work. If you happen to use other software programs which are different, you may find it will work with them also.

Notes:
Please use this margin for writing your ideas thoughts, inspirations and personal plan of action.

This Tutorial will then act as your route map to PR success!

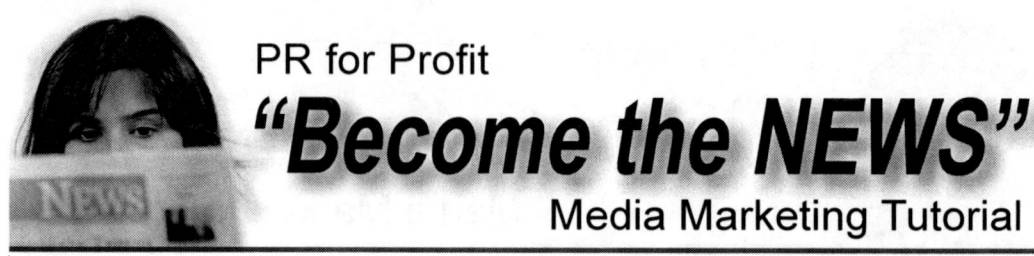

Relationship-building giants...

As I mentioned, ACT allows you to record your contacts' birthday details etc. Can you imagine just how powerful it would be to receive birthday greetings from someone with whom you have only dealt with a few times? ...I don't know about you, but if it happened to me I would certainly remember the name of the person who sent it for many years to come and deeply appreciate the sentiment and effort.

> *So does this technique work? As a matter of interest, I know someone who makes it her business to find out the birthdays of all of her customers and prospects, and for all I know, perhaps everyone she knows. She then of course ALWAYS sends them a hand written birthday card; she tracks all such personal information and sends a greeting. Unsurprisingly, she is NEVER short of business, and her clients are as LOYAL as can be! ...just because she shows she is INTERESTED.*

Even more simple, would be to send all your contacts a personalised Christmas email. If you were to create a special seasonal eCard, eMail, Video, etc, with ACT, it would only take a few minutes to add detailed personalisation and dispatch it to a list of thousands. But why stop at Christmas cards? ...with a little imagination you could use this facility to keep in contact with your favourite media personnel many times a year and perhaps bring a little smile to their faces. ACT makes all of this easy to achieve!

Final words of PR advice...

You now share the PR knowledge and the precise system which I use to make money from media exposure on a daily basis. Although our journey through this tutorial together is coming to a close, your PR journey is just about to start and you should be excited as with this tutorial to refer to when necessary, it should be a ***VERY BRIGHT*** one.

However, just knowing what to do will achieve you nothing; what you have to do is put what you have learned into ***ACTION***. The bigger the action, the bigger the results you can expect in return, so I suggest that you begin your journey by taking ***MASSIVE*** action to gain momentum and start your PR marketing ball rolling.

How quickly you start to profit from this material is ***TOTALLY*** down to you. As you progress you are going to encounter frustrations and make mistakes, perhaps lots of them, I know I did. However, from every mistake which I made, I learned a little more and advanced, and you will also if you stay with it; you will soon reach the position where you start to get results you can build upon.

As you experiment with what works for you and what does not, you will gain the experience and confidence you need to attract just as much business as you can manage.

However, now you know what is involved in obtaining ***QUALITY*** PR you may still want someone else to do it for you. Or even someone to help expand your ideas and advance your media campaign. If this is the case, Jeremy and I do a limited amount of PR consultancy on topics which we find interesting. If you would like to learn more please send us an email of your requirements, plus a telephone number, and one of us will get back to you. Please email us at: kevin@pr-forprofit.com

Notes:
Please use this margin for writing your ideas thoughts, inspirations and personal plan of action.

This Tutorial will then act as your route map to PR success!

Notes:

Notes:

Notes:

Notes:

Notes:

Notes:

Notes:

Notes:

Notes:

Notes:

Notes:

Notes:

Notes:

Notes:

Notes:

Notes:

Lightning Source UK Ltd.
Milton Keynes UK
17 March 2010

151512UK00001B/4/P

9 780954 920630